The Other Side of Suffering

The Other Side of Suffering

Finding a Path to Peace after Tragedy

Katie E. Cherry

Louisiana State University

OXFORD
UNIVERSITY PRESS

OXFORD
UNIVERSITY PRESS

Oxford University Press is a department of the University of Oxford. It furthers
the University's objective of excellence in research, scholarship, and education
by publishing worldwide. Oxford is a registered trade mark of Oxford University
Press in the UK and certain other countries.

Published in the United States of America by Oxford University Press
198 Madison Avenue, New York, NY 10016, United States of America.

Library of Congress Control Number: 2019052838
ISBN 978-0-19-084973-3

1 3 5 7 9 8 6 4 2
Printed by Sheridan Books, Inc., United States of America

CONTENTS

PREFACE

Humans are creatures of habit. Our routines of everyday living are ordered and predictable. We arise in the morning and daily routines fall into place without hesitation. A cup of coffee, maybe a bite to eat or a quick glance at the newspaper, and we are off to school or work. At the end of the day, we are home, wrapped in the comfort of the familiar. The events of the day—whether good or bad, ordinary or surprising, professional or personal—gradually slip away. Images of people and the echo of conversations with co-workers, friends, or family fade beyond awareness to be forgotten or maybe revisited later. We retire for the evening. Another day has gone, and a new one is coming tomorrow. And we smile as we remember the words of Ralph Waldo Emerson (1802–1883), the American poet and philosophical writer, who said, "Finish each day and be done with it. Some blunders and absurdities no doubt crept in. Forget them as soon as you can. Tomorrow is a new day. You shall begin it well and serenely. . . ."[1]

Peoples' daily routines are usually stable, as are their assumptions about the world in which they live. Assumptions are often outside of conscious awareness and seldom questioned, unless challenged by unexpected events. When a tragedy happens, peoples' assumptions about the rightness of the world are shaken. Nothing seems the same anymore. Daily routines and sense of normalcy are gone. People may worry about the well-being of friends and family. The world has changed suddenly, in the blink of an eye. Standing at the edge of a dark precipice, staring down an unbelievable, life-altering tragedy, people may begin to question the fairness of the world and the rightness of their life and its direction. Another day has come, but how do we get through the hour? And tomorrow may come, but what of serenity? That may be irretrievably gone, too. Feelings of anguish, confusion, and pain abound as one's spirit is simply overtaken by the totality of a tragic event.

What causes such emotional upheaval and comprehensive disruption of daily living? The answer is that many different events have the potential to serve as a catalyst for traumatic stress, which differs by degree from the stresses of daily living.[2] It may not be the event itself as much as the impact of this event on people's daily lives, routines, and sense of order. Such trigger events, ones that may threaten feelings of security and safety, can unfold on an international scale, as during wars, military conflicts, and terrorist attacks. Other events occur on a societal level, affecting entire communities: earthquakes, hurricanes, floods, tornadoes, wildfires, and chemical and oil spills. Trigger events may occur privately as well, devastating individuals and families. Personal tragedies can include events such as the premature or untimely death of a child, sibling, parent, or spouse; victimization due to violent crime or domestic abuse; industrial, automobile, or other accidents; or the onset of disease, disability, or health reversals. One common feature linking each of these disparate trigger events is the fundamental human instinct to survive.

Assuming that one manages to live through a tragic event, regardless of its source or the scope of impact, the next step concerns the process of healing, which means working through the loss. This clinical analysis seems strikingly simple: we are devastated and now we must "get over it." The problem is, it's not that simple. Unlike the mantra of well-meaning friends and acquaintances in the short run, things may not get better. In fact, sometimes things get worse. And one may not be able to "get over it." At least not right away. Anyone who has experienced a catastrophic event of any sort will tell you that, despite the assurances of others, it is not always possible to simply "get over it."

INTENT OF THIS VOLUME

The Other Side of Suffering provides a new look at the age-old question of how people find a pathway to peace and serenity after having experienced a tragedy. The central idea motivating this book is that a natural disaster, a categorically destructive and seemingly senseless event that surely *nothing* good can come out of, may shed light on the mystery of how the human spirit recovers after a tragedy. In the years after a disaster, survivors move on with the task of daily living. Experience may have taught them how to bridge the gap between the suffering associated with the natural disaster and resolution of this pain through healing.

As a developmental psychologist studying the impact of the 2005 Atlantic Hurricanes Katrina and Rita on health and well-being in later life, I have learned a few things about disaster exposure, loss, and the process of healing. This volume is written for the general public with the expressed intent of sharing both academic and experiential knowledge gained from a research project on post-Katrina resilience.[3] These data include structured interviews with more than 190 residents of two coastal parishes (counties) in south Louisiana. Some had evacuated prior to the storm. Others stayed behind by choice or by circumstance. Those who "stood for the storm" (a local term denoting the choice not to evacuate) experienced an unimaginable nightmare filled with death, destruction, and roof-top rescues. Narrative text from a Katrina survivor's personal journal provides a foundation for and unique glimpse into the hellish odyssey that began on the day of the storm and documents the Katrina tragedy suffered by thousands of US Gulf Coast residents.

This volume is organized as follows. In Part I (Chapters 1–4), the disaster experience is illuminated using the 2005 Atlantic Hurricanes Katrina and Rita as an example. In Part II (Chapters 5–7), six principles of healing are introduced in pairs: faith and humor, respect and gratitude, and acceptance and silver linings. Taken singly or as a whole, these principles can be flexibly applied to counter traumatic stress in daily life, support the healing process, and point survivors in the direction of a path toward peace after a disaster or other traumatic experience. In Part III (Chapters 8 and 9), the topics of grief, the "new normal," and life after disaster are examined.

The principles presented here offer a new way of thinking about traumatic stress and grief resolution from an adult developmental perspective. Direct quotations and illustrations from current and former coastal residents appear throughout this volume. Select findings from the research literature are also cited to strengthen the scholarship and academic rigor. Readers who are struggling with situation-specific despair due to circumstances beyond their control might relate to the Katrina tragedy. The long and painful journey forced on those who experienced Katrina's wrath directly provides an authentic and rich model for how survivors can heal and recover from a catastrophic, life-altering tragedy. Last, the value of these principles for promoting healing in the wake of tragedy should be addressed. To my way of thinking, the effectiveness of these principles as agents of change is realized simply—in *the experience of joy in everyday living* after a disaster or other tragic event. Joy, even if only fleeting, brings hope for a meaningful future and is a step taken in the direction of grief resolution and eventual healing.

A DEVELOPMENTAL PSYCHOLOGIST CONDUCTING RESEARCH IN A DISASTER CONTEXT

When the 2005 Hurricanes Katrina and Rita struck, my colleagues and I were in the third year of a multiyear program project grant funded by the National Institute on Aging to study the determinants of longevity and healthy aging from an interdisciplinary perspective. There was some urgency at the time to determine how Katrina had impacted those enrolled in the Louisiana Healthy Aging Study (LHAS), many of whom were nonagenarians (aged 90 years and older). LHAS participants lived in the greater Baton Rouge region in 2005, so they were indirectly affected with only minor hurricane damage, if any at all. Many were sheltering displaced coastal family members who had lost homes in Katrina. Because my colleagues from the New Orleans area were displaced, too, I was the lead investigator for the LHAS hurricane assessment.[4,5]

In the years after the Katrina disaster, I wondered what had happened to the displaced coastal residents that I had met during the LHAS hurricane assessment. Scaling it up just a bit, I knew that more than a million US Gulf Coast residents were displaced by Katrina in 2005—but where were they now? Did they go back to their devastated homes and communities, or did they relocate permanently inland to presumably safer ground? Knowing how disaster survivors were faring in the years after the 2005 Hurricanes Katrina and Rita was important to me. Although I had no prior training or experience in disaster science beyond the LHAS hurricane assessment, I decided it was time for a new study to compare coastal residents who returned to rebuild their communities and former coastal residents who relocated permanently inland to the greater Baton Rouge area after Katrina. This new study would provide valuable information on variables important to long-term disaster recovery. In this spirit, I set out to learn about post-disaster resilience from current and former coastal residents who had lost in Katrina everything they had acquired in life. Like a bumblebee who doesn't realize that she is not aerodynamically suited for flight (i.e., the tiny wings are disproportionally smaller than the bulky body: theoretically, the bumblebee is not a plausible candidate for flight), I took off in the direction of writing a new grant to fund a new line of research on post-Katrina resilience. I will always be grateful to the Louisiana Board of Regents for sponsoring my research project in the exploratory grant program for seasoned university researchers to embark on a new and possibly risky direction for programmatic research.

In early 2010, I was finalizing design decisions and collecting pilot data for this new study. I selected St. Bernard Parish as a data collection site based on objective considerations: the documented destruction after Hurricane Katrina and the poorly understood fates of the people who had lived there. Located five miles southeast of New Orleans, St. Bernard was devastated every bit as much as the great coastal city had been, but who other than locals and possibly Louisiana natives has ever heard of St. Bernard? News coverage, among other sources of public domain information, was scant. Media attention had focused almost exclusively on the city of New Orleans. Admittedly, I had never heard of St. Bernard until the fall of 2005, when two Katrina tragedies captured my attention: the paralyzed man and his elderly mother who drowned in their home waiting for the prearranged ambulance transport that never came and the St. Rita's nursing home tragedy, where 35 elderly residents drowned in a facility that did not evacuate before the storm (see Chapter 2). I knew I needed to educate myself before interviewing people who had lost everything in Katrina. Broadening my understanding of what had happened and the historic flooding that followed was a critical first step, but where to begin?

Logically, when one wants to learn about a particular topic, one considers going to school for this purpose or consulting with an expert who has a solid knowledge base on the topic of interest. To my way of thinking, it seemed fitting to do both, so I contacted Chalmette High School in St. Bernard Parish. I asked for an appointment with the Principal, Mr. Wayne Warner, who was himself a Katrina hero, although I did not know that at the time. I also had no idea how bad the devastation was, nor did I grasp the magnitude of the Katrina tragedy. In my naiveté at that time, I just didn't know.

On a sunny afternoon in April of 2010, I drove from my home to Chalmette High School, a 210-mile journey round trip, to meet with Principal Wayne Warner and Assistant Principal Carole Mundt. Mr. Warner's briefing on the events of August 29, 2005—the day Katrina made landfall—and the horrendous days that followed brought the Katrina tragedy into sharp focus for me. In short, my takeaway from this meeting boils down to one word: respect. Respect for the impact of this terrible environmental event on the people who experienced it directly. And respect for the longevity of pain that was still clearly evident so many years later. Without respect, outsiders like me who were not directly affected by Katrina remain uninformed and ignorant. Without respect, those people whose lives were forever changed by the Katrina tragedy can be locked in a place of frustration and pain for a very long time (see Chapter 6).

As an outsider looking in, Mr. Warner's selfless and thoughtful commentary helped me understand the Katrina disaster and appreciate all that was lost. I will always be grateful to Mr. Warner for his rich personal insights as a leader in the community, with his school serving as a shelter of last resort in August of 2005, and as a survivor who also lost his home in the floodwaters of Katrina. Listening to his in-depth explanation and personal knowledge of this storm and its aftermath prepared me well to embark on this new research project. His crystal-clear instruction helped me launch this study with a new-found respect and deeper appreciation for the Katrina tragedy. For the next two and a half years, I made weekly and sometimes biweekly trips to catchment sites for individual research sessions (two and sometimes more for each participant). Looking back, I drove more than 30,000 miles, crisscrossing coastal parishes to meet with Katrina survivors in their homes and listen to their experiences with the 2005 hurricanes, which constitute the primary data on which this volume is based.

KEY POINTS IN THE BOOK

The present analysis of suffering and healing after the Katrina disaster is based on four assumptions, which are incorporated throughout the book. These assumptions are as follows:

1. *Suffering happens.* One should begin by recognizing the inevitability of suffering, which is fundamental to the human condition. Consider the words of the late psychiatrist Viktor Frankl who said, "Suffering is an ineradicable part of life, even as fate and death. Without suffering and death, human life cannot be complete."[6]

Hurricane Katrina was an epic tragedy and the worst natural disaster in US history at that time. Katrina survivors recognize the loss and understand the impact of this disaster in a very personal way based on their lived experience. As discussed in Chapters 2–4, those who did not evacuate in advance of Katrina, either by choice or by circumstance, endured a terrifying experience, a living nightmare of the worst sort. In retrospect, many of the difficult and painful life experiences that can make us stronger and better people, we would not voluntarily undertake if we knew ahead of time how they would turn out.

2. *Suffering is not an end in and of itself.* Surely there must be some good thing that emerges after a comprehensive disaster which imposes such terrible suffering. These musings prompted the question which motivated this book: What is on the other side of suffering?

Looking to the natural world for answers, consider that, after a rainstorm, a beautiful rainbow can be observed overhead sometimes if one takes the time to look skyward. A rainbow is a natural event with a logical explanation that has something to do with water acting as a prism that splits light into seven separate colors. Rainbows are also quite lovely, however transitory they may be in a dark sky after a storm. But rainbows can be symbolic, too, holding different meanings for different people. Looking briefly at a rainbow, a sunset, or other phenomenon of nature from an aesthetic point of view may help people reconnect with the simple joys in everyday life, bringing a glimpse of hope and healing after disaster.

3. *The relationship between suffering and healing is not linear.* The infliction of pain and the process of healing that leads to successful recovery does not follow a predictable pattern: there is no A to B to C characterization. Rather, the relationship between suffering and eventual healing is perhaps more accurately described as bidirectional, like a two-way street.

As we step away from tragedy and the healing process begins in small, measured steps, we revisit the tragedy in our thoughts and memories. Other things happen. Life goes on. We take one step forward, but two steps backward sometimes. Kim Nunez once told me, "I'll give myself five years to get over it and then we close the book on Katrina." But the problem here is that healing really isn't linear. One may find that the pain of this experience continues to linger, resurfacing at certain times or on certain anniversaries, sometimes when least expected. This is why I suggest that the statute of limitations strategy for long-term disaster recovery may be helpful for some people, but not necessarily right for everyone.

4. *The suffering–healing relationship is dynamic.* Like plate tectonics, the gap between suffering and healing may shift over time, widening to a point where relief seems hopelessly out of reach. People may attempt to close this gap using healthy and effective coping strategies (e.g., social support seeking, therapeutic intervention under the direct care of licensed professionals) or destructive strategies (e.g., substance abuse).

Somehow, survivors find a way to lessen or manage the impact of a tragedy they have experienced in daily life as they move forward in the healing process, yet they will never forget the ordeal itself. Some days are better, some days are worse. And life is never exactly the same as it was before the tragic experience.

CAVEATS TO KEEP IN MIND

When it comes to disaster recovery (or overcoming a devastating event of any sort), finding the right steps to take will never be easy. A key point to keep in mind when reading this volume is that *one size doesn't fit all.* When it comes to healing, a principle that works well for one person may be ineffective for others moving forward after tragedy. One might wonder why this is so. "One size doesn't fit all? Why not?"

The answer is both simple and complicated. A contradiction in terms? Not necessarily. The simple answer to the question of why one size doesn't fit all is that people are unique: a tragic event will affect each person somewhat differently. Consequently, pathways to healing would be expected to differ from person to person as survivors learn how to live with an event as an unwelcomed but now indelible part of their developmental histories.

The complicated answer to the question of why one size doesn't fit all has to do with individual difference variables. People vary in age, gender, ethnicity, religious affiliation, educational attainment, and employment history, among other individual differences that will impact trajectories of healing. Understanding how individual differences affect the experience of traumatic stress and choice of coping strategies to counter disaster stress should be recognized. Stated differently, two people may experience the very same tragic event yet how they interpret, react to, and remember this event may be very different.

Thus, it should not be surprising that stress reactions to the same event differ among people. Variations in temperament, along with differences in preferred methods of coping, may also contribute to the duration of suffering after a tragedy. By definition, "temperament" pertains to the characteristic ways that individuals respond to the world, ongoing events, and others around them. The term captures the dispositional traits that shape our personality and make us unique as people. Temperamental tendencies, such as shyness and other signature styles of responding to people and events, are stable and appear very early in life. Temperamental tendencies may also affect an individual's experience and interpretation of a tragic event, choice of coping methods, and prognosis for recovery. When dealing with individuals who are suffering as a result of a tragedy, sensitivity and awareness of temperamental tendencies and how they may govern the pace and progression of recovery is a primary ethical concern.

To summarize, *The Other Side of Suffering* brings into focus the experience of community-wide destruction and catastrophic personal losses in the wake of a deadly hurricane. Of greater interest is the take-home message, which concerns the interplay between suffering that has seared souls forever and healing that may come long after a tragic event has fallen out of the public eye. No prior traumatic experience is needed to grasp the significance of the takeaway message of healing and hope after a disaster. Given the increasing frequency of natural disasters, among other tragedies,[7] this volume is a timely source of comfort for those who will survive disasters that have yet to happen. The voices of Katrina survivors from the coastal parishes of south Louisiana are here to tell us how to find our way through prolonged suffering and discover the principles of healing that lead to authentic recovery. It is time that we listen to their message and find our pathway to peace.

NOTES

1. Odelia Floris, *Inspiration and Wisdom from the Pen of Ralph Waldo Emmerson* (CreateSpace Independent Publishing Platform, June 2015), 6.
2. James I. Gerhart, Daphna Canetti, and Stevan E. Hobfoll, "Traumatic Stress in Overview: Definition, Context, Scope, and Long-Term Outcomes," in *Traumatic Stress and Long-Term Recovery: Coping with Disasters and Other Negative Life Events*, ed. Katie E. Cherry (New York: Springer International Publishing Switzerland, 2015), 3–24.
3. Katie E. Cherry, Laura Sampson, Pamela F. Nezat, Ashley Cacamo, Loren D. Marks, and Sandro Galea, "Long-Term Psychological Outcomes in Older Adults After Disaster: Relationships to Religiosity and Social Support," *Aging & Mental Health* 19, no. 5 (2015): 430–444.
4. Katie E. Cherry, ed., *Lifespan Perspectives on Natural Disasters: Coping with Katrina, Rita and Other Storms* (New York: Springer Science + Business Media, 2009).
5. Katie E. Cherry, Jennifer L. Silva Brown, Loren D. Marks, Sandro Galea, Julia Volaufova, Christina Lefante, L. Joseph Su, David A. Welsh, and S. Michal Jazwinski, "Longitudinal Assessment of Cognitive and Psychosocial Functioning after Hurricanes Katrina and Rita: Exploring Disaster Impact on Middle-Aged, Older, and Oldest-Old Adults," *Journal of Applied Biobehavioral Research* 16 (2011): 187–211.
6. Viktor E. Frankl, *Man's Search for Meaning* (Boston: Beacon Press, 2006), 67.
7. Katie E. Cherry, ed. *Traumatic Stress and Long-Term Recovery: Coping with Disasters and Other Negative Life Events* (New York: Springer International Publishing Switzerland, 2015).

AUTHOR NOTES

This book is based on the real-life experience of many people. The names of most people described in this book have been changed to protect confidentiality. There are a few exceptions, however. In these cases, actual names were used based on the individuals' (or surviving family members') stated preference. All real names included here are printed with written permission.

PART I

Natural Disasters

The Hurricane Katrina Experience

CHAPTER 1

࿓

Disasters and Their Human Impact

Natural disasters and severe weather events happen. With or without warning, geological and weather-related disasters can strike remote geographic areas as well as densely populated metropolitan regions. Occurring worldwide, hurricanes, floods, tornadoes, wildfires, earthquakes, tsunamis, snowstorms, and volcanic eruptions are frightening environmental events that can destroy entire communities. Property damage and loss of life can be considerable after a natural disaster. Homes and neighborhoods are often made no longer habitable, thus forcing residents of disaster-impacted communities to leave. Individuals and families are suddenly thrust into new circumstances without the benefit of anticipation or advanced planning.

After a disaster, the infrastructure of towns and communities is often challenged, with threats to public health and safety for those who live in disaster-affected regions.[1] The US Federal Emergency Management Agency (FEMA) has defined a natural disaster as "An occurrence of severity and magnitude that normally results in deaths, injuries, and property damage and that cannot be managed through routine procedures and resources of government. It . . . requires immediate, coordinated, and effective response by multiple government and private sector organizations to meet human needs and speed recovery."[2]

In contrast to FEMA, insurance companies take a different approach to the definition of a natural disaster. From an insurance industry point of view, the term, "an act of God" may be used to categorize claims filed by disaster survivors who seek monetary compensation for property damage and losses that can be attributed to the destructive forces of a natural disaster. At some level of abstraction, it probably makes sense to assign catastrophic damage to "an act of God." Perhaps some unknown cosmic force or faceless deity is at fault and can be considered the responsible party for geologic and weather-related events. Maybe this formulation works for a business model in the world of insurance.

In 2005, the Atlantic Hurricanes Katrina and Rita brought unparalleled destruction, forever changing the landscape and lives of people in the Gulf Coast region of the United States. Briefly, Katrina's swath of destruction stretched across Florida, Alabama, Mississippi, Louisiana, and portions of southeast Texas, with a death toll estimated at more than 1,800 persons. Less than a month after Katrina, Hurricane Rita made landfall on September 24, 2005. Also a destructive Category 3 storm, Rita demolished the western side of Louisiana and southeast Texas. From an insurance industry perspective, damages and losses due to the 2005 Hurricanes Katrina and Rita might be processed and filed under the "act of God" category; to my way of thinking, a loving and benevolent God would not set out to hurt humanity so comprehensively.

To broaden the discussion, consider the words of Rabbi Harold Kushner, author of the best seller book, *When Bad Things Happen to Good People*:

> Insurance companies refer to earthquakes, hurricanes, and other natural disasters as "acts of God." I consider that a case of using God's name in vain. I don't believe that an earthquake that kills thousands of innocent victims without reason is an act of God. It is an act of nature. Nature is morally blind, without values. It churns along, following its own laws, not caring who or what gets in the way. But God is not morally blind. I could not worship Him if I thought He was. God stands for justice, for fairness, for compassion. For me, the earthquake is not "an act of God." *The act of God is the courage of people to rebuild their lives* after the earthquake, and *the rush of others to help them in whatever way they can.*[3]

Current and former US Gulf Coast residents who lost homes and property in the Katrina disaster might agree with Rabbi Kushner. They can tell us in a very real way that rebuilding their lives after the costliest natural disaster in US history until that time required courage. During Katrina's immediate aftermath, medical personnel and other professionals from all over the country rushed to the severely damaged coastal towns and communities to provide disaster relief assistance. Those who lived outside of storm-ravaged areas and came quickly to offer their support might resonate with Kushner's "act of God . . . [as] the rush of others to help them in whatever way they can," as further discussed in Chapter 4.

*   *   *

The 2005 Atlantic Hurricanes Katrina and Rita were events of local and national significance. Natural disasters may also have global significance related to their economic and environmental impact. Some examples of disasters with global impact include the Haiti earthquake (January 12, 2010) and tsunamis such as those that struck in Asia (2004) and Japan (2011). As current events, natural disasters may capture media attention and may dominate the popular press for a brief time.

Catastrophic disasters, like Katrina, also invite continued thought and analysis by scientists and scholars in the years after these events. In fact, one can imagine at least four dimensions of interest for individuals as well as the world at large. Disasters may attract

- scientific interest, motivating research studies to examine disasters as phenomena of nature;

- political and economic interest related to disaster-specific planning, policy formulation, and implementation, as well as continued debate pertaining to issues of fiscal responsibility;

- epidemiological and public health interest owing to the large numbers of people affected and their well-being after disaster; and

- educational interest, informing the general public who may want to know what can be learned from disasters and how can individuals, families, and communities recover from and prepare for future disasters.

With disasters, as well as with mass shootings and other tragic events associated with loss of life, inquiries are often conducted in the months and years after these events. Investigative teams seek to uncover what went wrong. With meticulous care, prevailing circumstances are documented, along with possible errors in judgment that may have contributed to tragic outcomes. Investigative reports, sometimes quite extensive, are compiled and lessons learned are identified. In time, against the backdrop of knowledge generated, societies may develop better, more effective methods of security and precautions to ensure the safety of people and the communities in which they reside.

HISTORIC PERSPECTIVES ON DISASTERS

Disasters may hold a certain fascination for some people. Disasters may also find a foothold in our collective conscious, occupying a special niche in popular culture that persists over time and across generations. Some events have become legendary, a thread in the fabric of society so basic that they may be found in elementary schools. For instance, American school children may be familiar with the story of Mrs. O'Leary's cow, who allegedly kicked over a lantern that started the Great Chicago Fire of 1871.

Folklore notwithstanding, large-scale natural disasters may provide impetus for literary works as well. There are book-length volumes on geological events, such as the San Francisco earthquake of 1906[4] and the more recent Katrina disaster.[5-9] In addition to geological or weather-related events, disasters can also stem from technologically based incidents. Due to misfortune or lack of oversight, man-made disasters are typified by unintentional events, such as nuclear reactor accidents (e.g., Chernobyl, 1986; Japan, 2011) and oil spills (e.g., Exxon Valdez, 1987; Deepwater Horizon Oil Spill, 2010). Technological disasters, such as chemical and oil spills, threaten the environment and economy of affected areas with disastrous consequences and long-term health implications for local residents. Disasters born of human error also motivate books, sometimes with entertainment value. For example, the movie *Titanic* was a Hollywood rendition of the actual events that took place when this ocean liner hit an iceberg and sank off of the coast of Newfoundland in April of 1912, on its maiden voyage.

Conceivably, disasters may attract interest as events of national and political significance. That is, disasters may occupy a particular place in history that warrants continued attention and consideration, as do politically motivated tragedies, such as assassinations (e.g., Abraham Lincoln, John F. Kennedy, and Martin Luther King) and strategically planned, terrorist assaults (e.g., the 1988 Pan Am bombing in Lockerbie, Scotland; the 1995 Oklahoma City bombing; the 2000 bombing of the *USS Cole*; the terrorist attacks of September 11, 2001; the 2013 Boston Marathon bombing).

In addition to marking history, disasters may illustrate the limitations of contemporary principles of engineering. As an example, consider the fiery demise of the Hindenburg in 1937. This great German airship had made several successful transatlantic ocean crossings yet exploded into flame 200 feet above the ground as she made her descent to land in New Jersey, killing thirty-six passengers and crew members. The Hindenburg disaster was noteworthy for marking the beginning and end of the era of the great Zeppelin airships that were inflated with hydrogen, a highly flammable gas.

Human interest in disasters may also stem from the intrinsic emotional significance of these events. Disasters may evoke similar feelings of compassion for the victims of these events, as do other tragedies that cause the nation to weep, like mass shootings in public places (e.g., Columbine

High School massacre in 1999; Virginia Tech massacre in 2007; Aurora, Colorado, Movie Theatre massacre in the summer of 2012; and Sandy Hook Elementary School shooting in Newtown, Connecticut, in December of 2012). Continuing this line of thinking, disasters may also expose our naivety, forcing people to shed their innocence and assumptions of safety. Or, in some cases, what may be lost with disaster is not so much peoples' innocence as their arrogance. As an example, readers will remember that the *Titanic*, a carefully designed ocean liner, was touted as the "unsinkable ship." Nonetheless, this great ship tragically sank to the bottom of the Atlantic Ocean on her maiden voyage after a collision with an iceberg, directly causing the deaths of more than 1,500 people.

LIVES DISRUPTED: THE HUMAN IMPACT OF DISASTERS

As we consider the many and diverse implications of natural and technological disasters, we would do well to remember the human impact of a disaster. For survivors, the disaster experience can be a tragic event with losses that defy imagination. With comprehensive disruption of routines, the means for making a living, and social and friendship networks, among other catastrophic emotional and physical losses, disaster-related suffering can be immense and long-lasting.

Given the sudden array of disaster stressors to navigate, it is not surprising that there are many possible psychological reactions to disaster. At first, survivors may experience shock and disbelief. At the time, getting hit with a hurricane or other severe weather event may be overwhelming. Disaster exposure may be the impetus for a wealth of unpleasant thoughts and feelings that emerge over time for survivors, including (but not limited to) frustration ("no one understands"), unfairness ("why me?"), and perhaps isolation ("I am surrounded by strangers . . . I do not know where my friends are"). These psychological reactions and many more will be touched upon throughout this volume. To my way of thinking, there is great value in considering the life stories and experiences of people, young and old, who have been through a disaster. Why? Simply because disaster experiences are more common today than people may realize. From the US Gulf Coast region (Florida, Alabama, Mississippi, Louisiana, Texas) with its hurricanes and flooding; to the Midwestern states (Kansas, Missouri, Oklahoma) with their cyclones and tornadoes; California and the West Coast with its earthquakes, mudslides, and wildfires; the Northeast and New England with their snowstorms and blizzards; and the East Coast's Atlantic hurricanes, disasters claim lives every year in the United States.

Worldwide, disasters span the globe, claiming countless lives in distant locations that may not reach the news cycle threshold. Whether nearby or in a distant land, natural disasters are noteworthy events which may alter the course of development for those who survive them and sometimes for future generations, too.

To summarize, the experience of a natural disaster, among other negative life events, disrupts routines and alters the developmental context of life. This is why I believe that a lifespan developmental perspective on natural disasters is important.[10] Disasters, among other tragic events, will undoubtedly have differing impacts on children, adolescents, emerging and middle-aged adults, and elderly people. Trajectories of healing and long-term recovery are also likely to differ by life stage at the time of the tragic event.[11] For example, recent studies have shed light on significant long-term health consequences for children and youth who lived through the Katrina experience. Other evidence has shown that the number of elderly adults who perished in the aftermath of Katrina exceeded the number of deaths of all other age groups combined.[12] What this statistic does not capture are the sizeable numbers of premature deaths or early nursing home placements for elderly persons that cannot be unequivocally tied to the Katrina disaster yet are undoubtedly related to storm stressors and the disruption of healthcare or other medical services due to the storm. To appreciate the disruptive influence of a disaster on lifespan human development, it may be instructive to consider the distinction between normative versus non-normative developmental events, as discussed more fully next.

*   *   *

NORMATIVE VERSUS NON-NORMATIVE DEVELOPMENTAL EVENTS

A logical place to start is to consider the human condition from a lifespan developmental perspective. Briefly, healthy infants experience a sequence of predictable, normative events from birth through early and middle childhood. These events begin with basic reflexes and motor milestones. Soon after are the first utterances that lead to the acquisition of language. Emotional and behavioral self-regulatory processes follow, along with mastery of many cognitive and psychosocial developmental tasks. For instance, some tasks of early childhood include (but are not limited to) developmental gains such as understanding what is "mine" versus "yours," sharing, taking turns, and playing well with others. Social competence and awareness of a larger universe emerge as children enter the world of secondary education. From late childhood through adolescence and emerging adulthood, normative developmental events continue to unfold as social worlds expand. Teenagers anticipate entry into the adult world of responsibility. Career aspirations and new social opportunities present themselves as young people move away from the familiar circumstances of childhood homes and nuclear families.

For many people, these normative developmental events unfold like clockwork, without significant disruption or unforeseen detours on the road to maturity. Sometimes the occurrence of a traumatic event will disrupt this developmental context, spinning the individual into the depths of despair and forever altering normative trajectories of growth and change. In other cases, direct, personal experience of a tragedy strikes later in life, possibly in young adulthood, more likely by middle age, and certainly by late adulthood. Some individuals feel entitled to live an unblemished life, free of sorrow, regret, and misfortune. However, in reality, there are no such guarantees. Unanticipated tragedies happen. Sometimes lives are upended suddenly and needlessly: we never saw it coming—we never thought this would happen to us.

Suffering and prolonged despair are natural consequences of non-normative, negative life events. Finding oneself in the midst of a tragedy may seem unreal and unfair. Nonetheless, pain and suffering in this life are unavoidable and fundamental to the human condition. The more pressing issue concerns the question of how disaster-related pain can be managed so that one can move beyond it. Simply put, the question becomes how do disaster survivors recover from a catastrophic experience?

People who have been exposed to a natural disaster may want to get past the disruption and pain associated with catastrophic events and put it behind them. They would like to be on the other side of suffering, but how does one get there? While there may be no easy and satisfying answer to this question, Part II of the present volume presents six principles of healing to support the disaster recovery process. These principles are based on a program of research addressing resilience and long-term recovery in the coastal parishes (counties) of south Louisiana that were nearly destroyed by Hurricanes Katrina and Rita in 2005.

LIFE AFTER A NATURAL DISASTER: A WINDOW
TO HEALING AND LONG-TERM RECOVERY

What can we learn about long-term recovery from different types of tragic events by looking at the experiences of people who have survived a natural disaster? Do natural disasters really hold the key to understanding the dynamic relationship between traumatic stress and healing? How could excessive wind and water possibly compare to having suffered at the hands of a criminal? Or having watched a loved one become the victim of a violent crime? Doesn't the National Weather Service provide advance notice, forewarning of impending disaster, giving everyone the precious gift of time so that they can escape or avoid the onslaught? These are certainly reasonable questions that demand an answer. At a very broad level of analysis, at least in principle, the National Weather Service does provide warnings of impending weather hazards that may threaten our homes and our lives. On the surface, hurricanes and malevolent criminal activities, automobile or industrial accidents, and life-threatening illnesses seem very different indeed. At a deeper level of analysis, though, these events tend to converge. On closer examination, the surface dissimilarities among tragic events may disappear completely.

At the heart of any traumatic experience is a simple truth: our expectations have been not only challenged but severely violated. To illustrate, consider the following examples. "We never dreamed we would: (a) lose our home and our community (hurricane-related), (b) lose our innocence and sense of safety (criminal activity-related), (c) live the rest of our life on disability or in a wheelchair (accident-related), and/or (d) die before I reach old age (terminal illness-related)." Which one is more devastating or more painful? While it may be tempting to pick one option over the other based on personal knowledge of such events (or lack thereof), the answer is that each of these traumatic events is equally devastating in its own right. Each one of these events can bring excruciating, heart-wrenching pain that dominates our lives and scars our spirit. From this vantage point, we can see that suffering is soul-searing and profoundly painful. We seek healing and recovery in the short-term and over the long haul, regardless of the circumstances that brought us there.

THE SPECIAL CASE OF NATURAL DISASTER: COLLAPSE OF SOCIAL AND PHYSICAL WORLDS

Consider the dynamic relationship between the occurrence of pain and the resolution of pain through healing. The presence of physical pain in response to bodily injury seems logical and natural. So does the presence of emotional pain in the face of losses and disappointments that happen from time to time. Healing presupposes a wound or injury, either physical, emotional, or both.

With normative and anticipated events that are painful, suffering comes but healing follows. The suffering–healing dynamic often plays out within a calendar year of the event, sometimes sooner, sometimes later, depending on the individual and the circumstances. To illustrate, consider the experience of a death in the family. An elderly relative has passed away, and this saddens us. Our co-workers, neighbors, and friends offer support, send cards and flowers, and bring groceries or a casserole for dinner. Simple gestures such as these are comforting. We move beyond our pain, and, in time, we heal.

With non-normative and unexpected events like a natural disaster, the developmental context itself is disrupted, derailed, or destroyed completely. The pain and suffering that follow may be cataclysmic, unfathomable, and unimaginable. Ordinarily supportive friends and family are not available to help us. They are not there for us. No acts of kindness, no comforting words of encouragement or reassurance. No gentle hug or loving pat on the arm to sustain us. In short, our social world has collapsed. There is no one to bring the casserole. After a natural disaster, friends and extended family may be equally devastated or perhaps more so than we are. Due to widespread evacuations, they may be scattered geographically, holing up in distance cities, even in distant states very far away. Or, a more frightening prospect, those people so very dear to us, people who form our inner circle—that we have known and loved for years—may be unaccounted for. Did they survive? Where are they? What happened to them? We just don't know. Their fate may haunt us for months, possibly years.

In the case of a natural disaster, the physical world has collapsed also. Familiar landscapes have changed dramatically. Landmark buildings and structures that have been icons in the community for as long as we can remember are destroyed or damaged beyond recognition. We are dismayed with the sight that we see, either on television as the news cameras roll or on the return to our homes and neighborhoods after a disaster. Our jaws drop in disbelief. There are no words to capture this feeling. We are stunned, not only by the disfiguration of familiar sights, but also by the presence of profoundly damaged objects, structures swept off their foundations, and impossibly relocated vehicles. In the case of the Gulf Coast hurricanes, heavy metal roadside billboards were twisted into pretzel-like shapes. Large boats that should have been in the bayou or in the larger waterways or out in the Gulf were blown miles inland, impossibly lodged between houses in a neighborhood. Cars were upended, with hoods pressed to the ground and trunks reaching skyward. The roof and one side of a church were completely blown off, the once plush red carpet, carefully polished wooden pews, and an ornate altar and crucifix helplessly exposed and splattered with mud.

Cemeteries were disturbed, and unearthed tombs were scattered widely among other storm debris, desecrating what had once been hallowed ground. Ghastly sights such as these are all too common after a natural disaster. In time, storm debris may be removed and a semblance of order restored as the devastation is cleared away. Nonetheless, these haunting images remain in our collective consciousness for a long time, possibly forever.

At the thought of such disarray, anyone with an ounce of compassion can quickly anticipate that the survivors' emotional world will change as dramatically as their physical world has changed. From this point of view, it does seem natural and logical for survivors' emotional responses to swing as widely or be as terribly distorted as hurricane-tossed objects. In fact, how survivors react emotionally after such devastation may be as unrecognizable to close friends and extended family as the newly demolished landscape is to the community of people who had once lived there. In short, people who have experienced such a comprehensive tragedy will seek relief from the traumatic stress and unwelcomed pain that now permeate their daily lives. Depending on the individual and his or her circumstances, a simple phone call may provide the immediate relief and reassurance that comes with updates on the safety and whereabouts of loved ones. For others, relief from ongoing and relentless traumatic stress and suffering may be sought in more extreme ways, from substance use and abuse, to illegal drug use, to the ultimate release that may come for some with the act of suicide.

SOCIAL AND PHYSICAL RESTORATION AFTER A DISASTER: EMBRACING THE "NEW NORMAL"

To get back to the question of why natural disasters may hold the key to healing, remember the social and physical features that characterize them. With respect to social features, disasters rip relationships apart—from friendships and families, to neighborhoods and entire communities. As noted earlier, seeking social support is not an option because there is no one that we know and trust to provide instrumental support (e.g., bring a casserole) or offer validation support (e.g., "I had sixteen feet of water in my house, too"), at least not at first. A disaster, such as a hurricane, pulls the rug out from under our lives. Lifestyles, schedules, and routines are severely disrupted. How we make a living may be seriously compromised or gone completely. In fact, post-disaster life is a lot like *death*. Something has died. Well, actually, many things have died. These things are gone and will never come back. There is a mourning process and dark feeling of grief that begs for a resolution that may be pitifully slow and terribly long in coming. Regarding the physical features that characterize disasters, the outward appearance of normality is gone. Due to wind and water damage in the case of a hurricane, comprehensive destruction of homes and neighborhoods is all the eye can see. Nothing looks right. Nothing smells right. Nothing sounds right. There are no flowers, no green grass, no birds chirping merrily in the trees. In fact, trees are on the ground, sideways, amidst a hopelessly tangled web of fallen electrical poles and power lines. Countless limbs and trees are scattered for miles, stretching outward, crushing houses, buildings, and cars in their horizontal path of destruction. With such an appalling vision of chaos, it is hard to remember what the physical landscape used to look like before the storm.

Despite these grim circumstances, disaster survivors find a way to work through the pain of great loss. They return and rebuild their homes and restore their communities, or they relocate and establish a new life elsewhere. Five years later, a very different picture is emerging—one of growth, recovery, and *life*. Perhaps the experience of rebuilding and reestablishing one's home in a physical sense or establishing a new home elsewhere—in essence, putting things back together again—has a positive spillover effect on our spirit, our sense of rightness with the world and general well-being. For those who survived the tragedy and seemingly endless duration of adversity, there is a new normal to embrace. And life can be good again— certainly different, but good.

RESILIENCE AFTER A DISASTER

Despite the destruction of personal and public property that happens when a natural disaster like Katrina takes place, most people will manage the obstacles and difficulties. Responding positively to adversity, most will get on with the tasks of daily living.[13,14] Social scientists use the term "resilience" to characterize the process of returning to "normal" or baseline after a disruption.[15] In the adult development and aging literature, resilience has been defined as *the maintenance, recovery, or improvement in mental or physical health following challenge.*[16]

Contemporary views on resilience are historically traced to developmental psychology and studies of at-risk youth.[17,18] In brief, *risk* and *resilience* are core concepts that pertain to children's capacity to thrive despite environmental risks (e.g., poverty, low socioeconomic status, having experienced the death of a parent) and other adverse circumstances. From a dynamic systems standpoint, Masten defines resilience as the *capacity (potential or manifested) of a dynamic system to adapt successfully to disturbances that threaten system function, viability, or development* and also as a *positive adaptation or development in the context of significant adversity exposure*. For an individual to possess the latter definition, protective factors to buffer risk have been identified. Strong attachments and close relationships with others, autonomy (including people's agentic choices), ability to solve problems, social competence, and having a sense of future and perspective, among other factors, have been shown to help promote resilience when a person is faced with high risk or adversity. The greater the depth of these protective factors, the greater capacity of resilience one will have.[19]

SUMMARY

The experience of stress associated with disaster exposure, especially over a long period of time, can be detrimental to physical health.[20] As an example, there is evidence to indicate that prolonged exposure to traumatic stress can alter certain biological processes, including brain structure and function.[21,22] Prolonged traumatic stress may impact people's lives in other ways, having a negative impact on quality of life, whether or not they are aware of the source of this stress. Disaster stress disrupts the balance of social relationships and can challenge or compromise relationships with others, especially those closest to us. Consequently, the health status and well-being of hundreds of thousands of current and former residents of communities exposed to disaster must not be overlooked or forgotten.

In the years after a natural disaster, damaged houses and public buildings, such as schools, businesses and offices, places of worship, may be dismantled and removed or else rebuilt and restored. The local culture and traditions that gave life to a community, as well as characteristic lifestyles, may not be recovered or reestablished so quickly, if at all. The spirit of the community may be slow in returning or may never come back, at least not in the same form as before. The topic of community recovery after disaster will be discussed more fully in Chapter 9. In this context, I will make the point that remembering a tragedy through commemorative activities that mark the anniversary of the event may serve an important and valuable purpose for some people but possibly not for everyone.

Looking beyond Hurricane Katrina and other disasters of wind and water, one may realize that the human side of disaster-related suffering is perhaps best described as a universal phenomenon. We remember disaster survivors as we remember those who have suffered from other forms of tragedy. We consider how these persons are moving along on their path to recovery as the days, months, and years go by. We recognize that those who have been exposed to heart-rending tragedy, regardless of what happened and when, possess a certain knowledge. Through personal experience, disaster survivors can shed light on the mystery of how one goes from the depths of despair to a new normal that is meaningful, fulfilling, and enjoyable. Their insights or encouragement may offer inspiring new hope that can serve as a guide for other traumatized individuals. By example or instruction, disaster survivors can show others in a very real and authentic way how to heal and how to reach the other side of suffering.

NOTES

1. George A. Bonanno, Chris R. Brewin, Krzysztof Kaniasty, and Annette M. La Greca, "Weighing the Costs of Disaster: Consequences, Risks, and Resilience in Individuals, Families, and Communities," *Psychological Science in the Public Interest* 11 (2010): 1–49.
2. William E. Oriol, *Psychosocial Issues for Older Adults in Disasters* (Washington, DC: US Department of Health and Human Services, Substance Abuse and Mental Health Services Administration, Center for Mental Health Services, 1999), 6.
3. Harold S. Kushner, *When Bad Things Happen to Good People* (New York: Anchor Books, 1981), 68.
4. Simon Winchester, *A Crack in the Edge of the World: Earthquake of 1906* (New York: Harper Collins, 2005).
5. Douglas Brinkley, *The Great Deluge: Hurricane Katrina, New Orleans, and the Mississippi Gulf Coast* (New York: Harper Collins Publishers, 2005).
6. David L. Brunsma, David Overfelt, and J. Steven Picou, *The Sociology of Katrina: Perspectives on a Modern Catastrophe* (2nd ed.) (Lanham: Rowman & Littlefield Publishers, Inc., 2010).
7. Christopher Cooper and Robert Block, *Disaster Hurricane Katrina and the Failure of Homeland Security* (New York: Times Books, Henry Holt and Company, LLC, 2006).
8. Jed Horne, *Breach of Faith: Hurricane Katrina and the Near Death of a Great American City* (New York: Random House, 2006).
9. Chris Rose, *1 Dead in Attic* (New York: Simon & Schuster, 2005).
10. Katie E. Cherry (Ed.), *Lifespan Perspectives on Natural Disasters: Coping with Katrina, Rita and Other Storms* (New York: Springer Science + Business Media, 2009).
11. Carl F. Weems and Stacy Overstreet, "An Ecological-Needs-Based Perspective of Adolescent and Youth Emotional Development in the Context of Disaster: Lessons from Katrina," in *Lifespan Perspectives on Natural Disasters: Coping with Katrina, Rita and Other Storms*, ed. Katie E. Cherry (New York: Springer Science + Business Media, 2009), 27–44.
12. Jennifer Johnson and Sandro Galea, "Disasters and Population Health," in *Lifespan Perspectives on Natural Disasters: Coping with Katrina, Rita and Other Storms*, ed. Katie E. Cherry (New York: Springer Science + Business Media, 2009), 281–326.

13. George A. Bonanno, "Loss, Trauma, and Human Resilience: Have We Underestimated the Human Capacity to Thrive After Extremely Aversive Events?" *American Psychologist* 59 (2004): 20–28.

14. George A. Bonnano and Sumati Gupta, "Resilience After Disaster," in *Mental Health and Disasters,* eds. Yuval Neria, Sandro Galea, and Fran H. Norris (New York: Cambridge University Press, 2009), 145–160.

15. Margaret O'Dougherty Wright, Ann S. Masten, and Angela J. Narayan, "Resilience Processes in Development: Four Waves of Research on Positive Adaptation in the Context of Adversity," in *Handbook of Resilience in Children* (2nd ed.) eds. Sam Goldstein and Robert B. Brooks (New York: Springer, 2013), 15–37.

16. Carol Ryff, Elliott Friedman, Thomas Fuller-Rowell, Gayle Love, Yuri Miyamoto, Jennifer Morozink, Barry Radler, and Vera Tsenkova, "Varieties of Resilience in MIDUS," *Social and Personality Compass* 6/11 (2012): 792–806.

17. Katie E. Cherry and Sandro Galea, "Resilience After Trauma" in *Resiliency: Enhancing Coping with Crisis and Terrorism,* NATO Science for Peace and Security Series—E Human and Societal Dynamics, eds. Dean Ajdukovic, Shaul Kimhi, and Mooli Lahad (Netherlands: IOS Press, 2015), 35–40.

18. Ann S. Masten and Angela J. Narayan, "Child Development in the Context of Disaster, War, and Terrorism: Pathways of Risk and Resilience," *Annual Review of Psychology* 63 (2012): 227–57.

19. Ann S. Masten, *Ordinary Magic: Resilience in Development* (New York: Guilford Press, 2014), 308.

20. Paula P. Schnurr and Bonnie L. Green, *Trauma and Health: Physical Health Consequences of Exposure to Extreme Stress* (Washington, DC: American Psychological Association, 2004).

21. J. Douglas Bremner, "Effects of Traumatic Stress on Brain Structure and Function: Relevance to Early Responses to Trauma," *Journal of Trauma Dissociation* 6 (2005): 51–68.

22. J. Douglas Bremner and Lai Reed, *You Can't Just Snap Out of It* (Atlanta, GA: Laughing Cow Books, 2014).

CHAPTER 2

✎

Hurricane Katrina and Two Coastal
Parishes in South Louisiana

Dietrich Bonhoeffer (1906–1945) was a Lutheran pastor and German theologian who said, "Knowledge cannot be separated from the existence in which it was gained."[1] Bonhoeffer's words were voiced in a different era, under different social and political circumstances, yet there remains a certain timeless wisdom in his quote.

In the present volume, *knowledge* pertains to variables that matter for recovery after a natural disaster. In particular, six variables are presented here as healing principles that support long-term disaster recovery (see Chapters 5–7). The *existence in which this knowledge was gained* could cover a potentially wide geographic territory, beginning with the coastal parishes (counties) of south Louisiana. On further reflection, "existence" also implies survival. Many perished after Katrina. Those who survived have a breadth of life experience that is wider and possibly deeper than those who have yet to live through a disaster. To improve interpretability, we can think of the existence in which the present knowledge was gained on two levels of abstraction. At one level, *existence* will be interpreted to mean the historical and cultural milieu of two coastal parishes in south Louisiana that provide a context for the healing principles. At another level of abstraction, *existence* refers to the day-to-day activities of survival that more than 1 million displaced Gulf Coast residents faced after the 2005 Katrina disaster.

To illuminate the historical and cultural context in which the present knowledge was obtained, a brief overview of St. Bernard and Plaquemines

Parishes is provided next. Looking at the cultural heritage of this area provides a window into coastal residents' intergenerational understanding of severe weather events and hurricane preparedness tactics acquired over centuries of living in the bayous and natural waterways of south Louisiana. These coastal parishes are brought into focus here because they served as the catchment area for a research project on post-Katrina resilience (see Appendix A). Figure 2.1 provides a cartographic drawing of this region, which includes the major waterways and south Louisiana cities and towns referenced throughout this volume.

At another level of abstraction (where existence implies survival), one could argue that the disaster experience itself is a basis for the present knowledge. Later in this chapter and in Chapters 3 and 4, the Katrina experience will be revealed through the eyes of Mrs. Lori Hix, a forty-nine-year-old life-long resident of St. Bernard Parish. Together with her seventy-seven-year-old mother, Lori survived Katrina's onslaught and the difficult days, weeks, and months that followed. Lori is not only a Katrina survivor: she is a true model of resilience after disaster.

Entries from Lori's journal, though quite personal in nature, are likely to resonate with many US Gulf Coast residents who were directly impacted by the Katrina disaster. They provide in authentic, albeit painful, detail a day-by-day glimpse into a nightmare that began approximately 24 hours before Katrina made landfall (on Sunday, August 28, 2005) through their rescue the following week (on Monday, September 5, 2005). Throughout the fall of 2005, Lori's journal entries characterize in broad brush strokes the uncertainty, pain, and chaos of temporary displacement and work duties carried out in a different state; separation from family and friends; and eventual return to rebuild her coastal parish home in St. Bernard, Louisiana.

A GLIMPSE OF TWO COASTAL PARISHES

A very brief overview of the history and culture of St. Bernard and Plaquemines Parishes is given in the paragraphs that follow. A glimpse at these two coastal parishes prior to the hurricane season of 2005 is important as it establishes a pre-Katrina baseline. In other words, background information about lifestyles and traditions can be thought of as a measuring stick by which to gauge the disruption and the burden of suffering that continues to haunt some survivors so many years after the Katrina disaster.

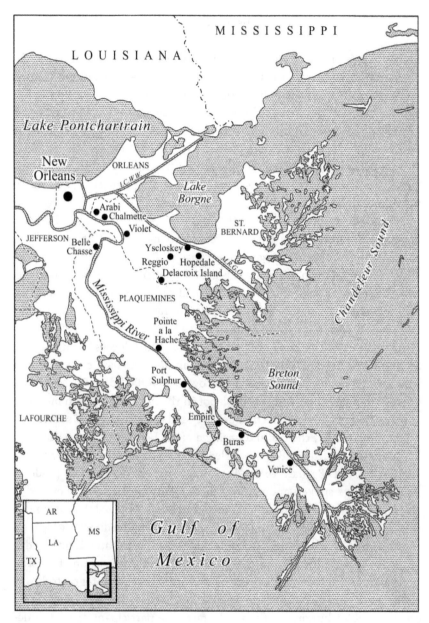

Figure 2.1 St. Bernard and Plaquemines Parishes in South Louisiana.
Courtesy of Mary Lee Eggart, Cartographer (2014).

St. Bernard Parish

Located approximately 5 miles southeast of the city of New Orleans, St. Bernard Parish is a suburban community with an estimated pre-Katrina population of approximately 68,000. The population of St. Bernard is smaller today; at the time of this writing, the current population estimate is 46,202.[2] St. Bernard has noteworthy historical significance because the Battle of New Orleans was fought here in 1815, during the War of 1812. From an economic perspective, St. Bernard has two oil refineries, industrial docks on the Mississippi River, and the world's largest sugar cane refinery, Domino's Sugar.

Perhaps best known for its world-class seafood, St. Bernard is largely a fishing community. Many people make their living catching fish or working in seafood sales or processing in some capacity. As a marina owner and operator whose family has been in this area for generations explained to me, "the water is a way of life." This is no small statement as the commercial fishing industry in southeastern St. Bernard traces its roots to the Isleños from the Canary Islands who came to south Louisiana in the 1780s.[3,4]

As documented in the *Good Pirates of the Forgotten Bayous*,[5] southeastern St. Bernard is home to multigenerational families who have caught shrimp with nets on double riggers and fished oysters on flat boats since the days of wooden rakes and backbreaking labor in the hot sun. Modern methods and mechanized dredging techniques are used to harvest oysters today.

As noted earlier, the cultural heritage of St. Bernard dates to the early Isleño settlers in the 1780s. The Isleños' presence is still strongly felt in southeastern St. Bernard today. For some, Spanish remains the predominant language spoken among families of Isleños descent. St. Bernard is also home to the Los Isleños Museum and an annual festival that celebrates the Isleños' ways of life. When I visited this museum, the director gave me a copy of a book she authored, which includes fascinating and decidedly different home remedies, among other tidbits of Isleños culture and folklore.[6]

In addition to fishing, trapping and hunting are also integral to life in St. Bernard. Self-sufficient and resourceful, coastal residents have lived off the land for hundreds of years. In fact, one participant of Isleños descent gave me a homemade duck call, along with a lesson on how he made it and a demonstration of how it works—an interesting window into his world where hunting in the backwoods and bayou marshes is a favorite pastime. In earlier days, hunting was not a leisure activity; it was a necessity, a means of survival. People ate what they hunted or caught—deer, duck, alligator, fish—and they sold the pelts of animals they trapped.

Throughout the course of conducting interviews for the 2010–2012 study (Appendix A), I was warmly welcomed into many homes. Whether participants returned to rebuild homes in St. Bernard Parish or permanently relocated inland because of Katrina-related devastation, the people I came to know are gracious, thoughtful, and kind. Participants served an assortment of delicious refreshments, from walnuts and cranberries to freshly baked brownies and homemade apple pie, to artichokes and toasted bread with cheese and garlic, to name a few. Commercial fishers sent me home with pounds of freshly caught Gulf shrimp, the best I have ever tasted. Still other participants provided helpful documentary evidence, including resources and materials, such as books, photographs, CDs and DVDs, and newspaper clippings. All gave their time and attention to the questionnaires and survey measures associated with the study. They also shared remarkable stories based on real-life experience. Together, these stories detail in a very rich and relatable way what happened to them in 2005 and in the years after the storm. A warm and personable community, St. Bernard also has a unique intergenerational aspect, where families have grown up together as neighbors and friends for decades.

Plaquemines Parish

Located on both sides of the Mississippi river (see Figure 2.1), Plaquemines Parish extends in a southerly direction and is bordered by the Gulf of Mexico. The population is smaller than St. Bernard, with current estimates at the time of this writing at 23,348.[7] Plaquemines Parish is home to several refineries and a Naval Air Station in Belle Chasse. From an agricultural perspective, Plaquemines Parish is rich with citrus farms and orange groves. Citrus farming was once a larger industry from World War I to the 1960s, although freezing weather and two hurricanes—Betsy in 1965 and Camille in 1969—have taken their toll, destroying the groves in lower Plaquemines Parish.[8] Today, the citrus industry is still strong in upper Plaquemines Parish. Orange farming is honored in the annual Orange Festival held in early December at the historic Fort Jackson located at the mouth of the Mississippi River approximately 70 miles south of New Orleans.

Oyster farming is an important agricultural component in Plaquemines Parish. In the 1950s, the Louisiana Oyster Dealers and Growers Association was formed to collectively lobby and promote the development of the oyster industry. Today, oyster farming remains a significant industry in Plaquemines and in other coastal parishes in south Louisiana, although the 2010 Deepwater Horizon Oil Spill severely threatened this industry, as discussed in Chapter 9.

Plaquemines Parish is another Louisiana coastal community with a unique cultural heritage and is home to a multigenerational Croatian community.[9] As documented in *Yugoslavs in Louisiana*,[10] the first Croatians settlers came to south Louisiana in the 1800s and lived in camps on the bayous in Plaquemines, Jefferson, and Lafourche Parishes. Croatian men immigrated to south Louisiana and made their livelihood by oyster fishing, leaving their families, wives, and children in the old country. In the middle to late 1800s, the United Slavonian Benevolent Society (USBA) was formed. The USBA established a graveyard—one in Buras and one in the city of New Orleans—to allow proper burial for Croatian immigrants who died here. Today, the Croatian American Society is an active group who meet regularly in Jesuit Bend.[11]

In conducting research interviews, I had the pleasure of meeting several families of Croatian descent. They are fourth-, fifth-, and sixth-generation oyster farmers who travel to Croatia annually to spend time with family and friends in the old country. As has been my experience in St. Bernard, the people I met in lower Plaquemines have been kind, thoughtful, and generous. They provided a unique glimpse into the world of oysters, from farming to harvesting and processing.

One Croatian family who owned an oyster processing and sales business in the city of New Orleans prior to Katrina had courtesy copies of a recently published oyster cookbook to which they had contributed. Along with the many recipes, the history and culture conveyed in this cookbook is fascinating, with beautiful pictures of Croatian oystermen at work in earlier times on boats with wooden dredging tongs.[12] This family gave me a copy of the oyster cookbook to use for reference and to share with my students, for which I was very grateful.

Another Croatian family had white linens and a beautiful table runner stretched neatly across a dining room table. This participant's mother had made these linens by hand, a common practice among Croatian women. She also served the most delicious blueberry cobbler—in a moment of self-indulgence, I ate two pieces of cobbler on that day. Thinking of other culinary treats, I also sampled *krustula*, a tasty Croatian cookie that takes a full day to prepare.

In addition to the Croatian community and oyster farming, Plaquemines Parish is also significant as the site where Hurricane Katrina made landfall. Packing 150 mile per hour winds, the eye of Hurricane Katrina covered a 30–50-mile swath, from Buras to Pointe a la Hache (see Figure 2.1). The levee surrounding this part of south Louisiana was not breached; it was overtopped, bringing a devastating 30–40 feet of water into south Plaquemines. With unrelenting force, the water then punched a hole on the other side—a levee breach from the inside out—leaving a gaping 150-foot hole straight into the Gulf of Mexico. I was told that the flooded towns in south Plaquemines experienced a tide—the water coming in and going out—bringing all manner of sea life from the Gulf of Mexico directly into people's front yards.

BEFORE THE STORM

Current and former coastal residents are well acquainted with hurricanes and other severe weather events that happen routinely in this part of the country. They know about the threat of severe weather and possible consequences of environmental events for homes and property. According to the National Weather Service, the Atlantic hurricane season begins on June 1 and continues through November 30. Year after year, hurricane season comes and goes, sometimes with great activity churning in the Gulf of Mexico, other times more quietly, with less activity and relative calm. In the vernacular, one could say that the coastal residents are hurricane savvy. Storm preparations, anticipation, and the storm experience—*hunkering down and riding out the storm*—are fundamental. A skill set often ingrained early in life, the reality of severe weather and how to respond are life lessons that begin in childhood for many coastal residents.

Residents of the US Gulf Coast know that storms come and go. Storm-related devastation may be especially upsetting for children, adolescents, and emerging adults with scant hurricane experience. On the contrary, well-seasoned coastal residents talk about hurricanes that destroyed the area before storms were named. Older research participants often spoke of losing everything and having to rebuild homes on up to three different occasions. As an example, The Unnamed Storm of 1947 took one woman's first home on Delacroix Island (see Figure 2.1). She lost her second home to Hurricane Flossy in September of 1956. Flossy was a Category 1 storm that damaged the oil rigs in the Gulf of Mexico and directly caused fifteen deaths. She lost her third home to Katrina in 2005. At ninety years of age, this participant spoke of rebuilding homes and reestablishing routines of everyday living as a part of life, something one does without hesitation or complaint. She was grateful for the financial assistance she had received from the federal government following Katrina, noting that she never had help before. As she explained, her new home was in many ways nicer than the home she lost in Katrina (see Chapter 6).

Another older person shared a similar story of loss and reconstruction in southeastern St. Bernard: Hurricane Flossy in 1956 destroyed her first home in Hopedale, she lost her second home in Yscloskey to Hurricane Betsy in 1965, and Katrina took her third home in 2005. Listening to these older adults talk about losing everything and rebuilding multiple times without litany, self-pity, or blame, one gets the sense that *resilience* (referring to the tendency to bounce back from negative life events) is a developmental characteristic acquired over time through experience and repeated exposure to adversity (see Chapter 1).

Storms associated with flooding and significant property damage stand out in memory, serving as reference points against which future storms are judged. Middle-aged and older participants spoke of Hurricane Betsy that struck on September 9, 1965. Betsy caused flooding in New Orleans and some parts of St. Bernard. Several participants in south Plaquemines Parish described severe water damage and childhood homes lost in Betsy. Some people referenced Hurricane Betsy when considering their evacuation plans for Katrina, reasoning that they made it through Betsy, so Katrina should be no different.

At some level of awareness, most people know that the city of New Orleans, among the many coastal towns and communities in south Louisiana, is situated below sea level and that a storm of the magnitude of Hurricane Katrina would devastate the region. In the weeks before this storm, weather forecasters and public officials knew of the impending danger. Preparations began at the local and national levels. President George W. Bush declared the region a disaster area in the days before the storm to secure federal assistance in advance of landfall. Integral to storm preparations is the decision-making process as individuals and families formulate their plans to stay put or evacuate to other destinations for a brief period. For those who left, three days of summer clothing and maybe a few other personal items were all they packed. That is all they had ever needed for a hurricane evacuation. In retrospect, no one anticipated being away from home for more than a few days. In reality, some people were displaced from their home for two or more years. Others never returned, relocating to nearby cities or states to establish a new home elsewhere, as discussed in Chapter 4.

An estimated 6,000 individuals stayed in St. Bernard, choosing to shelter in place rather than experience a lengthy evacuation in the August heat. There are many reasons why people stayed: history and tradition, family circumstances, personal preferences, expense (evacuations are costly, and it was the end of the month when many month-to-month laborers were low on funds), and possibly the late call for a mandatory evacuation in St. Bernard, which was issued on Sunday, August 28, 2005, less than 24 hours before the hurricane made landfall.

For those who stayed, sandbags were made available and shelters of last resort were established at local high schools. Essential personnel and their spouses—first responders, elected officials, and other St. Bernard Parish workers—reported for duty at their designated locations: the Government Complex, the Civic Center, and the Water Board, among other places. For those in the commercial fishing world, large shrimping and oyster boats were moved from southeastern St. Bernard to the Violet Canal (within the levee protection system) for safety. Who would have ever thought that these austere and commanding sea vessels would soon become a safe haven, a place of shelter and refuge for hundreds of storm-ravaged strangers rescued from rooftops or plucked from the fetid floodwaters by first responders and beneficent citizens using their personal or commandeered boats to ferry these victims to safety?

KATRINA'S IMPACT AND THE FLOODING THAT FOLLOWED

On August 29, 2005, Hurricane Katrina made landfall as a Category 3 storm. Katrina passed over a very large area, estimated to be as big in size as the United Kingdom. In the last moments before landfall, the hurricane took a turn to the east. At landfall, 150 mile per hour winds and a 30-foot tidal surge pummeled the coastal towns in lower Plaquemines Parish, with the eye of the hurricane covering a 30–50-mile swath. In St. Bernard Parish, estimated 120 mile per hour winds rocked buildings as horizontal rain fell during the night.

The next morning, people came out to survey the storm damage. At approximately 10:30 A.M. on Monday, August 29, 2005, a monstrous wall of water pushed through St. Bernard. With unimaginable force, water from the levee breaches in New Orleans and water coming in from the Gulf of Mexico swept cars off roads and homes off foundations. The flooding was intense and stunningly fast. It was a horrific and unwelcomed surprise in the hours *after* Katrina had passed, when people thought they had made it through the worst of the storm.

No one expected the fierce flooding, which brought unspeakable suffering and loss. Looking back, some of the hardest stories to hear concern the plight of the most vulnerable: disabled residents at home and those in hospitals and nursing home facilities in precarious circumstances—some under the care of administrators who did not follow protocol, others in the care of those who did but were faced with impossible situations in the eleventh hour. Either way, many of the most vulnerable coastal residents perished. Some drowned. Other died in transit or while waiting for assistance in the stifling August heat.[13]

*   *   *

There are countless, heart-rending stories of doom and peril associated with the Katrina disaster throughout the US Gulf Coast. For me, tears of compassion still form when I consider two tragedies that happened in St. Bernard on August 29, 2005. The first tragedy concerned a paralyzed man and his elderly mother. At eighty-three years of age, Mrs. Dorothy (Dot) Hingle had cared for her fifty-four-year-old son, Russell Embry, for more than thirty years since an accident left him nearly completely paralyzed and with limited speech and mobility. They were registered for special needs assistance with St. Bernard Parish and had a contract with an ambulance service that routinely evacuated them in advance of hurricanes. Despite the assurances of the service, they were left behind, waiting for the prearranged evacuation assistance that never came to their home as planned. As the raging flood waters quickly consumed their home, they drowned together on that day.[14]

This particular tragedy has lingered in my heart for many years. I have often thought about the devotion this mother exhibited toward her son, a large man who needed an ambulance team of paramedics to move him for his annual doctor visits. Thirteen years after this tragedy took place, I had a unique opportunity to meet Mrs. Dot's daughter and Russell's sister, Sally Viada.[15]

Sally told me about her family, filling in details that completed the picture I had always imagined: a portrait of a loving and devoted mother whose children came first in her life. Earlier that year, Mrs. Dot had given Sally her cache of treasured family photographs. From a different era, these pictures included a headshot of herself as a young woman and one of her son, Russell, as a child riding a pony. In the weeks before Katrina made landfall, Sally spent a day scanning these images into a computer. An avid genealogy enthusiast, Sally's plan at the time was to share the multigenerational family photographs with others who would be interested. Little did she know that these precious pictures would be later lost in Katrina. Nor could she have known how deeply moved I would be to see her mother's picture in the summer of 2018. In a round frame with the brown sepia tones characteristic of earlier days, I saw for myself a picture of courage—the face of a loving mother who took care of her son no matter what the cost, staying right there by his side until the end.

Looking back, Sally told me that she called her mother after work on Saturday, August 28, 2005, the day before Katrina made landfall. She offered to stay with them, but her mother refused, saying that only two were permitted in the ambulance. As Russell's primary caretaker, she would evacuate by ambulance with her son. Her mother reassured her that they would be fine the last time they spoke. For well over a decade, the ambulance service had picked them up like clockwork, taking them to Ruston, Louisiana, so there was no reason to expect anything different for this hurricane, Sally said. With no knowledge of their whereabouts after the storm, the family searched frantically for information. Agonizing days and weeks passed with no news of where they were. Finally, the husband of a co-worker searched the house on his own. On September 23, 2005, he found their bodies in the back bedroom, side by side, with Mrs. Dot's arm protectively around her son. The next day, Hurricane Rita made landfall. Another Category 3 hurricane, Rita reflooded parts of St. Bernard Parish and complicated the recovery process. On September 26, 2005, the bodies of Mrs. Dot and her son were removed from their home and taken to St. Gabriel, Louisiana, where the Disaster Mortuary Operational Response Team (DMORT) operations were located.

The second tragedy that defined the Katrina disaster for me occurred at St. Rita's, a local nursing home in St. Bernard Parish that did not evacuate prior to the storm. Flood waters quickly filled the facility on August 29, 2005, claiming the lives of thirty-five elderly residents, some of whom were wheelchair-bound with no chance to escape the onslaught. A certified nursing assistant who survived spoke of plastic-covered mattresses floating to the ceiling. In water up to her neck, she struggled to keep an elderly resident atop of the floating mattress and out of rushing flood waters. Elderly survivors were pulled from the water and hoisted onto the roof by nursing home staff and the owners' son through the wind and stinging rain. They were later transported by boat to a nearby school.[16] Those who perished were left behind. As I was told, they were eventually carried out of the facility on doors: there were not enough body bags or stretchers to accommodate those who perished.

Four months later, those who died at St. Rita's were identified and released to their families for burial. The couple who owned this facility faced criminal charges of negligent homicide related to the deaths of thirty-five residents and twenty-four counts of cruelty to the infirm for residents who survived. Their ill-fated decision to shelter in place was thought at the time to be less risky than to move frail residents in a lengthy evacuation. Defense lawyers argued that there was no state or local mandatory evacuation order and that the facility would have been fine had the levee protection system surrounding St. Bernard Parish not failed. Two years later, the owners were acquitted of these charges by a six-member jury in West Feliciana Parish.[17] The empty brick building that was St. Rita's was still standing in 2010–2012 while I was there— a dark and somber reminder of what happened in 2005. The haunting structure of the flooded nursing home was eventually replaced with a new senior living facility that opened in June of 2018. Life goes on—as will be discussed in the final chapter of this volume—yet painful memories undoubtedly remain for Katrina survivors who lost loved ones in the St. Rita's tragedy on August 29, 2005.

*   *   *

One individual who survived the Katrina disaster shared her written story with me. Through journaling in the first year after the storm, Mrs. Lori Hix committed her terrifying ordeal to paper. Doing so helped her frame this experience in a manner that allowed her to put it to rest and go on with her life. Sharing her story is a simple, yet deeply moving gesture that speaks of grace, generosity, and a truly unselfish spirit. Reflecting intellectual honesty and humility, Lori's story conveys in a very real way the essence of the Katrina experience for thousands of south Louisiana coastal residents who sheltered in place. In the paragraphs and chapters that follow, her story is presented in segments to illustrate the sequence of events which began in late August of 2005: from pre-hurricane preparations to the storm's passing through St. Bernard Parish with estimated 120 mile per hour winds and the devastating flooding that followed. She describes this terrifying event from the vantage point of her escape through a bedroom window, being swept down a street in rushing flood waters, clinging for her life to a telephone pole, and eventually making her way to a rooftop.

In painful detail, Mrs. Lori's story as a whole illustrates the frightening and agonizing events that typify the Katrina tragedy: getting to safety; getting out of St. Bernard parish with assistance from the US Coast Guard; being transported by school bus with a US National Guard escort, then by a coach bus; being taken to distant places; and then the long road back to what was left of home. Here is her story (with pseudonyms to protect anonymity).

*   *   *

MRS. LORI'S JOURNAL

Sunday, August 28, 2005

I woke up Sunday to the news that Hurricane Katrina was going to hit close to us. My sister and nieces were evacuating. I thought about the traffic and decided to stay put and since I was staying, my mom decided to stay with me. I knew we could handle the wind so I thought we would be okay. As far as the water I thought maybe some street flooding, but never in my wildest imaginings did I think water like we got. I called [my friend] Flo to see if she wanted to go get some sand bags just in case. We went to the barn by the port and got about 25 bags. When I dropped Flo off, we started unloading some of the bags. After, we went into her house and James was sitting there staring at the TV. He was very nervous since he had been looking at it all morning. We both tried to convince him it would be okay, but it was like he knew.

When I got home, I unloaded my [sand] bags. Me and my mom started to pick things up and put them in the garage and I was trying to put the sand bags in places that I thought might get a little water—like in front of the door to the garage, on the side of the carport where we usually got water when it rained. I put them by the front door since I was thinking street flooding. After we finished we both decided that we better take baths in case we lost electricity later. As the day wore on, we were calm. We ate a light snack played some cards. I think we might have even looked at a movie. I talked to a few people on the phone assuring them that we were okay.

It wasn't until almost dark that I began thinking that maybe I made a very bad judgment call. All of the news people were predicting a huge amount of water, but in my ignorance of water and houses I thought I had a waterproof house. How dumb I feel now. During the night as conditions got worse we played cards sometimes by candle light and sometimes we actually had lights, but we soon got tired. I had just bought a battery operated black and white TV, and we looked at it the whole night. I guess both of us were a little scared to go to sleep. My mom talked to Mrs. Laura across the street to see if all was okay over there. She told them to remember us if they left during the night.

Monday, August 29, 2005 (day 1)

Monday morning I talked to my sister, Peggy, and Bobby telling them that all was okay. I even told Peggy that I would go check on her dogs after the wind died down. I talked to Flo to see how they were faring, and she told me they went to her brother's house on Meraux Lane. She said things were blowing around the yard, but that was all. As I was talking to my sister the second time, I was looking out the window in my utility room at my mom's car and as I was talking to her, part of the roof of the garage flipped over onto the roof of the patio and knocked it down on top of my mom's car. (The kicker about that was we parked her car close in that corner because of Michael's rickety shed that we didn't think would hold up to the wind.)

Not long after hanging up with my sister, things went south. I was walking down the hall when I heard the water in my mom's toilet gurgling and I thought that didn't sound good. My mom was in my bathroom and the water started coming up the floor drain in the utility room. When we met at the door to my room she saw my face and I saw hers at that point we knew something was very wrong. We both went into the kitchen and saw water by the back door. We got a couple of bath towels and put them down to sop up some of the water, but still we didn't have a clue as to what was going on outside. As I was walking to the hall, I happened to look over to the side of the living room only to see water there and I thought, "Gee, how did it get there from the door?"

Kind of still thinking "how did that happen," I looked out the back door to see the water was already one-quarter of the way up the door. I tried to open it, but the pressure had already built up so much I couldn't open. I turned to look at my mom and she was right there. As I realized what was happening I kind of lost it and started to cry that I didn't have flood insurance. Now that I think about it I was still kind of naïve, not once thinking that we were in real trouble for our lives. My mom calmed me down saying that we would handle that later, but right now we had to save ourselves. Lucky for us that my niece's husband left us life jackets as a joke. We quickly put them on got our purses, important papers, picked up shoes and put them on the bed so they wouldn't get wet. I went to one of the windows in my mom's room thinking that we were going to Mr. Tommy and Mrs. Laura's house since they had a boat and they were closer than my nephew, Jeff.

By this time, the water was just under the window sill; by the time I went out the window and turned to help my mom the water was flowing in the house over the sill. Still in our naiveté we still thought we were going across the street, but the current was so strong and the wind was blowing so hard we really didn't have a choice where we were going. We were swept away so fast. My mom was hanging on to me by my neck and I was trying to grab onto anything. The first thing I saw was a van and I tried to get there, but we just went by too fast. I did manage to grab on to a phone pole and we held on, but the water was still rising so fast that we had to keep scooting up the pole. My mom was kind of on top of my shoulders. I had to keep telling her to scoot up. Both of our legs were wrapped around the pole holding on. There were a few times that tree limbs in the water hit my legs and I almost lost my grip. We held on to that pole for about 20 or 30 minutes. We saw the van that I tried to get to float past us, and I was so thankful that God didn't let us grab that van. We were praying so hard for God to help us and not to let us die. (Come to think of it we were praying quite a lot that morning. My mom who is scared of water said later that she had absolutely no fear of going out that window into the water. I can only think that God had a hand in that thankfully.)

I saw a jet ski across the street that I for some reason thought that we could reach. I told my mom that we had to let go. We were so tired and cold from holding on that pole we had to try something. Again thinking that we could do it, we let go and of course we again were swept down the street so fast we didn't have any way to get over there. I tried to keep us close to the house, and once we shot over Margaret Lane I managed to guide us to the corner house and they had a big fence that was still standing and we managed to get over a spot in the fence that was down. We held on the fence until we were high enough to reach the eave of the house. We were a little protected by the fence that was still standing close to the house. Once we grabbed the eave, we held on until the water was high enough to climb onto the roof. While we were holding on I saw all kinds of bugs. I am sure all know of my bug fear. Well let me tell you there was some HUGE ROACHES in this house all looking for someplace dry to go. One of them crawled on my mom. I grabbed it an threw it off her! OH MY GAWD!!!!! You know, now that I think about it, that is the thing that creeps me out the most through all of this. Silly huh?

It wasn't long before we were able to climb on the roof; by this time the wind had died down and the water wasn't rising as fast. We were up and out of the water, but we were shivering cold; that was when it hit me that if the water continued to rise we would have a lot of company on this roof. All kinds of bugs, mice, and rats: it gave us a different kind of chill. Thankfully two houses down was the Melerine's two-story house, and they stood like us. John and his friend, Bill, had a boat. They spotted us and came to get us off that roof. At the Melerine's house they had two sheets tied together and we had to climb up that makeshift rope into the house. My mom crawled up with no problems, but I was so tired and cold I just couldn't get my feet to scoot me up. Bill came and picked me up to help me get into the house.

John asked if there was anybody else on our street that needed help. I immediately thought of our neighbors, Mr. Tommy, Mrs. Laura, Adam, and my nephew, Jeff. I told them about the Smiths, but said that Jeff had his own boat. They went to check on the Smiths and overshot them to end up by Jeff's house. He was on the roof with no boat. John and Bill was in Jeff's boat. I am not sure how it ended up on Margaret Lane but I am so thankful to God that it did. So Jeff was rescued with his own boat. On the way back from Jeff's they pass the Smiths, and Mr. Tommy said that the wind was still too strong and if they could come back after it died down, but to not leave them there over night. Close to dark they went back to get them and Mr. Tommy and Mrs. Laura made it into the window okay, but when Adam came in he fell and landed on his knees. Luckily he was okay.

On one of John's boat rescues, he fell into something in the water. He cut his leg pretty bad. It was bleeding and of course nobody had anything to put on it for infection. Then I remembered that I had a tube of Neosporin in my water-logged purse. I guess it was a good thing that I took my purse. Although all my important papers, cell phone, and wallet fell out of my purse when I went out the window. We stood with the Melerine's that night and ate fold-over jelly sandwiches. The water finally stopped rising, but it wasn't going down either.

SUMMARY

In this chapter, the history, culture, and lifestyles of two coastal communities in south Louisiana were considered. The exclusive focus on St. Bernard and Plaquemines Parishes was intentional as this region was the catchment area for a two-year research project on post-disaster resilience (see Appendix A). These coastal communities constitute the existence in which knowledge for this volume was gained. Interviews with current and former residents of these two coastal parishes gave rise to the six principles of healing that serve as the central theme of this volume.

The journal entries presented here and in Chapters 3 and 4 offer a unique glimpse into the Katrina disaster and the terrible suffering that followed. They capture in a very real and relatable way the ordeal that many survivors experienced. A careful read of Mrs. Lori's journal also reveals several lifespan developmental themes that warrant brief mention, from pre-hurricane preparations that are routine for coastal community residents (sandbags placed strategically to protect property from street flooding) to the devotion among family members and friends looking out for each other in advance of the storm (sharing news reports, offering life jackets). One might also sense the protective bonds of parental attachment coming into play before Katrina made landfall (Lori's mother did not want her to ride out the storm alone). Attachments, being bidirectional in nature, work both ways—parent to child as well as child to parent. With a fierce survival instinct, Lori kept herself and her seventy-seven-year-old mother alive as they were swept away in the rapid current, nearly drowning together on August 29, 2005.

Disaster resilience is also evident in the journal entries here. As an example, consider the intergenerational loyalty among life-long friends and neighbors who survived the first day after Katrina's landfall. Further evidence of disaster resilience will be revealed in Chapters 3 and 4 as Lori's journal entries chronicle their long and arduous trek to safety. The Katrina disaster and its historic flooding brought unprecedented destruction and loss of life, with suffering and pain for some survivors that is still evident at the time of this writing. The focus in the next two chapters is broadened to cover the first days after Katrina made landfall. These chapters cover the perilous circumstances of total destruction across the Gulf Coast in the wake of the worst natural disaster in US history at that time.

NOTES

1. Dietrich Bonhoeffer, *I Want to Live These Days with You: A Year of Daily Devotions* (Louisville: Westminster John Knox Press, 2007), ix.
2. US Census Bureau, *QuickFacts St. Bernard Parish, Louisiana*, 2017, retrieved on August 8, 2018, from https://www.census.gov/quickfacts/fact/map/stbernardparishlouisiana,US/PST045217
3. Katie E. Cherry, Loren D. Marks, Rachel Adamek, and Bethany A. Lyon, "Younger and Older Coastal Fishers Face Catastrophic Loss After Hurricane Katrina," in *Traumatic Stress and Long-Term Recovery: Coping with Disasters and Other Negative Life Events*, ed. Katie E. Cherry (New York: Springer International Publishing Switzerland, 2015), 327–348.
4. Samantha Perez, *The Isleños of Louisiana: On the Water's Edge* (Charleston: The History Press, 2011).
5. Ken Wells, *The Good Pirates of the Forgotten Bayous* (New Haven, CT: Yale University Press, 2008).
6. Cecile Jones Robin, *Remedies and Lost Secrets of St. Bernard's Isleños* (St. Bernard Village: Los Isleños Heritage and Cultural Society, 2000).
7. US Census Bureau, *QuickFacts Plaquemines Parish, Louisiana*, 2017, retrieved on August 8, 2018, https://www.census.gov/quickfacts/fact/map/plaqueminesparishlouisiana,stbernardparishlouisiana,US#viewtop
8. Carolyn E. Ware, "Croatians in Southeast Louisiana: An Overview," *Louisiana Folklore Miscellany* 11 (1996): 67–85.
9. Carolyn E. Ware, "Neda Jurisich, Eva Vujnovich, and Mary Jane Munsterman Tesvich: Three Generations of Croatian-American Women in Louisiana" in *Louisiana Women: Their Lives and Times, Vol. 2*, eds. Shannon Frystak and Mary Farmer-Kaiser (Athens: University of Georgia Press, 2016), 149–172.
10. Milos M. Vujnovich, *Yugoslavs in Louisiana* (Gretna: Pelican Publishing Company, 1974).
11. Carolyn E. Ware, "Louisiana's Croatian American Society: A Case Study in Adaptation and Resilience," *Louisiana Folklore Miscellany* 23 (2013): 97–128.

12. Jerald Horst and Glenda Horst, *The Louisiana Seafood Bible: Oysters* (Gretna: Pelican Publishing Company, 2011).
13. Katie E. Cherry, Priscilla D. Allen, and Sandro Galea, "Older Adults and Natural Disasters: Lessons Learned from Hurricanes Katrina and Rita," in *Crisis and Disaster Counseling: Lessons Learned from Hurricane Katrina and Other Disasters*, ed. Priscilla Dass-Brailsford (Thousand Oaks, CA: Sage, 2010), 115–130.
14. Keith Spera, "Katrina's Lives Lost: The Life Stories Behind the Storm Victims," *New Orleans Times-Picayune*, October 20, 2005.
15. Sally E. Viada, interview by Katie E. Cherry, Denham Springs, LA (2018, June 20 and July 5).
16. Mikel Schaefer, *Lost in Katrina* (Gretna: Pelican Publishing Company, 2007).
17. Emily Kern, "Manganos Not Guilty," *Baton Rouge the Advocate*, September 8, 2007.

CHAPTER 3

✧

Total Destruction

By the end of the day on August 29, 2005, Katrina had passed through the coastal towns and communities of south Louisiana. An estimated sixteen feet of water covered most of Chalmette and the nearby suburban neighborhoods of St. Bernard Parish. Vehicles parked in the streets were completely under water. Rooftops of one-story, single-family dwellings were barely visible. Farther "down the road" in the southeastern portion of the parish, the estimates of water ranged between twenty and thirty feet from Katrina's storm surge.

In south Plaquemines Parish, an estimated thirty feet of water demolished the land. Built to sustain hurricane-force winds, the water tower in the town of Buras had crashed to the ground. Nothing was left of homes and fishing camps except for a handful of pilings sticking up from the ground in some places. Docks were splintered or destroyed completely. Boats were swept ashore in a tangled mess of rigging and broken masts. For coastal residents who had thirty feet of water on their property, all that was left were timbers scattered widely, cement steps leading to nowhere, and a mountain of endlessly thick and tangled marsh grass. Where one's property ended and another's began was difficult, if not impossible, to discern. The coastal communities were simply gone.

I have tried many times to imagine what so much water could look like. I have also wondered where everything went. Blown out to the Gulf of Mexico perhaps, yet some participants talked about finding assorted treasures, such as the living room recliner blown far away and lodged in a neighbor's tree and a wedding dress wrapped tightly around some lumber that used to be a doorframe. Other items were partially buried in the mud—a clay slow-cooker, some silverware, and even a handful of glass marbles were recovered in time, cleaned off, and kept in a kitchen jar in a home in Yscloskey.

From the spring of 2010 to the fall of 2012, I made scores of trips to the catchment area for research visits with Katrina survivors. They recounted their experiences in vivid detail. They also shared personal photographs in a gracious effort to help my students and me understand what happened to their homes and communities. Driving along the two-lane highway that leads to the fishing communities of southeastern St. Bernard, I pass by what I have termed the "dead tree forest." Magnificent live oak trees, yet now they are completely bare. Reaching skyward, the huge trunks with thick, stately branches speak to the longevity of these trees. Some are spotted with tattered veils of dead Spanish moss that move gently in the breeze. A forest of driftwood, these trees died owing to the intrusion of saltwater accelerated by the 2005 flooding. Haunting, yet beautiful in their own right, dead tree forest stands today as nature's monument, a stark reminder of Katrina's deadly aftermath. As I look closely, I also notice the patches of green near the bottom of these magnificent trees: some new growth among the ghostly dead trees, some signs of life as nature recovers its own. I know this one, yet there are many dead tree forests throughout the remote areas of southeastern St. Bernard and Plaquemines Parishes.

IN THE WAKE OF KATRINA: DEATH AND LIFE

As the years since 2005 have passed, I have heard many different descriptions and terms used to characterize this epic storm and its devastation, yet one stands out for me. A unique blend of secular and sacred, this characterization did not come from a priest or church official. Rather, Arthur Bronson was a fireman. He was a first responder who experienced Katrina's wrath directly, placing his life on the line to save others. Sitting at Art's kitchen table on a bright and sunny afternoon in 2011, we worked through the research surveys. This is what he said: "People claim that this [Katrina] was an act of God. It was not an act of God. It was an act of the Devil, and God protected His stuff."

This courageous man, along with his colleagues in the St. Bernard Fire Department, spent countless hours and long days in search-and-rescue operations, which are documented in detail elsewhere.[1] They saved the lives of people who were trapped in attics or stranded on rooftops. Sadly, many individuals did not survive the flooding. Rescue for those who perished meant recovery and spray painting the all too familiar symbol of death—the X code[2]—on the outside of houses to indicate bodies for the Disaster Mortuary Operational Response Team (DMORT) to collect.

"Katrina was an act of the Devil," Art Bronson said. For those who experienced this soul-crushing disaster directly, yes, certainly such suffering could be ascribed to a malevolent, supernatural force. I suspect that many US Gulf Coast residents could relate to this view, nodding in solemn agreement. From across the nation, the countless others who witnessed the pain and anguish brought on by the storm from afar might agree with this assessment, too.

Art also said, "And God protected his stuff." Now this *is* an interesting remark—different, but very curious, inviting contemplation.

When this first responder voiced his characterization of Katrina, I knew instantly what he meant. His belief statement, "God protected His stuff," resonated with other information that I had received from current and former coastal residents who lost homes in Katrina. Other participants had spoken about sacred objects found intact after the flood water receded. One could interpret the discovery of personally meaningful objects intact, though mired in the mud, as a chance phenomenon or fluke. For the more spiritually minded reader, one might also say these objects were *heavenly symbols of hope* amid the devastation.

Thinking about sacred objects unscathed by the forces of wind and water calls to mind the research interview I had with an elderly couple who did not evacuate from their home in St. Bernard before Katrina. On the morning of August 29, 2005, this Catholic deacon and his wife had gone to their church in Chalmette to secure the communion hosts and sacramental records because the priest was out of the country at the time of the storm.[3] In Roman Catholic tradition, the Eucharistic Host is the Body and Blood of Jesus Christ and is kept in an ornate and delicate vessel known as the *monstrance*. The couple had carefully placed the host in two plastic bags and secured the records when they noticed water coming into the church. Seeing the floodwater pushing against the side of the church's glass windows, they strapped on life jackets that they had brought for safety. They promised each other that if one of them didn't make it, the survivor would not feel guilty or responsible for other's death. Within minutes, raging floodwater burst into the sanctuary with such force that the pews were swept off the floor and swirled in a spiral pattern as the water continued to rise. As they scrambled to get out of a window, the communion host fell out of the deacon's hands. Struggling to hold on to the edge of the building and each other, they scrambled to the roof. There, this brave couple rode out the storm, sheltered behind a large air conditioner unit. They were eventually rescued by a neighbor in his boat. Later on, the monstrance and sacramental records were retrieved from the mud-filled church, legible and intact. As the deacon and his wife explained to me during a research interview, the communion host was found in perfect form—it was not even wet.

* * *

Returning to my visit with Art Bronson in the spring of 2011, he joked lightly that he only had nine inches of water—in his attic! We chuckled briefly over the clever description of his Katrina-flooded home. Inches of water in the attic meant at least sixteen or more feet of floodwater had breached his house, a funny way to think about the fate of one's home after Katrina. Art's joke is another example of dark humor as a coping strategy deployed in the tragic days of Katrina's immediate aftermath, as will be discussed in Chapter 6.

In his line of work with the St. Bernard Fire Department, Art explained that humor was a necessity—a helpful tool to get through the grim circumstances and unpleasant discoveries that firefighters sometimes encounter. I thought about the implications of "nine inches of water in the attic" (i.e., intense flooding, structural damage due to wind and water). The home and its contents would surely have been destroyed. Would anything be salvageable? I thought probably not.

Art told me what he saw when he first looked into his livingroom after the floodwaters had receded. Everything was in disarray, smashed and demolished—*except the statue of St. Joseph.* I was amazed at what I heard. Incredibly, his St. Joseph statue was still standing in its original place on a rolling table. The entertainment center had fallen on top of the rolling table, but St. Joseph stood upright in the midst of it.

As he described the perfectly positioned St. Joseph statue, I remembered what Patsy Shapiro had told me concerning a similar statue in her daughter's house that survived Katrina's intense flooding. Patsy recounted her daughter's discovery when she surveyed her ruined house for the first time.

> It was the St. Joseph statue, about three to three and a half inches high, in [my daughter's] house that stayed on the mantle five feet above the floor covered in nine to ten feet of water. A medicine bottle of Holy Water from Easter also stayed on the mantle. All other things, such as her wedding goblets, pictures in frames and other mementos were washed away and ended up on the ground in the three feet of muck that covered the floors of the house.

Art Bronson and Patsy Shapiro were not the only ones who spontaneously referenced meaningful objects they had found unscathed despite Katrina's fury. Another participant described four crosses perfectly positioned inside her flood-ravaged home—one cross hung above the front door, and others were located above each of her three children's bedroom doors. Despite the forceful intrusion of water that crashed into this family's home, swirled to the rafters, and eventually subsided, these four crosses remained perfectly fixed in their original locations. Seemingly untouched, each cross hung prominently above its door in the original spot, as they had been since the day she had first placed them there.

Farther "down the road," in southeastern St. Bernard, Doogie Robin spoke of his two fiberglass statues, St. Joseph and the Blessed Mother, along with a round, mahogany family seal. A precious heirloom, this seal was hand-carved in Honduras, bearing the family name along the top and the names of his four sons who run the oyster and seafood business along the bottom. These items were originally located in his office at the oyster shucking facility. Katrina's thirty-foot tidal surge had demolished this building. All contents were lost except for these three items, which were blown miles away. The statues and the seal were recovered in time and returned to him, perfectly intact.

In south Plaquemines Parish where Hurricane Katrina made landfall, nothing was left of Neta Valen's camp except for five of the original pilings *and her statue of the Blessed Virgin Mary*. Her son was the first to return to the family property. He found this statue in its original location outside of the camp, although lying on her side with some minor damage. He also recovered a treasured family heirloom, his mother's orange cake plate, partially submerged in the mud yet perfectly intact. As Neta explained to me, this precious plate was *a sign from God that she had something to return to.*

I thought about this special cake plate that had belonged to Neta's Croatian grandmother, an heirloom passed along from a different generation, a different place in time. Clearly, this was not an ordinary plate for Neta. Rich with emotional significance and personal meaning, this plate could be described as a symbol of faith—*the knowledge of things unseen and the hope of things to come* (see Chapter 5). Within the first year after the storm, her son rebuilt the family camp, incorporating the surviving pilings to preserve a part of the original structure, amply reinforced with new timber to provide a strong and secure foundation.

Illustration of Death and Life: "The Scent of Roses"

Nicholas "Duke" Collins, who worked in law enforcement, and his deputy were patrolling in the days after the storm. They came to St. Bernard Church, a quaint Catholic church in the southeastern part of the parish. This beautiful little church with stained glass windows and a rustic, black iron fence sits on one side of a two-lane road. On the other side of the road is the Terre-Aux-Boeufs Cemetery, a historic graveyard with tombs dating back to the 1700s. According to the placard at the entrance, this St. Bernard Catholic Cemetery was established in 1787 by Canary Islanders after Pierre Philippe Marigny parceled this land under the regime of Governor Bernardo de Gálvez (for whom the parish and St. Bernard Church were named). The first individual buried in this cemetery was Joseph Mesa on June 6, 1787.

With unspeakable force, Hurricane Katrina and its terrible flooding had desecrated this hallowed ground. Tombs were unearthed and caskets were floating amid the debris. The deputies rounded up the floating caskets and secured them to the iron fence surrounding the church.

The deputy worked his way through the storm debris into the church. In awe, he called to his partner, "Come here, Duke, you have got to see this." As the two men walked into the sanctuary, they were overwhelmed by a powerful, floral sent. In the midst of death and destruction, this beautiful church that withstood Katrina's fury was filled with a magnificent floral scent. As Duke spoke of this event five years later, I thought about miracles. I also thought about divine signs of hope that defy the boundaries of human reason and logic.

"The scent of roses," Duke Collins said, "is the symbol of a Catholic Saint." Intrigued, I looked into this when I got back to the university. What I learned is that the floral scent is the symbol of Saint Thérèse of Lisieux, a French Carmelite nun who was born in 1873 and died of tuberculosis at age twenty-four. Known by Catholics as "the little flower of Jesus," the experience of "a shower of roses" is thought to indicate her heavenly influence on earth.[4]

Thinking about roses reminded me of a participant who evacuated to Tomahawk, Wisconsin. Still in Wisconsin in February of 2006, her neighbor in St. Bernard relayed an intriguing property update. This participant's red rose bush was blooming brightly where nothing else was growing—another sign of life amid death. I thought about this solitary rose bush blooming brilliantly despite the environmental circumstances, which included at least three feet of mud in some places. I also considered what Duke Collins had told me concerning the unmistakable floral scent in the little church encircled by death and destruction in 2005. Both reports struck me as highly consistent with the fireman's unique characterization and his belief statement that "this [Katrina] was an act of the Devil and God protected his stuff." And a scriptural reference came to mind: "O death, where is thy sting? O grave, where is thy victory?" (KJV: 1 Corinthians 15:55).

THE NEXT FOUR DAYS: A LIVING NIGHTMARE

The days after Hurricane Katrina made landfall were insufferable, with no relief in sight. People were stranded after the intense flooding without adequate drinking water, food, and medical supplies. Trapped on the roof of a shopping center complex, one participant watched a bag of Cheetos float by, a tantalizing snack yet out of reach from his perch on the roof. His parents told me that they hoped their son had not seen the dead body that had floated by earlier in the day. Sadly, so many people who had survived Katrina's wind drowned in the terrible flooding after the levee breaches. At this point, however, the focus was on survival. Local firemen had launched door-to-door search-and-rescue operations, chronicled in greater detail elsewhere.[5] As I was told, the first outside assistants to arrive in St. Bernard Parish were Canadian.

> They had some people from Canada that came down, emergency response people from Canada. They were the first ones that got in the parish. I think [elected official] always says the Canadian Mounties. They weren't Mounties, but they were Canadians.

Stranded storm victims were brought by boat to St. Bernard and Chalmette High Schools, the designated shelters of last resort in the hours before Hurricane Katrina made landfall. School administrators and first responders worked tirelessly through the night to care for them. Recall my 2010 conversation with Mr. Wayne Warner, the principal of Chalmette High School (see Preface). As he explained, his school, which had begun as a temporary shelter for a few dozen people, turned into a staging area brimming beyond capacity with more than 300 people by the end of the week. In April of 2010, when he and I met, I had no idea that Mr. Warner had risked his own safety to save the lives of hundreds of people right there in his school. I was deeply moved by the valuable insights that Principal Warner gave me when we met on that April afternoon in 2010. My respect for the Katrina experience enlarged greatly, as did my gratitude for the information conveyed. *Respect* and *gratitude*, two fundamentally different psychological constructs, yet aligned side by side. Both have a role to play in the healing process in the years after a catastrophic, life-changing environmental event, as will be discussed in Chapter 6.

Looking back to late August of 2005, it is impossible to grasp how dire this situation was at Chalmette High School unless one had experienced it directly. Lori Hix and her mother did, as chronicled in her journal. I return now to her story. Recall that they had spent the first night after the storm with neighbors in a flooded neighborhood on the second floor in a two-story home. The next day, they headed to Chalmette High School, as did hundreds of other storm victims.

MRS. LORI'S JOURNAL

Tuesday, August 30, 2005 (day 2)

The house on the highway side of the house had a gas leak and during the night, depending what way the breeze was blowing at the time, the gas smell got so strong. My mom got sick. Mr. Tommy went to the bathroom and he was little off balance and fell in the tub. I think the gas was getting to him also. I guess we were thankful we had a bathroom. No water or plumbing, but we did have a bucket to dip out the second floor window for water to flush. I realized that morning that we couldn't stay there because of the smell, and the Smiths needed medicine.

So when they suggested that since they didn't have medical supplies that some had to leave, I volunteered us to go first. I guess we could have stayed with my nephew Jeff, but I figured that the Smiths needed us more. We got into the boat for the ride to Chalmette High School. Going down Margaret Lane we saw a lot of gas leaks, houses that were floating, we had to watch for low-hanging wires and trees that might be under water. It was really amazing how much damage water can do to a brick house. When we got to Judge Perez Drive and started down the street, it hit us all over again. I saw the tops of vans and trucks, saying a prayer that there was nobody in those cars. The devastation was overwhelming. We saw people in boats trying to get into K-mart, but the water was too high to fit under the hanging, but there was all kind of things floating in the water you could just reach down and grab things as you passed by. It was the same way by Rite-Aid.

When we got to Chalmette High School the water was still kind of high. We pulled up and there were people on top of the breezeways, there were people hanging out the windows of the second floor. The gym door had a truck back up to the double doors, and they had a little passage on either side of the truck, but the back of the truck was loaded with people. They pulled the boat as close as they could and we got out. I rounded up my group and we went into the Gym. That was when it really hit me what we were up against. It was sobering sight. The Gym was nasty. The entryway still had water or sewer . . . I am not really sure what it was. People had their pets there, that is what made me think it was the potty room for the pets since there really was no dry land outside for them to go do their business. After we walked carefully through the entry and went into the Gym. People were everywhere. There was a little medical place for bandages and diapers for the baby. The Smiths stood in line to see if they had any of their meds that they needed.

Me and mom went to find a seat, but as we were walking to sit I saw a line forming to get something to drink. They were handing out little cups of punch and chips. The Smiths joined us, and after we went to find five seats together. On the way we saw all kinds of animals. Birds, dogs, cats, pigs it seemed like it was a regular zoo. We just sat and watched the people. After watching for a while I realized that the only food that was coming in was stuff that was looted, but we were thankful for it.

When a boat came back from looting, the police would line people up across the Gym and they would pass all to the stage where they were holding the food and drinks. We walked to the front doors a few times since we couldn't just sit all the time. That is when I realized that the reason people were sitting on the back of that truck is because the boats coming back came there, and they got first pick and also as much as they wanted.

Sometimes after the boat left they would hand out things to us sitting. They would do it by sections, and the people would get up and stand in line to get a bottle of water and maybe a bag of chips. Sometimes it would be a cup of punch; it would just depend on what the boat would bring in and how much it would bring. I guess it was a good thing that we didn't get too much to drink since the bathroom left a lot to be desired. There were two rooms on the side of the stage that they had cut a barrel in half and you had to hover over the top with no light (unless you had a flashlight . . . which we didn't). Of course since there were no lights it was hard to judge. It smelled so bad that I held until I couldn't do it anymore, and then there was a line all the time and of course no toilet paper. Of course the way my luck was going I happened to get my period that afternoon. I had to go to the medical stand and ask if they had any pads. Thankfully they happened to have two. I used one then and the other the next morning. It was horrible.

Late on the afternoon that we got to CHS, the police wanted us to walk in water almost chest deep to St. Bernard Highway, which he said was dry and we would be picked up and taken to the ferry. At the ferry they would take us to the Naval Air Base . . . you know hot water, air condition all the comforts of home. I didn't think it would be a good idea since it was getting dark, the water was still so deep and there was things swimming around. Well we stood there that night and it got very dark. I stayed sitting after the sun went down, but Mr. Tommy had to keep going to the bathroom. One time he fell so hard on his butt he fell back and banged his head on the hardwood gym floor. I am sure he slipped on water. We heard all kinds of noises, but you really couldn't see anything.

The Water Department Building is located on St. Bernard Highway, not far from Chalmette High School. Water Board employees were out in boats trying to carry out their job assignments, but they stopped to participate in rescues along the way. One Water Board employee, Joseph Lopez, reflected on what he saw in those first days.

They had people that were living there [in Chalmette High School], but they were under really bad conditions. We were a little bit luckier because we had generators. And so we were able to have our fans and things like that. But, we knew that they had people, people had died in the school, in the gym. And they had just placed them on the side.

One of the things that I remember . . . it just stays in my mind . . . We had to live on the second floor [of the Water Board Building]. If we went out onto the balcony, it was a roof. And I would watch people. It was amazing how many people stayed in the parish; and they were coming from down the road . . . they were just carrying the little things that they had, whatever they salvaged. And they would carry them in buggies [grocery carts] and whatever they could find.

And it was just endless people coming and passing by, and I know that there was supposed to be like a staging area where they were sending them to, I think Baton Rouge . . . amazing how many people stayed back. It's just watching these people go by, and go by, and go by, for days and days and days.

Five miles away, in the city of New Orleans, outside disaster relief assistance had arrived. At the city's hospitals, patients were airlifted out by helicopter. At Methodist Hospital in New Orleans East, Ray Martin helped load patients into a helicopter in the sweltering heat. As he was securing the lift for an elderly woman in a wheelchair, she reached lovingly toward him. With the edge of the hospital sheet that covered her, she gently mopped his sweaty forehead. A simple gesture during an intense moment, he remembered it vividly so many years later. Gratitude, despite her circumstances in a terrifying and chaotic situation, has left a lasting and meaningful impression (see Chapter 6).

Returning to the written record of these harrowing days, Mrs. Lori, her Mom, and neighbors spent the second night of their ordeal at Chalmette High School, a shelter of last resort that would close on Thursday, September 1, 2005. I return to her story, picking up where we left off.

Wednesday, August 31, 2005 (day 3)

When the sun came up and we saw what the Gym had turned into, I thought we couldn't stay there any longer. I guess a bunch of people left that night and they left their pets. There was animal pee and poop all over the gym floor. My mom being a school cafeteria worker got upset when she saw that someone had taken the milk box and put their pets in there to roll them around in. I thought, "Do you see the Gym? How can you get upset with that when everything else looks like this?"

When the police came back and said we should all start to walk to St. Bernard Highway to the Parish Jail, I talked to Mr. Tommy and said I thought we should leave. It was just going to get nastier and nastier here. He didn't think he could make it, but I told him there really was no rush since we didn't have anything else to do that day. We would walk and rest, then walk a little more and rest. He agreed and we start out the door. I went first and told them all to stay close to the school since it was higher ground than the sidewalk (which you couldn't see anyway). The water by this time was about thigh high against the school. I would walk a little and look back to make sure they were okay. I told them to follow as close to my steps as possible. If I ran across something that might cause problems, I would tell them to be careful here. At one time I looked back and there were about 10 people following.

Once we got to Palmisano Blvd., it got a little easier. We just went slow. The closer we got to the highway the lower the water was. About three-quarters of the way up Palmisano, the street was dry. We rested right there by Rebel Park on the back of someone's trailer. We got to the library and rested on their planters. We sat there for a while. Once we rested in the shade enough, we started down the highway. We just kept walking slow. We made it to Gallo's veggie stand, and we decided to sit there a spell only to discover RED ANTS!! We brushed them off as best as we could and started to walk again. As we were leaving there some people were walking back down to CHS and they said the jail was real bad. People were getting sick and dying. I said that as bad as CHS was getting people were going to start dying there also.

We knew what we left, but I wasn't taking anybody's word on what was ahead. When we got to Paris Road, we sat on the bench for a spell. After resting again we continued down to the jail. At the jail they waved us on and said to go to the ferry landing. Mr. Tommy said he didn't think he could make it. I said I would pull him up that darn ramp if I had to, but we were going to continue. Once we got up the levy we sat on the railings with a bunch of other people waiting, for what we weren't sure. I took a walk down the ramp and it was pretty badly tangled, and I thought what kind of boat would be able to dock there much less pick us up. There was barges on top of the levees. It was kind of amazing to see those big barges washed ashore like blocks. As I was looking around, I saw the Coast Guard boats coming. They were a welcome sight. I went back to the beginning of the ramp and told them we had to get up and start walking down to the river edge, that boats were coming to get us.

The Coast Guard guys were so nice. They helped us on board and gave us seats (I guess it was for our safety also). They brought us to the battlefield and left us off the boat. We were told by a police officer to walk along the levy to the port. When we got there they led us to this big warehouse that had pallets of plywood stacked up to the ceiling in some places. They had pallets set out with four rows across then a big walkway then four more rows. It was a big warehouse with all of these pallets set up. There were people there before us and every group grabbed a pallet. Me and my mom thought we would be smart and get a pallet next to the big walkway that went down the center of the warehouse. The Smiths took two on the next row. Well that night the birds would pass over and poop on us. My mom got pooped on a few times. That whole day there were helicopters landing and taking off. I guess they were dropping off supplies.

Thursday, September 1, 2005 (day 4)

The bathroom situation didn't improve by much. Remember I was still on my period and had no more pads. I asked the medical station they had set up and all they had was a big bandage that I managed to cut in strips. It worked out okay . . . well it was better than nothing.

There were five port-a-lets and one handicap. The first day there, I had to ask the policeman for toilet paper, and he handed me four little squares. I asked him if he was kidding? That wasn't even enough to wipe the seat. He said they had to ration it since when they got there the toilet paper was plentiful, but people started to take rolls of it and since then they are handing it out four squares at a time. I made the best of it.

After that first day, they had to tape two of the port-a-lets shut. Well later the first day they started to hand out MREs [Meals Ready to Eat]. They did it in sections also, and you better not get caught going when it wasn't your section's turn. One night one of the many policemen came looking for someone that went when it wasn't his turn. They were shouting and saying that he was stealing from us and all that stuff. I guess someone pointed him out, and he had a little baby in his arms and they took the baby out of his arms, handcuffed him, and took him off someplace. That was when I realized that the power of the moment had gone to the police officer's head or it could have been just the stress of the situation. I am sure they were very worried about their families and their welfare, and I guess they were kind of aggravated that they had to be there taking care of us because we didn't follow the evacuation orders.

At first they were handing out one MRE to every two people, but that worked out for me and my mom since neither one of us was very hungry. I guess we were just too overwhelmed by the whole thing to be very hungry. When they started to give us each a MRE, we were just so used to eating one that we were still splitting one between the two of us and saving parts out of the other one and giving some to Mr. Tommy; since he was a man we figured that he would probably need more to eat than one MRE.

The second night at the port, Adam had a seizure and the medics came to help; they ended up taking Mrs. Laura and Adam off to the hospital at the jail, but they left Mr. Tommy. We really felt for him since he couldn't find out anything about how his son, Adam, was doing, if he was okay, where they were. We started to kind of take care of him now that his wife, Mrs. Laura, wasn't around. The food we saved from our MREs we would give him some of it, but not until the next morning since we really didn't know how long it would be before we would get another one. Also they had powdered drinks in the meal, but they would only give you one water, and you need part of it to heat up your meal and the other part was for drinking. It was so hot, but once in a while there would be a breeze blowing through.

When we would get up we would check on Mr. Tommy and see if he wanted something to eat, then me and mom would go for a walk around the outside of the building and sit by the water, but that got hot also. I saw a friend from work there, and she happened to have a whole set up on the side of the warehouse. She had soap, she had toilet paper, and a battery-operated TV. She let us look at the TV for a little while, but it was everything about New Orleans and it was kind of depressing. After about five minutes of watching I just turned it off and waited until Rachel came back to get it. Now that I think about it, she didn't offer any of her toilet paper. Hmmmm . . . what kind of friend is that?

We met some other people we knew, and thankfully Mr. Tommy ran into a friend from his Kaiser [Aluminum] days that they kind of stuck together. That was very good since he kept Mr. Tommy busy. One of the guys that was at the Nunez's house that Monday, but he split up and went to another house down the street since the Nunez house was overflowing. I can't remember his name, but him and his wife were very nice people. He had a guy that would leave and get him supplies. One time he told us that he had some soap if we wanted to use it when it rained. I took a little piece, but it never did really rain after that. He did ask us if we wanted to go to the river when he took his wife so we can get a little clean, but we never did get to do that either.

So here we were in our funk for days and no way to clean. Each day someone would pass by and say today was the day we were leaving, but it never did really happen. At one time there was guards all around the building we were in because we were told that inmates broke into Jackson Barracks and stole a bunch of guns and they didn't want anyone to know we were there. When the army arrived, the meals got a little regular and the water hand-outs were more frequent. It just seemed like we were settling in.

GETTING OUT OF THE CITY: "IT WAS HARDER THAN YOU THINK"

For hundreds of thousands of people, the difficulty encountered in getting out of the flooded communities and towns of the greater New Orleans area defies imagination. Toward the end of the week, medically challenged patients were airlifted by Black Hawk helicopter from the dock in Chalmette, Louisiana. Elizabeth Abadie was a nurse who was there on the dock, tending to injuries among survivors, having only the medical supplies that firemen and other first responders could salvage for her. She described a heart-rending scene: there on the dock was an elderly gentleman who was recovering from a recent surgery, with his wife by his side. It was his turn to be airlifted to a nearby hospital, but the medics were only taking the gravely ill, four at a time, by helicopter to the nearest medical facility. He refused to leave his wife behind, a decision which meant a certain death for him in the insufferable August heat. Sensing another needless tragedy about to unfold, Elizabeth stepped in. This brave nurse looked at the medically compromised man and called for transport, adding that the woman near him (his wife) "was suffering from chest pains and shortness of breath" and she must be taken to the nearest medical facility, too. The medics loaded the man and his wife onto the helicopter together and off they went. Through Elizabeth's compassion for this elderly couple and her unstoppable tenacity in a disaster situation, six were airlifted to safely instead of four on that day.

On the outskirts of the city, a bridge was used as a staging area where Katrina evacuees waited for transportation to shelters in distant locations, including Houston, Texas, and in Oklahoma. One participant who had voluntarily used his own private boat to rescue people stranded on rooftops in his flooded St. Bernard neighborhood spoke of his ordeal. After turning over his boat to first responders who carried out search-and-rescue missions that week, he set forth on foot, walking a great distance to the bridge. With no shoes and badly blistered feet, he finally made it to the bridge. There, he was treated harshly, like a criminal, he said.

Ashley Bowen spoke of her nightmarish experience on the bridge. She was a healthcare provider with proper credentials. Based on her medical background, she was asked to prioritize storm victims for transport. Unwilling to leave medically compromised victims by the wayside to die of exposure in the heat, she refused. In a strange turn of events, her medical background evolved from a burden to a blessing as her credentials enabled her to secure transport for herself and her family to Baton Rouge by ambulance. In time, the bridge was emptied as thousands of Katrina evacuees were taken by bus to shelters in different cities and states.

Returning to Mrs. Lori's story, she and her mother and friends spent the first four nights in St. Bernard. On the fifth day, they left the parish, first by ferry, then by school bus with a National Guard escort. They were finally transferred to a coach bus and driven to Oklahoma. I pick up her story at the warehouse by the port in St. Bernard.

Friday, September 2, 2005 (day 5)

On Friday morning, they finally said it was official: we were leaving for some place better. Of course at that time they said we were going to Baton Rouge. I got with Rachel, whose daughter lived there in Baton Rouge. She gave me her cell phone number, and I gave her my sister's cell number. She was going to have her daughter pick us up wherever it was we landed in Baton Rouge. Of course it didn't quite work out that way. We were in different sections, and when they loaded us on the ferries they did it, of course, by sections. One section at a time would line up outside, and there were ferries there to take us to safety. Once the ferry was full, they would leave and another would pull up. We didn't know where they were going, but I figured it had to be better than where we were. When it was our turn, I knew Rachel was no place that I saw. Still thinking we were on our way to Baton Rouge, I figured it still might work out. It was finally our turn to get on the ferry. It was air conditioned . . . it was heaven! By this time, there were five to our group. Me, mom, Mr. Tommy, his friend Mr. Ray, and Mrs. Lucy; we all sat together, and we made sure we stood together. I didn't want to lose anybody else.

When we got off the ferry at Algiers Point, there were school buses there ready to take us someplace. We were searched before we were able to get on the bus. They asked if we had any kind of weapons. My mom had a fingernail clipper in her purse; she didn't think it was a big deal, but they took it from her anyway. The five of us got on a Handicap School bus with a National Guard riding with us. He advised us he was locked and loaded. Us not being familiar with military terms asked him what that meant. He said he had a bullet in the chamber and was ready to shoot. The bus we were on had to back up and go a different route. The National Guard man told us, if he told us to duck, we were to do it and not ask any questions.

Once we were clear of that neighborhood, he told us that we had to go a different route because on the next block over from where we got on the bus, there was a shootout. After that we never questioned his orders. From the ferry landing we went to the Airport in Kenner. As we were sitting in the bus in the heat, we saw people arriving at the airport on Jefferson Parish buses and they were going into the building. We pulled up like we were going to get off the bus, but we sat there for hours. We were told that we could not get off the bus to go to the bathroom. He had a bucket with a blanket to hold up around us if we had to go. After some of the people started to fuss, he talked to his other people and they decided they would let us go a few at a time. Some of the older men went, but we had to stay on the bus until they came back. When they finally came back, we were told that they could not let anyone else leave the bus, and if we got off the bus they would not let us back on. One of the younger guys started to get a little crazy, and he demanded to get off the bus. They let him off, but when he tried to leave the airport Kenner police wouldn't let them leave and made him get back on the bus. They let him and his mom back, on which was good, but we all wanted to get out and go for a walk. We sat there till dusk. They had MREs, and we choose two different meals since I knew Mr. Tommy had to eat something. I gave him part of one, and we ate part of one, saving the snacks until later.

When we finally left the Airport, we sat on the overpass for a while right there on airline highway. They had someone shooting at the buses, and we were told. We had to stay in the buses again. Which I guess made sense. The bus driver and guard man was very nice. When it finally was clear, they let us get out for a short time in groups. The driver let us try to use her cell phone, but it wouldn't work. From there we went to the weigh station on I-10 in LaPlace and sat there for a few hours. It was so hot. At that stop we could not get off the bus at all. It was very dark out and a bunch of buses was sitting there in line. We inched closer to someplace, a little at a time during those hours. In the middle of the night, we were put on Coach buses. AC AT LEAST!!! The seats were a little more comfortable. We only had MREs that we took from the School Bus. I gave Mr. Tommy a little more to eat, and we snacked a little.

Saturday, September 3, 2005 (day 6)

On the coach buses, we were alone (no guards), so I guess it was safe at this time. Of course we did have a State Police escort. At first we heard we were going to Baton Rouge, but we passed that. Then we were told we were going to Shreveport. I thought, "Thank God." Mr. Tommy had relatives there. We stopped someplace outside of Shreveport, and they let us get off the bus and go in the little store to go potty and buy something if we had money. We went to the potty and got to actually use soap and running water!! When we got out of the bathroom, the line was so long and there was no phone to call anyone. We stood outside until we were told to get back on the bus. Once we were all there, we pulled out. I remember we kept asking the driver where we were going, but he said he didn't know. I finally slept for a little while. I woke up right before we got in Waskom, Texas. We had driven right through Shreveport. When we got off the bus at Waskom, it was around 8:30 P.M. They had hot dogs, chips, cookies, water, and other drinks for us provided by the people in Waskom.

I immediately saw the pay phone, so I dug around for some change and called my sister's cell phone, but for some reason it didn't ring. Thank God I didn't lose my money. The next call I made was to Bobby at work. When I heard his voice I kind of started to cry. I told him where we were and at that time we were told we were going to the Mesquite Convention Center. I asked him to come and get us. I also asked him to call my sister and let her know we were okay. After I hung up with him thinking our nightmare was almost over, we ate, then got back on the buses and headed to Mesquite. When we pulled into the parking lot, they told us we could not get off the buses. Thinking we were almost rescued, I was okay. I kept looking around for his [Bobby's] little blue truck, but I never did see it.

Once we sat there for a while some people started to get up and leave the buses to go over to the little market to buy some fresh fruit. I got off the bus and walked around looking for Bobby, but I never could find him. We were sitting there for a while now, and I started to get nervous. Mrs. Lucy's cell phone worked some of the time at this point and I asked to use it to call Bobby's work to see if he left, if maybe they knew where he was. I talked to the guy that took his place and he said Bobby was looking for us, but if he called back he would get more info. I talked to my sister and my niece, Monica, by this time and they had talked to Bobby also. Well Bobby never did make it to the convention center . . . which turned out to not be a convention center since Mesquite didn't have a convention center. The bus driver that took us all that way refused to drive further like they all wanted him to. So we had to sit there waiting for another driver. Nobody could tell us where we were going yet.

When we left Mesquite, I lost it and started to cry and cry. After I managed to get it together again I finally found out where we were going and of course I got it confused. We were told we were going to Bragg. I thought it was Fort Bragg, you know the army base. When I got that message to Bobby, he looked it up and found out that Fort Bragg was in California. He didn't think we were going that far. We ended up in Bragg, Oklahoma, at Fort Gruber. We got there in the middle of the night after riding for two days and not stopping to eat.

When we got there, they processed us by the bus load. Since it was so late we got snacks to eat. We had to register, and they assigned us to beds and barracks. They had one barracks for older women, one for young women, one for older men, and one for younger men. They were going to put my mom in one barracks and me in another, but they made an exception since we were together. So me, mom, and Mrs. Lucy were in one barracks and Mr. Tommy and Mr. Ray in another one. When we got in ours, we were the only ones there, so we quickly went to take a shower at last. Unfortunately it was an open shower, but at this time it really didn't matter—we had already been through so much. We stripped down washed ourselves and finally our hair. We tried to wash our clothes, but once we did that we had nothing to wear. We wrapped sheets around us and put our clothes close to the fan to try to dry them before we went to sleep. Once our underwear was close to being dry, we put them back on and slept in our undies.

RECEIVING CITIES AND THE NEWLY HOMELESS

Across the nation, many cities and towns became receiving communities, a destination for evacuees and not necessarily by choice. Baton Rouge, the capital of the state of Louisiana, became a temporary home for an estimated 250,000 people who had been displaced by Katrina. The influx of evacuees during this time had a dramatic impact on the demographics of this area, making Baton Rouge the largest city in the state.[6]

In a suburban community northeast of Baton Rouge, a local physician spoke of his experience in the first days after Katrina made landfall. Coming home one afternoon, he noticed a school bus filled with evacuees headed to where he wasn't sure. Concerned that some of the passengers might need medical attention, he followed the bus to its destination, North Park in Denham Springs, Louisiana. As he soon discovered, there were no medical provisions at the park. On his own initiative, this dedicated physician set up a medical triage. With no assistance from the Red Cross or from a national pharmaceutical chain, he persuaded a local family-owned pharmacy to donate medical supplies to meet the pressing needs. He stayed at this shelter for days, providing assistance and appropriate medical referrals. This physician's story is one of many that illustrate the dire circumstances evacuees faced in Katrina's immediate aftermath as the infrastructure of the region was strained beyond capacity.

By this time, medical personnel and other professionals from all over the country hurried to storm-ravaged areas across the US Gulf Coast to provide disaster relief assistance. Laypersons and professionals alike went to extraordinary lengths in 2005 to make a difference in the lives of Katrina survivors who had suddenly lost everything. Faith-based communities and local churches made substantial contributions to the relief effort, sheltering storm victims and disaster relief personnel. As I was told, church-based disaster relief efforts lasted up to two years in some communities. Local universities and schools also quickly stepped in, providing direct care and hands-on assistance with the relief effort. Louisiana State University (LSU) in Baton Rouge established the largest disaster field hospital in US history in the Pete Maravich Assembly Center, which was used to treat and triage more than 20,000 people. LSU also housed a Special Needs Shelter by converting the Maddox Fieldhouse on campus to a temporary, 800-bed field nursing home.[7]

In the fall of 2005, jobs changed in focus and intensity for people in the receiving cities who had been indirectly affected by Katrina. As a professional with Catholic Charities in Baton Rouge, Todd Hamilton explained to me, "my job changed." With a staggering case load that demanded long hours, he went through nine pairs of Rockport shoes after the storm. He reflected on those long and difficult days, recalling an evening when he had a stunning realization: this will shorten my life, but there is more to do—our work isn't finished. In his own words, Todd said,

> Driving home one night, mid-December [of 2005], I was casually talking to the full moon that illuminated the highway after another day of disaster response, nearly four months post-Katrina. I was startled to remember that I had held a similar conversation with the moon on the way in to work that morning. Winter days may be short, but work days were still really long. Remembering I'd just marked a birthday, a realization came so sharply I said out loud, "this is going to affect my life expectancy." And a reply came back, almost audibly, "it's not your life." That was the moment I realized my life didn't belong to me. I was serving a cause, and the work that was so demanding, day in and day out, was a gift.

As Todd spoke, I marveled at his dedication and willingness to go the extra miles for strangers in the wake of a catastrophic natural disaster. I also found myself in agreement with his flash of insight. Katrina has taken a toll on peoples' lives. A different toll for the indirectly affected, but a toll nonetheless for caring and concerned individuals who contributed in their own way to the disaster relief effort. A toll over the long term for professionals whose jobs are now inextricably linked to disaster response and preparedness, forever altered as a result of 2005 Hurricane Katrina.

*   *   *

A stark realization dawned on many evacuees from the coastal parishes of south Louisiana during Katrina's immediate aftermath: I have no home and no place to live. The experience of being suddenly homeless after Katrina was a terrible jolt. I remember a conversation I had with a gentleman whose family owned a local marina. A multigenerational family business owner and marina operator, Ronald Campbell was an individual for whom water was a way of life (see Chapter 2). Ronald referenced homelessness in his response to an open-ended question concerning the challenges he faced after the storm. In his own words (emphasis added), he recalled,

> Well, the first struggle was finding somewhere to live. And then there was getting back to work . . . after I accomplished those two, then I was getting back into the [marina] business and rebuilding those buildings. And then once people started fishing again and we just knew everything was going to be okay, you know? *The biggest thing was getting, having a place to live. My biggest fear is being homeless.* That's a major setback when you, when you realize you lose everything.

The disaster experience left residents across the US Gulf Coast standing in long lines at designated shelters to register for disaster relief assistance. For independent, self-sufficient people, having to ask for help was beyond the realm of their personal experience to that point. Perhaps it was the first time in a family's history that they were in the position of seeking public assistance. To illustrate, consider the words of Kim Nunez, a dedicated and hard-working professional employed by the state of Louisiana in the local office for needy families and children. She said, "There were some very challenging times. For me, doing the kind of work that I do, it was very tough for me to be on the other side." Kim spoke of the first days after Katrina, using the term "fog," an apt metaphor for capturing the uncertainty of this time and the difficulty of seeing the next steps ahead. She said,

I think the thing I wanted to say most is that for the first few days after, a good five days after [Katrina made landfall], it was just a fog. You know, there wasn't really any coping at that point. It was just . . . I can't believe everything I owned, that my daughter and I owned, fits in the trunk of my car! [laughs] You know, that was kind of like just a fog, so I don't know that there was any coping at that time. It was probably a sense of shock, "What am I going to do?"

As she spoke, I wondered how it would feel for a professional with a career dedicated to serving others in need to suddenly become a "client" in need herself? In her own words, Kim explained,

I was not a good receiver. I'm a much better giver than I am a receiver. So it was very, very difficult for me to be in the food stamp line and the Red Cross line. . . . And all I kept saying to myself while I was in line was, "I'm glad that I can look back and say I treated everybody with dignity that I handled [my clients in St. Bernard] because this is . . . boy, when you were on the other side of it, it is not a good place to be at all. I had a very difficult time . . . not the lines so much as the process, that I had to do that.

Patsy Shapiro spoke of her experience in a shelter in Texas. As her daughter was filling out the intake forms for her family, she paused to think about one of the questions, "What is your monthly income?" As she began to calculate the answer, the shelter worker asked her where she was from. She answered, "St. Bernard," to which the worker replied, "You have lost everything and you do not have a job anymore—leave it blank." At that point, the painful realization of the reality of their situation struck full force, and the daughter began to cry. In time, this family was taken under the wing of a wealthy family from Texas who cared for them.

Across the US Gulf Coast, Katrina's immediate aftermath brought unparalleled challenges for individuals, families, and communities. For those directly affected by the hurricane and horrendous flooding after the levee breaches in New Orleans, the first challenges were meeting basic needs, almost primal in nature. *Where do we stay? Where do we eat, shower, and sleep?* Participants spoke of many different temporary accommodations: living in other people's homes, apartments, and college dormitory rooms. Some stayed in hotels and motels. Others stayed in campers, RV parks, and Red Cross shelters. Faith-based communities provided shelters in church gymnasiums and classrooms. One family spoke of staying in an air-conditioned storage unit for a few weeks. A shelter, yes, but beyond what most would consider a habitable home environment for a family to live.

Among the basic needs to be met during this time were locating displaced loved ones. *Where is my family, and when will I see them again?* Battling dark thoughts of destruction and possible death, many people spent endless hours consumed with worry and searching online for parents, siblings, and children. Sometimes families were joyfully reunited weeks and months later, like Pam Mones and her family who had evacuated to Panama City, Florida. She and her mother told us how they found an uncle at the New Orleans Airport in Kenner (a staging area) after having seen him on television. In her own words:

> Somebody saw them on TV or something they were showing people at the place and one of his sons or somebody said, "That is Uncle Bubba [pseudonym]," as we call him. And they said, "You are crazy." And they said, "No, look—that is him! He is at the airport." So they called [his son in Houma, Louisiana] and some kind of way got in touch with him and they went and picked him up.

In other cases, knowledge of family members' whereabouts was devastating. One elderly participant had begged her adult son to evacuate with her and his sister from their home in St. Bernard. As she waited on a crowded school bus in a parking lot staging area the day before Hurricane Katrina hit, she knew he would not leave his girlfriend who chose to stay in St. Bernard. Several days later, at a shelter in Oklahoma, she told her daughter she had a very bad feeling about her son. Call it mother's intuition maybe, but somehow, she knew. Hours later, FEMA contacted her with the news that her son had drowned in St. Bernard. They asked her what she wanted to do with his remains. Sitting in a lonely evacuation shelter among dozens of strangers, she accepted FEMA's offer to have her son cremated.

*   *   *

Returning to Mrs. Lori's story, they spent the sixth night of their ordeal at the shelter in Fort Gruber, Oklahoma. On the seventh day, Mr. Tommy's daughter Lisa came for them. They left the shelter with her, soon to be welcomed and cared for by Lisa's extended family in north Louisiana. Here we pick up her story at the shelter.

Sunday, September 4, 2005 (day 7)

The next morning, I went looking for a phone to call and see if someone could come and get us. Bobby was going to rent a van to come and get my bunch, but he talked to my sister who was in contact with Lisa, Mr. Tommy's daughter, and they were on their way from

Shreveport. Mrs. Lucy was in contact with her daughter, and Mr. Ray was in contact with his son, so they were taken care of. It was just the three of us left. We spent much of the day walking around checking things out when Lisa arrived later that day.

I was never so happy to see someone as I was at that time. I hugged and hugged her; my mom didn't want to let her go. Once we finally got it together, I brought her to Mr. Tommy's barracks and pointed him out. They had a happy reunion. Mr. Tommy wouldn't leave until he found Mr. Ray, but I told him remember he contacted his son and was making arrangements.

It was a good thing we were leaving the time we were because a bunch of the New Orleans' rough people were arriving all the time. We drove all afternoon and into the night. Once we arrived at Mr. Tommy cousin's house, she brought me and my mom to her mother's house for us to stay there. Mrs. Annette was very nice to us after we arrived in the middle of the night. Her and my mom talked while I took a shower first, but I realized I had no clean undies or clothes, but she has night shirts for us to wear. Once we both finished taking a bath and settling in, Mrs. Annette finally went to bed.

Monday, September 5, 2005 (day 8)

The next morning, her daughter JoAnne came to see what we needed in way of clothes and sizes so she could go shopping. Mrs. Annette, her husband, JoAnne, and her two girls were our angels. They day we arrived happened to be Labor Day and thankfully things were open. We both got clothes and clean underwear. That afternoon we all went to Mrs. Laura's relative's house for good old red beans and rice. It was delicious.

I finally got in touch with my work, and they wanted to fly me to Houston, but I didn't know what to do with my mom. I had planned to go with her to Stone Mountain in Alabama, then go to see Bobby, but my work had other plans for me. I had to put my mom on a plane to Alabama. After she left, I had a little time before my plane left. JoAnne was a huge help. I was very upset that I had to leave my mom. My employer threatened me that if I didn't go to Houston, I wouldn't have a job anymore and since I knew what home looked like, I figured that I did have that left at least, so off to Houston I went. We worked out of the Houston office for about two months.

SUMMARY

Disaster stressors have been comprehensive for individuals and families across the US Gulf Coast region.[8,9] Those directly affected by the 2005

Hurricanes Katrina and Rita lost homes and property and possibly witnessed death. They were separated from their families due to job circumstances or because of having taken different evacuation routes. There was little direct communication at this time owing to loss of telephone service in storm-ravaged areas.

The influx of hundreds of thousands of evacuees into nearby cities and neighboring states was a disruptive event at many levels. The sudden population growth in neighboring cities and towns brought different challenges for local residents—from infrastructure issues, such as dramatically altered traffic patterns, to changes in school and work environments. Many people who were indirectly affected by Katrina made sacrifices, both personal and professional, to accommodate displaced family and friends who needed assistance or a place to stay. Katrina-related circumstances also led to permanent changes in jobs and the focus of professional responsibilities for some people. While storm-related challenges may have been less comprehensive for indirectly affected people by comparison, they are part of the Katrina story that could be overlooked or easily forgotten.

In the years since 2005, there have been many changes for those people impacted by Hurricanes Katrina and Rita—from the means of making a living to access to healthcare, businesses and services, schools and daycare centers. Sadly, Katrina recovery may not be fully complete at the time of this writing for the many people who directly experienced this epic storm and its historic flooding, which crippled New Orleans. Long-term threats to the cultural heritage of the region are becoming more apparent over time as well.[10] Even leisure activities are different now. The repercussions for routines of daily living were profound in 2005 and can still be felt today, as will be discussed more fully in the last chapter of this volume.

NOTES

1. Michelle Mahl Buuck, *Firestorm: Hurricane Katrina and the St. Bernard Fire Department* (Xlibris Corporation, 2007).
2. Dorothy Moye, "The X-Codes: A Post-Katrina Postscript," *Southern Spaces* (August 26, 2009), accessed July 24, 2018, http://www.southernspaces.org/2009/x-codes-post-katrina-postscript#content_top
3. Peter Finney, Jr., "Prince of Peace Deacon Tells Harrowing Tale of Survival," *Clarion Herald Archive* (August 26, 2006), 9.
4. John Beevers, *The Autobiography of St. Thérèse of Lisieux: The Story of a Soul* (New York: Doubleday, 1957).
5. Buuck, *Firestorm.*
6. Katie E. Cherry, Priscilla D. Allen, and Sandro Galea, "Older Adults and Natural Disasters: Lessons Learned from Hurricanes Katrina and Rita," in *Crisis and*

Disaster Counseling: Lessons Learned from Hurricane Katrina and Other Disasters, ed. Priscilla Dass-Brailsford (Thousand Oaks, CA: Sage, 2010), 115–130.

7. Renee Bacher, Teresa Devlin, Kristine Calongne, Joshua Duplechain, and Stephanie Pertuit, *LSU in the Eye of the Storm* (Baton Rouge: Louisiana State University Press, 2005).

8. Katie E. Cherry, ed., *Lifespan Perspectives on Natural Disasters: Coping with Katrina, Rita and Other Storms* (New York: Springer Science+Business Media, 2009).

9. Ryan P. Kilmer, Virginia Gil-Rivas, Richard G. Tedeschi, and Lawrence G. Calhoun, eds., *Helping Families and Communities Recover from Disaster: Lessons Learned from Hurricane Katrina and Its Aftermath* (Washington, DC: American Psychological Association, 2010).

10. Katie E. Cherry, Loren D. Marks, Rachel Adamek, and Bethany A. Lyon, "Younger and Older Coastal Fishers Face Catastrophic Loss After Hurricane Katrina," in *Traumatic Stress and Long-Term Recovery: Coping with Disasters and Other Negative Life Events,* ed. Katie E. Cherry (New York: Springer International Publishing Switzerland, 2015), 327–348.

CHAPTER 4

✑

Picking Up the Pieces

Trauma invites us to learn about our strength, endurance, and hope after it visits.
—Elisabeth Kübler-Ross

People will remember seeing photographs of the historic flooding after Katrina. On the covers of magazines and the front pages of newspapers across the nation were haunting pictures of survivors peering out from attics and stranded on rooftops surrounded by water. Other images captured the desperation of survivors walking slowly through the deep and fetid water, sometimes up to their chests. Chaos, mayhem, and rampant looting in the streets of New Orleans were among Katrina's iconic images, too.

Readers may recall what the flooded city of New Orleans looked like in the days after Katrina. Listening to newscasts and investigative reports at the time also taught us about the unprecedented levee breaches and failures that caused the horrific flooding on August 29, 2005. An equally important question, however, is one that has received far less media attention by comparison: Just how did the city officials in charge get all that water out of the city?

Throughout the course of conducting research interviews, I had the unique opportunity to talk with several professionals who worked for the Water Board in St. Bernard Parish. In conversations with a gentleman who oversaw the Lake Borgne Basin Levee District during the storm, I learned something about the horrendous challenges they faced. Now a regional director, Robert Turner spoke candidly about what was involved in getting the water out of his flooded levee district. In his own words:

Our organization was charged with providing flood protection for St. Bernard Parish. After we were flooded, we had a job to do, as far as getting water out of the parish, and then re-establishing some type of a perimeter protection in case something else happened to come along. . . . I relied heavily on the employees that worked for the district who I thought were heroes in this thing. I mean, they did just a superb job, a very selfless job, of doing whatever it was that I asked them to do.

The regional director explained in broad brush strokes about the control sectors in the bayou district that had sustained structural damage. As I learned, a fifty-six-foot wide sector gate, which was underwater at the time, would have to be opened manually. Bob reflected,

Well . . . you can't get the water out until you can open up this gate to let that water flow out into Lake Borgne, and the marsh and all that . . . we tried to find that structure the night after the storm. The storm hit actually on Monday morning.

Monday during the day when we first got out, we spent most of our time in rescue operations. And then, my big challenge was to get this sector gate open to try and get some water out into the lake system. So we made it down to our shop, got our boat, with one person, met up with a couple of our other people in the district, and went out to try to find the structure.

And, everything was flooded. Houses were floating, there were no landmarks anymore. And this eight-mile trek out to where the structure was . . . because we had spent so much time on the rescue stuff, it got dark on us by the time we were going out to the structure. And so, we couldn't find it . . . one of the guys that was with us swore up and down, still to this day swears up and down, that we went right over the top of it when we were out on Lake Borgne.

The next day, next morning, at first light, we went out there to open the structure up, and of course, the water was still very high on the inside. It was low on the outside. And it had washed out on one of the ends, so you couldn't even get the boat on one side because the current was so strong, we were afraid it would swoop somebody out to sea. So, we went to the other side . . . and they have to release a brake in order to manually operate this gate. I had to have one of my employees dive down in this pit, feel his way around, release the brake, and we were able to open the gate. That's just one example. I mean, we had people [levee district employees, pump station operators] that really did extraordinary things in an effort to relieve some of the flooding that had occurred in that parish.

Conditions were deteriorating rapidly in St. Bernard during the first days after Katrina made landfall. With no sign of outside assistance in sight, the local sheriff deputized select essential personnel and other heroic citizens. Following an impromptu swearing in, these persons were given a badge and firearm and instructed to uphold order in a manner befitting of the office of deputy. The regional director of the levee district was among those appointed to serve as a "deputy." Bob reflected on that experience.

And I remember . . . the second day . . . some people had [a concern about] being able to keep themselves safe. The St. Bernard Parish Sheriff's Department, [the] Sheriff himself, had commandeered these big old front-end loaders from Murphy's sand pit, and built this huge wall of cars along the parish line. I mean, stacked them up one on top of the other . . . to separate the lower ninth ward from St. Bernard Parish, and have only little controlled access points to come into the parish.

I think it was the second day or third day, I walked into the EOC [command center], and one of the deputies said, "Okay raise your hand." And I said, "For what?" And he said, "Okay, now you're a deputy." And he handed me a .357, Smith and Wesson, and a box of hollow point bullets . . . I said, "Well, where is the holster?" "Well, we don't have a holster." And all I had was a pair of [donated] camo pants because my clothes had rotted away, and they were about two inches too big in the waist, so this heavy firearm kept dragging my pants down around my knees . . . I had to find a piece of rope to tie them up! [Laughs]

You know, luckily I didn't have to fire the gun the whole time that I had it, and the only time I ever considered firing it was that Thursday when we really didn't have anything to eat for those few days. And there was a deer sitting on top of a car near one of the pump stations, and I was contemplating, "Hmm, should I take this deer? And have something for the guys to eat?" And I said, "Oh, I'll let it go one more day." And sure enough we got the MREs [Meals Ready to Eat].

*   *   *

Toward the end of the week, the US National Guard arrived in St. Bernard with supplies and disaster relief assistance. At that time, a directive was issued for citizens to clear the area. Although essential personnel and parish officials remained in place for many months, residents were ushered out of the parish by the end of the week. Doogie Robin, a commercial fisher who rode out Katrina on his sixty-five-foot shrimping boat moored in the Violet Canal, told us:

After the storm passed, we stood there in the Violet Canal for six days on our boats, and then after the six days, they made us get out. I wind up in Baton

Rouge in one of our deer camps. . . . And I spent there six months before I got a little trailer from FEMA [Federal Emergency Management Agency]. . . . When I came back, they put the little trailer down here from FEMA. It was a nice little trailer, a little push-out.

A cruise ship was brought to the industrial dock in St. Bernard that served as headquarters for some essential personnel and disaster relief assistance workers. The Red Cross established a disaster relief center where tents were set up in a parking lot with food, supplies, and donations. One participant who owned and operated a local bar spoke of a beer company that sent him bottled water and ice to distribute. His bar, one of the very first establishments to open after the storm, became a community distribution center where he gave away ice, bottled water, and food.

ESSENTIAL PERSONNEL WORKING BEHIND THE SCENES

During the fall of 2005, checkpoints were set up to restrict access to St. Bernard Parish. At first, only those with a Homeland Security Access pass were allowed to enter the parish. The essential personnel at that time were local law enforcement officers, elected officials, and employees with the Water Board and Levee District. As I learned in conversations with Bob Turner, the executive director of the levee district in St. Bernard, levee district employees had nowhere to stay at first. In his own words:

So, the first three weeks, we made make-shift shelters at the drainage pumping stations, and lived there with our employees. Out of eight drainage pumping stations, we had three that were destroyed basically, so we had access to five of those stations. We split up into the groups into five [with twenty-four people across five different groups]. We had post-guards at night, we had to take turns sleeping at night because of, at least in the first three or four days, because all the animals were just like us. They were trying to get out of the water, so they'd run to habitate with us in the pump stations.

So we'd have to have somebody stay awake and keep the animals away from the people that were sleeping. . . . It was dogs. It was nutria, muskrat, hogs, skunks, all the regular vermin that you think of, plus the domesticated animals, because many people had left their pets behind. So you had dogs and cats, and things like that.

Actually some of the dogs acted like watch dogs for us. . . . We learned early on that if we were nice to the dogs that came up, and fed them, they would keep the other animals off the pump station for us, you know, barking.

Joseph Lopez, an employee at the Water Board, described those first weeks with limited communication: no telephone land lines and severely limited cell phone signals. Here is what he said:

> We were there. . . . Before I was able to leave and see my family, any one of my kids, I want to say, it was at least four to six weeks . . . Just being able to talk to them on the cell phone, it was the only time, in the evening where we got a little reception. It was so frustrating, because sometimes we would get reception and sometimes we wouldn't . . . and we had a limited amount of cell phones, and we were trying to share as many as we could.
>
> And finally, I believe the parish got us a phone, but everybody was on that phone. Luckily, I had mine that I was able to salvage, my phone. But we would get out on the highest part of the roof. I used to climb a ladder even higher to be able to get reception. And it was so exciting to be able to hear from my kids. And they would tell me how they were living.

Joseph told us about working in the parish under desperate conditions. Daily life after Katrina was a challenge with no amenities—no electricity, no running water, and no plumbing. Living in a storm-ravaged area called for creativity and resourcefulness. Joseph continued:

> Like I said, every day, it was something new. . . . We would work as much as we could, and then the guys we had, a certain crew would go out. . . . It's amazing how enterprising people can be. We salvaged two washers and two dryers from Wal-Mart. They were high up. And they used to have to take a boat to get there. And we brought them back to where we were, and we hooked them up, and we washed our clothes and things like that. We set up a shower outside because we had this big ole, it's called a clarifier. It's a big, big giant tank where we had our reservoir of clean water.
>
> We set up this shower, and . . . we had this little pump and we hooked it up, and the water would come up the top, and we all took showers out there. We were able to get clean, you know.
>
> We used to go out in the field, and we were full of mud . . . so we were able to get clean. And we were also able to use that reservoir to clean our clothes. . . . It was scary . . . trying to get clean, trying to stay clean. Um, and then, just the things that we needed, shampoo, soap, toothpaste, things like that. . . . It took a while before we started getting supplies. We had to go out there and, I'm ashamed to say, but we had to go to these stores and take what we needed. It's embarrassing, but we . . . we had to do it. We weren't taking anything that was not necessary. We just took what we needed.

Water Board employees worked tirelessly around the clock to restore water service to the parish by October of 2005. Dave Brubaker, who also worked for the Water Board, explained:

> My work duties and all the people that worked for us completely changed, whether you were in upper management or not, and everybody was out in the field. That lasted at least six to eight months. We had about 100 people that worked with the Water Department, and we were only able to retain about thirty to thirty-five of them afterwards . . . we didn't have as many people back, so our main job was repairs and getting the water system up and working properly, testing everything. . . . We had regulations we had to follow before we could open areas for drinking water so it wasn't a situation where you could just turn the system on and, "Okay, now we have water."

As he explained, there were sixty locations throughout St. Bernard Parish that had to be tested for water safety after Katrina. Dave told us:

> They required us to test all the same locations [that were tested before Katrina], and it had to pass the bacteria test before we were allowed to open up an area. So we had to shut down the system, the water mains, the main shutoff valves in all of the different areas. You might be able to isolate, say, a three- or four-square-mile area, and once we got the water system going and we were ready to open up an area, we sent water to that system.
>
> Then we had to go and check every home in that area to make sure that water wasn't leaking out of the houses, and, if it was, we had to shut the meters down or shut the water off to the house. . . . We actually had the National Guard and Army and the Marines come and help us with that.

Later on, during the fall of 2005, FEMA trailers were provided for essential personnel in a camplike situation. Joseph Lopez, an employee with the Water Board, told us what it was like when the FEMA trailers arrived. In his own words, Joseph explained:

> We started hearing rumors that they were going to get the trailers for us. We had no idea what these trailers looked like, what they were, whatever; but, we started working in this area where we would work, and we started cleaning up and just setting up the pipe, the water, the waste, well everything setting up. And then they started coming in dribs and drabs. Ah, that was so great, it was like, "Wow, finally!" because we were living together. As a group, I like these guys, but I don't want to be with them twenty-four hours a day . . . it's nice to be with them at work, but I want to come home.

So finally when we did get our trailers, and we had the alone time for ourselves, it was emotional. There's got to be something psychological healing, I mean I don't know how to put it in words, but it was so nice to be able to have our trailers, and they designated one trailer for each family. Whoever had children, they could come live with them. So that also helped out. Because my son . . . I believe he was a senior in high school, and taking care of him and making sure that he was okay, and finally when he came back to living with me, was I guess as close as you can get to normalcy.

At this point in the conversation, he asked me if I had ever been in a FEMA trailer, and I told him no, that I had not. Joseph reflected (emphasis added):

We lived in the trailer together . . . they're small, but it was great. *To me, it was a palace.* We had our own little place, so we had to start buying pillows [Laughs]. I don't know how to describe it, buying a new place and you have to buy pillows, you have to buy, even our own clothes because we had no clothes. We were going to places like Target and buying clothes, shoes, small TVs because you can't fit big TVs in there. And it was nice. I finally had something that was mine.

AFTER THE FLOOD WATERS RECEDED

Post-disaster assessment of Katrina's catastrophic damage was an unpleasant reality that coastal residents had to face. After several long weeks, residents were given access to St. Bernard Parish to survey the damage to their homes and property. A valid driver's license to confirm pre-Katrina residence was required for entry into the parish. During the first weeks after the storm, there was no color—everything was gray. There was also a very bad smell. One participant suggested that a museum exhibit, like the sensory exhibits at Epcot in Disney World, is needed to capture the sensory aspect of Katrina's devastation so that others could know what this experience was like for survivors who experienced it directly.

Looking back to the fall of 2005, Kim Nunez spoke of those difficult weeks when residents with valid identification were permitted to return to assess their homes. One day, while she was working outside of her home, sorting through the mud and mess, she noticed a tour bus filled with strangers surveying Katrina's damage. As the tour bus rolled by, she saw these strangers looking at her. She described the feeling of being studied with interest like an animal in a zoo habitat. Surely, this is what zoo animals must feel when tourists file by with their noses pressed tightly against the glass, peering into an animal's enclosure. I wondered how it would feel to be gawked at by strangers while sorting through what was left of my home. Devastation or no devastation, homes are still homes. Homes have meaning—they may be associated with a lifetime of memories for the people who lived there. Respect for what was someone's home is an important element of assessment and post-disaster recovery, as will be discussed in Chapter 6.

As for tour buses, most would agree that assessments in the early phases of disaster are a necessity. From an operations point of view, the US Department of Homeland Security FEMA follows a standard protocol to collect information needed for a disaster declaration, a necessary step for granting federal disaster assistance. From a practical perspective, homeowners also make an assessment and decide whether to relocate permanently or rebuild their ruined homes and resume a coastal lifestyle, albeit under the changed circumstances that constitute a "new normal" (see Chapter 8). Regardless of personal choices and preferences, a certain number of houses and public places, including schools and churches, were razed eventually. Crushed by the undiscerning arm of an industrial-size backhoe, these structures were bulldozed into spiritless piles of splintered timbers and rubble, another casualty of the storm.

Picking Up the Pieces

Residents of Chalmette and the nearby neighborhoods of Meraux and Violet described what they saw when they returned: homes washed off their foundations, thick mud everywhere, with snakes and other denizens of the dark lurking about, both inside and outside of homes. Unfamiliar objects were washed up in their yards or into their houses: one participant spoke of a child's Big Wheel tricycle on the stairs leading to the second floor of her home—whose tricycle it was, she will never know.

Homeowners came to salvage what they could, but they had to leave by nightfall owing to a parish-wide curfew implemented in the fall of 2005. They faced the Herculean task of clearing flooded property and cleaning out mold, ruined furniture and appliances, and other household contents. Participants spoke of the disheartening task of going into their homes and reclaiming what was left during the long weeks after Katrina. Sorting through the wreckage was arduous and painful. "Save what you can" was Jane Tesvich's mantra as she and her husband, John, worked through their mud-filled home, sorting through soiled clothing and mud-caked belongings. John added, "Some things I saved at the time, like socks, because I didn't want to make a decision at that moment. I kept a lot of things

I ended up discarding later because *I didn't want Katrina to take them from me.*"

Participants described their resolve during the cleanup and recovery process using terms which personified Katrina as a wicked and sinister force that took precious things away. To me, it seemed like the determination and sheer grit required to recover property and reestablish the home place was fueled by an almost primal urge to protect oneself from a malevolent being. Or perhaps survivors' recovery efforts were driven by a deep-seated desire to set right that which a menace of nature had laid waste. Recall the first responder, Arthur Bronson, who described Katrina's aftermath in diabolical terms, "Katrina was an act of the Devil" Art said (see Chapter 3). Intellectually, we know that the 2005 Hurricane Katrina was an environmental event: this was a storm and not an evil entity. Yet it is conceivable that survivors may find it easier to think or talk about Katrina's destruction when personified in that way.

Catherine Serpas described the experience of reclaiming her flood-damaged property in St. Bernard in the fall of 2005. She looked at the mess—fallen trees with limbs everywhere among the storm debris. In her own words, Cathy told us:

> The yard was so bad, I asked my husband "how we going to clean this up?" He said, "We got to pick up one stick at a time." So we cleaned it up. We cleaned it up one [stick at a time] . . . of course it was more than sticks. It was like wheelbarrows and [other storm debris]. . . . But we cleaned it up a section at the time. . . . Every day we worked, we worked from sunup to sundown, and I guess the work and knowing that, we were going to get this done. We knew it.
>
> And I think the fact that we had the house to work on . . . we still had something. It wasn't like a lot of people, their house was totally destroyed and they didn't have a house to work on. We constantly . . . worked on our house and that is what helped us to cope with every day . . . our challenges, we just went about every day. Whatever we seen had to get done, we did.

As she spoke, I began to sense the magnitude of the task at hand. After the floodwaters receded, the post-Katrina cleanup process would take months, if not years to complete. A daunting reality to face, I wondered just how survivors were able to overcome dark thoughts and dread and perhaps a paralyzing fear that this cleanup effort would be simply too much to accomplish, more than they could handle? I remembered a conversation with John and Jane Tesvich, a Croatian couple from Plaquemines Parish where Katrina had made landfall. As John explained, the levees were not breached; they were overtopped, which brought the Gulf of Mexico directly into homes and neighborhoods in his community. In conversation about the post-disaster cleanup process, John referenced a Croatian proverb, *Oči su strašljive, a ruke grabljive.* As he explained, this saying from the old country directly translates to "(the) eyes are fearful while hands are grasping." I could appreciate the idea: When all one can see is catastrophic devastation—overwhelming and far too much to take in or process—stop looking (or stop thinking) and start moving, picking up pieces "one stick at a time."

CHALLENGES AND SETBACKS IN ST. BERNARD

Many who returned to this coastal parish applied for and received FEMA trailers, which were set up in their front yards while they restored their homes. As I learned from the research interviews, many participants told us that living in a FEMA trailer was a challenge in itself. A local bank was set up in a trailer, and Small Business Administration (SBA) loans were made available for residents to purchase lumber and supplies to clean up and repair their flood-damaged homes. The priest and parishioners of Our Lady of Prompt Succor Catholic Church in Chalmette held Mass under a tent with donated folding chairs. Commercial fishing boats equipped with kitchens and sleeping areas provided a safe haven for fishers who worked tirelessly to clean out the bayous and salvage ruined boats and equipment.

Chalmette High School (CHS), where hundreds of storm victims were sheltered in those first days, was cleaned and prepared for students. Through the strong leadership, resourcefulness, and tenacity of the Superintendent of the School Board, along with the tireless efforts of the school's principal, Mr. Wayne Warner, and other dedicated administrators and teachers, St. Bernard Unified School (SBUS) was opened in November of 2005. Completing the circle from a vibrant and successful public high school before Katrina to a shelter of last resort, to a dark place of despair and death in the days after Katrina, CHS evolved into SBUS, a beacon of hope for the children and families of this coastal community.

Cleanup and restoration efforts were complicated by many setbacks in the fall of 2005. Several participants spoke of becoming injured during the cleanup process and of having no urgent care clinic available for treatment. One participant received first aid for an injured foot while lying prone on a cot on the CHS football field. Other setbacks included additional environmental events in the fall of 2005. At Murphy Oil USA, a refinery located in St. Bernard proper, a crude oil storage tank was severely damaged by Katrina and the extensive flooding. Approximately 1 million barrels of oil spilled into flooded neighborhoods nearby. Affecting more than 2,000 houses, the Murphy Oil spill was the largest residential oil spill in US history at that time.

Adding to the chaos of those early days was a second major environmental event just four weeks after Katrina: Hurricane Rita struck southwest Louisiana and southeast Texas on September 24, 2005. Also a destructive Category 3 storm, Rita demolished the western side of Louisiana and southeast Texas. Evacuees who had found temporary living arrangements in these geographic areas were uprooted and displaced for a second time, only a month after Katrina. In St. Bernard Parish, Bob Turner, the regional director of the levee district, reflected on the difficulties they faced with Hurricane Rita.

> When I think back on that, some of the obstacles and setbacks that we had . . . obviously [there were] obstacles we couldn't get around very easily. The setback was Rita because, just as we had gotten the parish dried out, pumped out, all of a sudden we got flooded again.

As I learned, Rita reflooded areas in St. Bernard in close proximity to the Mississippi River Gulf of Mexico Outlet (MRGO; see Figure 2.1 in Chapter 2) and contributed to further destruction in lower Plaquemines Parish. The American Red Cross opened new shelters across the state for those displaced by Hurricane Rita, adding to the thousands of shelters already in place for Katrina evacuees. At the time, media coverage was still focused intensely on Hurricane Katrina and the devastation in the city of New Orleans. The disproportionate focus on Katrina has all but eclipsed Rita, a phenomenon that residents have termed "Rita Amnesia."[1]

*   *   *

Returning to Mrs. Lori's personal journal, a narrative which began in Chapter 2, she described her first trip back to St. Bernard after relocating to Houston, Texas, for her job.

MRS. LORI'S JOURNAL

On my first trip back to the parish with Bobby was right after Hurricane Rita passed and it was so weird and sad. There of course was no plumbing so there was port-a-lets lined up on the neutral ground in different places. There was very few people. We went down to the house with me crying on and off as I looked at what had become of my home. When we pulled up in the driveway and got out to start looking around. It was so quiet; no birds, no people. The wind would blow once in a while and there was piece of siding hitting the mailbox and every time I heard it, I jumped.

We put on the protective clothing, boots, and gloves to go in. We pried out the front door, but it was like someone had filled my house with mud and water and shook it up. The task at hand was very overwhelming, but Bobby said to do it little at a time and we could get it done. If it wasn't for him being with me I don't think I could have handled everything.

The Red Cross came around offering us water. We only saw two other people that day. My friend's husband and my nephew. We talked to them for a few minutes; after they left I had to potty, and since there was nothing around I had to go in the back of my neighbor's house. Me being me, I had to take my pants and panties off, but there was nobody around so I felt safe. Bobby rooted around in the mud and muck in my bathroom until he found a bunch of my jewelry. There was a ring that my dad gave my mom and she gave to me. I was so happy when he found that. It was like I had part of my old life back.

Before we left to go back to Houston, I had to go to the cemetery to make sure my dad was where we left him. We checked his gravesite and it was not disturbed. That was a relief. Odd, huh? When we left we went towards Slidell, but the traffic wasn't moving so we decided to go through the city and go back to Houston through Baton Rouge: well that was even worse. It took about five hours to get to Baton Rouge. A trip that normally takes about an hour. We drove all night to get to Houston. Once there we slept for a few hours then Bobby left to go back home.

In late October of 2005, Mrs. Lori came back to St. Bernard Parish and lived with a friend until she received her FEMA trailer. Returning to her story:

My office all went back to the New Orleans office right before October 31st. I lived in a half of a double with one of my very best friends, Flo, for about two months. My mom moved down and lived with us for about two weeks before we got our FEMA camper on December 23. We moved in December 24. It was kind of depressing living in a disaster area and facing it each morning, but we were closer and able to do things in the evenings. I know it was very depressing facing it each evening. There were very few people around and we heard all kinds of strange noises at night. One of the families living down the street said there was wild pigs rooting around at night. So I guess that was what we were hearing.

Bobby arrived on December 31st with his dogs, washer, and rifle. We slept in the camper, but my mom went to visit her sister for a few weeks and it was just me and Bobby. While I was at work, he started to gut the house. On the weekends, I would put my boots on and root through some of the stuff looking for anything salvageable. Bobby found my mom's jewelry. She was so happy when we showed it to her. A lot of it was stuff my dad had given her, and it was nice to see that she still had it since she lost everything else she had of his. We kept working to clean the house out and pull down everything that was still standing. We had to pile it in front of other houses since we had no room in our yard. Once we finished gutting it, me and Bobby used a Steel brush and scrubbed each two by four to get the mold off. Then we sprayed bleach twice. Once that was dried, we sprayed the Termite proof. It all took a very long time with us working each weekend and sometimes in the evening.

We are finally in the house after much trials and tribulation, and it is so nice to have this much room. I guess after all we went through, thank God for the help and various donations we received along the way from all of the many organizations that is down here helping.

THE DISPLACEMENT EXPERIENCE: SURVIVORS SCATTERED IN DIFFERENT CITIES

Over a million US Gulf Coast residents were displaced after the Katrina disaster. Survivors faced many challenges in an uncertain and chaotic post-disaster environment. In the days before Katrina made landfall, coastal residents had evacuated by car, with a few possessions and two to three days of clothing. No one realized that they were leaving their homeland for good, with all their earthly possessions in the back seat of their cars.

A pressing dilemma is where to live when one's home and way of life has been destroyed in a disaster, as discussed throughout this volume and elsewhere.[2] Evacuees stayed in Baton Rouge, among other Louisiana cities, and in different states in temporary situations for months on end.

Circumstances of everyday living were tense and stressful. Day after day, hassles imposed by the storm were mounting: displacement and struggling to live without a home, a job, a daily routine, and separation from family and friends. Gina Buchanan, a former school teacher, explained to me, "You make a list . . . I made a lot of lists during that time [of recovery]." There were actionable items to check off in the series of "to do" lists in the fall of 2005. Priorities that required immediate attention came first. Telephone calls to the insurance company, applications to fill out for disaster relief assistance, along with many other things to do as survivors moved forward into a new post-disaster reality. This teacher also told me that she slept in a shelter with her phone on her neck so she would hear it and awaken if FEMA called while she slept in the night. Seemingly endless paperwork and wrestling with insurance companies over claims were among the many burdens piling up during that time.

Displaced coastal residents faced an exceedingly difficult decision of whether to relocate permanently and start over somewhere else or return to coastal parishes and rebuild homes despite the devastation, hardships, and crippled infrastructure. One environmental reality that coastal residents must face and that factored into the decision-making process is that hurricanes contribute to coastal land loss.

As climatologists will tell you, hurricanes contribute to the erosion of coastlines, a perennial problem in south Louisiana. Sadly, Katrina accelerated the insidious problem of coastal erosion—miles of marshland are now replaced with water as far as the eye can see, allowing the next hurricane to destructively penetrate even further inland. For those in southeastern St. Bernard, the decision to rebuild or not was further complicated by the uncertainty surrounding whether their property would be designated a "green zone." The "green zone" designation refers to land set off-limits as nonhabitable. As a result, utilities and services would not be restored to these areas: there would be no returning to rebuild homes for people who lived there before the storm. Whether or not one's ancestral home-land would become a "green zone" added to the uncertainty. Return and rebuild? Relocate to higher and presumably safer ground? Just move somewhere and figure out a new game plan for life later? Such decisions were heart-rending and quite difficult to make at the time.[3] For some, the "return versus relocate" decision was made for them when their hometowns were declared nonhabitable green zones.

Many factors, interpersonal, economic, and historical, likely influenced the decision to relocate permanently inland versus returning and rebuilding flood-damaged homes.[4,5] Some families solved this dilemma by purchasing a new home within driving distance of their former coastal home. They relocated in a strict sense of this term, yet they returned to the parish to work during the week or participate in social, recreational, and/or civic activities. As I was told, relationships were strained during this time, sometimes to the breaking point, over differences of opinion regarding the relocate or return decision. Sadly, this fundamental question of return or relocate was a deal breaker for some couples. Marriages ended over differences of opinion concerning where to live, yet others said that coming home and picking up the pieces after the storm strengthened relationships, bringing couples and families closer together.

Moving to a New Community

The relocation experience, whether temporary or permanent, was challenging and understandably stressful. Several participants talked about hurtful remarks made by strangers in public places, making them feel out of place and unwelcome. Ashley Bowen shared her frustration with heartless comments made during Katrina's immediate aftermath. She told us

> I have found that some of the comments made right after Katrina and Rita made me sick. Like this one: "If I have to listen to one more Katrina story, I'm going to scream." That person is truly clueless or just plain insensitive to the plight of people who are just trying to put their lives back together one day at a time. I can't tell you how many times when I would start to say something about the struggles we were going through, only to have someone cut me off in the middle of a sentence . . . how sad.

Other stressors included difficulties obtaining medical care. Survivors in different cities had to find new healthcare providers, a nontrivial task during the chaotic times that defined the Katrina experience for many people. There were other obstacles to overcome related to having medical records lost in the flood. From routine activities such as prescriptions to refill to the extreme, like postsurgical care and physical therapy regimens to resume, many survivors were challenged in the healthcare arena.

For displaced families with school-age children, a major challenge in the fall of 2005 was finding a school and getting enrolled. Circumstances were complicated: there were different uniforms, books, and supplies to obtain; curricula to match, where skill levels and age-appropriate grades did not always align; and the nontrivial issue of transportation. Some displaced students were forced to live miles away from their parents, staying with relatives or friends in different cities and seeing their parents on weekends only.

Displaced students in new schools faced multiple stressors on a daily basis. Students accustomed to small class sizes in small-town schools were forced into larger schools with hundreds of classmates. Looking on the bright side, Ralph Grayson told me about landing a role in a school play in Texas. For him, a larger school meant more opportunities that he benefitted from. Another young man spoke of fierce competition in the high school sports program as local students resented displaced students vying for positions on the varsity teams.

One young woman told me about her Katrina experience. They were staying with twenty-nine relatives, and her younger brother looked to her for support. She said he threw up every day because he didn't want to go to his new elementary school. Her experience as a displaced high school student at the time sounded no different. She spoke of a biology teacher who treated the "evacuees" like vermin in her opinion. The kids at this school made fun of her accent, goading her to speak with "Say, cucumber!" "Say, water!" How humiliating. Adding insult to injury, the principal told the students not to talk about water around the evacuees as it might upset them. She summed up her situation simply and articulately with "No one had a clue."

For many displaced students, the angst of adolescence that characterizes the middle school and high school years was intensified by the Katrina experience. I will never forget the conversation I had with Lauren Denley, who was a freshman in high school when Katrina struck. She and her family had evacuated to Tupelo, Mississippi, where they stayed in a hotel at first. Later on, they would be taken in by a family who gave them a cabin to live in during their displacement. Lauren told me about the daily stressors she faced while trying to fit in at a new school in a different state. She tried to find clothes at a Red Cross donation center that would fit in with what the kids wore at her new school. The local students were unkind. They asked her, "Why are you wearing that shirt that doesn't match?" And she said, "Because it is the only one I have." They dressed up at this school, so she found donated pumps that did not quite fit. She walked across campus for a Katrina relief luncheon in shoes that hurt her feet.

As a part of the research interview, I asked Lauren, "What kinds of things did you do to establish a new daily routine?" At first, she spoke of going to school in St. Bernard before and after Katrina.

> Hmm . . . I guess I just, I woke up, went to school, came home, did homework and went to sleep. My routine never really changed from before Katrina to after Katrina, except for the time that I was in Mississippi. When I came back down here [to St. Bernard], it was pretty much the same because I was in high school. [There] wasn't really too much else to do . . . except for go to school. And when I was in Mississippi, that was the only time that my routine was completely messed up, because I was trying to get out of going to school, because I hated it at Tupelo.

Lauren went on to describe her daily routine, which included a very creative strategy for getting out of going to the school in Mississippi. In her own words:

> When I was in Tupelo, I would wake up, go downstairs [in the hotel], and they had the big, I guess it was the continental breakfast that the hotels give out, they

have for free. So I'd go downstairs, and I'd make myself like five waffles because they took a while to cook, so I'd make five of them just so that I could sit there and say that I had to cook my waffles . . . and I wouldn't eat them all, I'd just make them all to take up time, and then I'd go sit there and eat like one waffle and a little bowl of grits and then by the time I was done, I'd go outside and be like, "Aww, I missed the bus. I missed the bus. Oops!"

Listening to her story made me smile. Personally, I thought Lauren's strategy for deliberately missing the bus was brilliant. I asked her, "Did your parents catch on?" Here is what she said:

Oh yes. They went and met up with my school counselor, who actually became a good friend of ours. . . . When we go up there [now to visit] we meet her all the time. She's like my little granny. But [back then], my Mom went and met up with her; and at first, from what my parents say, she didn't like us very much because she thought that, I don't know, I guess she just thought that I was a bad kid for trying to skip out of school. And my Mom explained to her everything that was going on. . . . And then we just became close friends.

As I learned, Lauren and her family connected with a family in Tupelo who provided a cabin, a safe haven from the stresses of hotel living and an opportunity to attend a different school. This school was pre-kindergarten through twelfth grade, so Lauren and her younger sister attended school together during Katrina's immediate aftermath. In December of 2005, the family returned to St. Bernard to rebuild their coastal home. What a welcomed relief to be home and attend SBUS with familiar students and teachers. Looking back, Lauren does not let present-day challenges upset her. In her own words,

It was a lot better for me to have gone through that [experience] because now whenever something bad comes up, I say, "Well, if I could handle going to Tupelo High, I can handle this."

I learned that her parents eventually purchased the cabin where they stayed during Katrina as a home away from home, affectionately dubbed their "hurri-cation getaway." I recently learned that the "hurri-cation getaway" has transitioned to a new home for this couple, who relocated permanently to Tupelo after retirement. And their daughter, who at one point employed a strategic waffle trick to get out of going to an unfriendly school, has since graduated from college and is now a successful young professional who lives in her original home in St. Bernard Parish.

AFTER THE KATRINA DISASTER: PSYCHOLOGICAL
REACTIONS AND PATHWAYS TO HEALING

In her last book, *On Grief and Grieving*, Elisabeth Kübler-Ross said: "Trauma invites us to learn about our strength, endurance, and hope after it visits."[6] This quote was made in the context of death under specific circumstances, covering disasters and other mass casualties. To my way of thinking, her point aptly applies to the Katrina experience.

Resilience, pertaining to a natural tendency to bounce back from adversity, varies among individuals. After a natural disaster like the 2005 Hurricanes Katrina and Rita, some people seem to recover relatively quickly. They regain their footing, develop new routines, and move forward in a new normal (see Chapter 9). In contrast to people who bounce back with seeming ease, others may take a more circuitous route, possibly cycling through destructive coping strategies that do not promote recovery.

Social scientists, among other health and wellness professionals, realize that psychological reactions to disasters vary from person to person. The cascade of emotions may include (but are not limited to) anger, resentment, and a pervasive sense of sorrow. In the long days and months after a catastrophic event, crying spells and other emotional reactions in connection with a disaster may lessen in frequency and intensity. While emotions may spike and subside over time, the stress imposed by a disaster, both physical and psychological, can be persistent and overwhelming for people whose lives are forever changed by catastrophic environmental events.

Taking their toll, a multitude of disaster stressors can threaten well-being and shorten lives. In October of 2010, Stephen Wilson-Oakley ("Oates" to his friends) told me, "the stress from Katrina is still taking lives, still adversely affecting people." As this local businessman spoke, I thought about courageous people who survived the hurricane, evacuation, and lengthy displacement yet died soon after. Surely those deaths were premature, an unfortunate result of having one's world turned completely upside down by the forces of nature. Oates went on to share his observation of the increased frequency of death in St. Bernard after Katrina. In his own words:

> I was in the funeral parlor at least a couple days . . . a few times a month after Katrina for at least four years. We had to go to a funeral at least once or twice a month. Customers, friends . . . I've never been to a funeral more in my life than in that period of time. Before that, it was very rare you went to

a funeral, but after that you became a regular at the funeral parlor. And that room over there at St. Bernard Memorial Gardens, I've been there quite often since Katrina.

Traumatic stress, which differs from the stresses of ordinary daily life by degree, may become an integral aspect of everyday living for disaster survivors. For those whose lives have been impacted by a disaster or other tragedy, telltale signs of stress may be evident in appearance and demeanor. Traumatic stress may be experienced inwardly, too, in the form of somatic (bodily) complaints such as headaches, stomachaches, and disrupted sleep. The burden of traumatic stress may be felt in all areas of life, although people who live through a disaster will not necessarily develop a psychological disorder. Symptoms of distress are likely for those who have experienced a disaster, although such reactions do not necessarily indicate the onset of a clinical disorder.

Some people are aware of the toll that traumatic stress may be taking on their lives. For others, the experience of traumatic stress may be more insidious. These individuals soldier on, ostensibly unaware, doing the best they can to meet daily responsibilities and obligations. They experience the negative effects of traumatic stress yet attribute their difficulties to external factors, such as work and family dynamics. In fact, one participant told me she had mistaken disaster stress effects for the possible onset of Alzheimer's disease, a neurocognitive disorder with symptoms that include dysfunction in attention and memory in its early phases.

Most would agree that the presence of traumatic stress disrupts one's sense of well-being. Those who have suffered a tragedy live in a world of pain, where sadness predominates and joy may be short-lived and sporadic, if present at all. Depending on the individual and his or her circumstances, traumatic stress related to a tragic event may vary in intensity and duration. For people with limited prior experience, the first occurrence of a tragedy marks the onset of traumatic stress as a new and darkly foreign feeling. For others whose life experiences include prior trauma(s), another tragic event merely adds a layer to the mix of ongoing and/or resolved traumatic stresses. Even though tragic events may have happened decades ago, prior traumatic experiences are relevant to current life circumstances. Awareness of the impact that tragic events of long ago may have on people's current well-being is fundamental, having implications for social and family relationships. Co-existing stressors related to prior negative life events (also known as *cumulative adversity*) may haunt the present, as will be discussed more fully in Chapter 8.

Post-Disaster Stress: Temperament and Individual
Differences Matter

Temperamental tendencies can buffer or exacerbate stress reactions. By "temperament," I am referring to individuals' characteristic ways of responding to the world, ongoing events, and to others around them. Temperamental tendencies are likely to affect an individual's experience and interpretation of a tragic event, choice of coping methods, and prognosis for long-term recovery.

The term "temperament" describes the constellation of dispositional traits that shape personality and make us unique as people. We are born with certain traits or behavioral propensities along with the capacity to experience a wide range of emotions. Temperamental tendencies, such as shyness and other signature styles of responding to people and events, are apparent very early in life. The fact that healthy infants display a full range of emotional expression within their first year of life suggests that there is something very fundamental, almost primal, to emotions and how they are expressed. Recognizing the natural variation in peoples' emotional responses (and that we may be hardwired to differ one from another) is an important consideration in a disaster context. When dealing with individuals who are suffering as a result of a tragedy, sensitivity and awareness of temperamental tendencies and how they may govern the pace and progression of recovery is a primary concern.

In addition to temperament, there are other individual difference variables that characterize people, such as age, gender, ethnicity, religious affiliation, educational attainment, and employment history, among others. Understanding how individual differences such as these may affect the experience of traumatic stress and choice of coping strategies to counter traumatic stress is important. Two people may experience the very same event, yet how they interpret and react to this event in the immediate aftermath and over many years may be very different. Different routes to recovery and variations in time tables for healing are all too common after a tragedy, sometimes causing friction among family and friends—or, if not friction, these differences certainly provide grist for frustration and harsh judgment among people who presumably care about each other.

Respect for individual differences among survivors and variations in their time tables for healing is imperative. The topic of respect as a principle of healing will be addressed in Chapter 6, where I make the point that the relationship between trauma exposure and long-term recovery is multifaceted and dynamic. How this relationship plays out over time may depend on a combination of temperamental tendencies and individual characteristics, such as the age of the individual and where he or she may have been in the life course when the tragic event took place (e.g., a child, a young adult just starting out, a middle-aged adult contemplating retirement, or a senior facing later-life issues such as health, finances, independence). In short, it may take much longer for survivors to reach closure after a disaster than people who have not experienced a disaster would expect.

A "One-Size Doesn't Fit All" Approach Is Called For

When it comes to recovering from a disaster or tragedy of any sort, finding the right steps to take to overcome this event can be difficult. A critical realization for survivors is that *one size doesn't fit all*. In other words, a "one-size" approach to patterns of recovery and trajectories of healing is not appropriate or consistent with the scientific record.[7] With disasters, as with other negative life events, a coping strategy that works well for one person may be ineffective for a different individual at any given point in time, as noted in the Preface of this volume.

People are unique: a tragic event will affect each person somewhat differently. Thus, one would expect that pathways to healing may differ from person to person as each survivor learns how to live with this event as an unwelcomed but certainly now indelible part of his or her developmental history. People may deny or minimize the reality of their circumstances, but the truth is that no one can change the past.

The challenge, then, becomes finding a way to integrate negative experiences while accepting the new circumstances in which survivors now find themselves after a tragedy. For some, acceptance may be a bitter pill to swallow—a cold slap in the face with the dawn of each new day that comes after a tragedy. We resist the notion that we must accept the occurrence of an event that was not supposed to happen. Maybe such an event could happen to strangers who we read about in the newspaper, but not to us—not to our family and not in our lifetime. Herein lies the rub: acceptance of a tragedy may set survivors on a higher spiritual plane. Paradoxically, acceptance may bring survivors closer to healing, becoming whole again, and freed of the relentless sorrow that weakens the spirit. The topic of acceptance as a principle of healing is addressed in Chapter 7.

SUMMARY

By now, Hurricane Katrina's devastating impact across the US Gulf Coast is a familiar story. Katrina brought unparalleled destruction and losses, forever changing the landscape and lives of people in the Gulf Coast region. Hundreds of thousands of people felt the impact of this epic storm, including those outside of the severely damaged Gulf Coast towns and communities. The loss of life was substantial, making Katrina one of the costliest disasters in US history. With widespread destruction and property damage estimated in billions of dollars, no one doubts that Hurricane Katrina typifies the catastrophic nature of a natural disaster. Forever etched in our collective conscious, Katrina will be remembered as a ferocious hurricane with unprecedented flooding that followed the catastrophic levee breaches throughout the region. Katrina has inspired numerous literary works and motivated changes in local, regional, and federal hurricane preparedness and response tactics, as noted in Chapter 1 and elsewhere.[8–12]

Most would agree that natural disasters are associated with property destruction and great personal losses. They also bring many stressors for individuals, families, and communities. While disasters may capture media attention briefly, disaster-related challenges and setbacks may remain for survivors long after the spotlight of media attention is directed elsewhere. We also remember those who are indirectly impacted by these events. Multitudes of family members, friends, and sometimes complete strangers in receiving cities opened their homes to those displaced by the Katrina disaster. In some cases, receiving cities have become a final destination for displaced coastal residents who relocated permanently.

Looking beyond the 2005 Katrina tragedy, survivors' lives are impacted in many ways by disasters and severe weather events across the nation and the globe. Some disaster-related changes can be anticipated, like the financial impact of replacement expenses (e.g., purchasing new items lost in a disaster; replacing vehicles, furniture, and household appliances; and new construction costs or the expense of relocating). Other changes after a disaster may be less predictable, such as the social challenges of relocating to a new community (or staying in place after a disaster has struck) and shifts in population size and density, which happen for both directly and indirectly impacted communities.

Whether expected or not, the many changes set in motion by a disaster will play out on multiple levels over time. Disaster-related suffering can be crippling for survivors when these events occur. Painful memories, sorrow, and perhaps regrets in connection with disasters may reach forward in

time as well, having lasting effects for survivors that are felt across generations. Bridging the gap between suffering and inner peace then becomes a
vitally important challenge for disaster survivors as for everyone whose life
has been touched by tragedy.

In the next part of this volume, I begin with an overview of different ways
of knowing about the world in which we live. These different approaches
to knowledge of the world are important for the reader to consider in the
context of post-disaster life. Why? The reason is simple: there is more than
one way to think about, understand, or embrace the "new normal" after a
disaster. By "new normal," I am referring to the world in which people may
find themselves after a disaster or other calamitous event has taken place
(see also Chapter 9).

In the overview that follows, I make the point that most individuals'
understanding of the world is based on *personal observations*: what they
see, think, and believe to be true based on real-life experience. In contrast, philosophers view the world based on a more scholastic approach
that includes *rational argument* and the application of logic. Last, scientists
know about the world based on *scientific facts* that have been discovered
in an objective way through the process of conducting basic research. In
short, the overview presented next is offered as a prelude to the healing
principles that constitute the central focus of this volume.

This overview will set the stage for a discussion of six evidence-based
principles that support the healing process and long-term recovery in the
years after a disaster. For expository convenience, these principles are
presented in pairs: faith and humor, respect and gratitude, and acceptance
and silver linings. Each principle begins with a brief introduction, includes
illustrative case examples, and ends with a crisp summary. This formulation is intentional, allowing these healing principles to stand alone or to
be considered flexibly in combination, as dictated by the readers' need and
personal preference.

In summary, illustrations and direct quotes from Katrina survivors
are interspersed throughout the next two parts of this volume. Having
suffered catastrophic losses in 2005, current and former coastal residents
of south Louisiana have lived through the Katrina disaster. Collectively,
their voices bring the six principles offered here to life in an authentic and
relatable way, offering hope for better days ahead and promoting healing
after tragedy.

NOTES

1. Mark Hancock, "Many in Louisiana, Texas Lament Rita 'Amnesia,'" *USA Today* (January 25, 2006), accessed October 18, 2018, from https://usatoday30.usatoday.com/news/nation/2006-01-25-rita_x.htm

2. Trevan G. Hatch, Katie E. Cherry, Keri L. Kytola, Yaxin Lu, and Loren D. Marks, "Loss, Chaos, Survival, and Despair: The Storm After the Storms," in *Traumatic Stress and Long-Term Recovery: Coping with Disasters and Other Negative Life Events*, ed. Katie E. Cherry (New York: Springer International Publishing Switzerland, 2015), 231–245.

3. Keri L. Kytola, Katie E. Cherry, Loren D. Marks, and Trevan G. Hatch, "When Neighborhoods Are Destroyed by Disaster: Relocate or Return and Rebuild?," in *Traumatic Stress and Long-Term Recovery: Coping with Disasters and Other Negative Life Events*, ed. Katie E. Cherry (New York: Springer International Publishing Switzerland, 2015), 211–229.

4. Jacques Henry, "Return or Relocate? An Inductive Analysis of Decision-Making in a Disaster," *Disaster* 37, no. 2 (2013): 294–316.

5. Yoshinori Kamo, Tammy L. Henderson, and Karen A. Roberto, "Displaced Older Adults' Reactions to and Coping with the Aftermath of Hurricane Katrina," *Journal of Family Issues* 30 (2011): 1346–1370.

6. Elisabeth Kübler-Ross and David Kessler, *On Grief and Grieving* (New York: Scribner, 2005).

7. James I. Gerhart, Daphna Canetti, and Stevan E. Hobfoll, "Traumatic Stress in Overview: Definition, Context, Scope, and Long-Term Outcomes," in *Traumatic Stress and Long-Term Recovery: Coping with Disasters and Other Negative Life Events*, ed. Katie E. Cherry (New York: Springer International Publishing Switzerland, 2015), 3–24.

8. Douglas Brinkley, *The Great Deluge: Hurricane Katrina, New Orleans, and the Mississippi Gulf Coast* (New York: Harper Collins Publishers, 2006).

9. David L. Brunsma, David Overfelt, and J. Steven Picou, *The Sociology of Katrina: Perspectives on a Modern Catastrophe* (2nd ed.) (Lanham: Rowman & Littlefield Publishers, 2010).

10. Christopher Cooper and Robert Block, *Disaster Hurricane Katrina and the Failure of Homeland Security* (New York: Times Books, Henry Holt and Company, 2006).

11. Jed Horne, *Breach of Faith: Hurricane Katrina and the Near Death of a Great American City* (New York: Random House, 2006).

12. Chris Rose, *1 Dead in Attic* (New York: Simon & Schuster, 2005).

PART II

———————— ⌇ ————————

Principles of Healing

A Bridge Between Suffering and Peace

OVERVIEW

People know about their world based on personal experience. Philosophers tell us that there are different world views and different ways to know about the world in which we live. Scientists know about the world based on theory, hypotheses, and evidence that can be measured or inferred. A *theory* provides a conceptual framework for generating testable hypotheses that can be confirmed (or disconfirmed) by objective data. To appreciate a scientific approach to knowing, one must first recognize that any theory, by definition, is *logically falsifiable*. What this means is that a theory can be shown to be probably (or at least possibly) true or probably false based on research outcomes. This is why scientists conduct basic research—a series of carefully designed experiments conducted within the parameters of the scientific method—to objectively evaluate a theory. By doing so, scientists generate knowledge that can address theory-based research questions and provide direction for further inquiry. From a practical point of view, the scientific enterprise not only informs theory but also provides objective information that is useful for end users and, ultimately, society at large.

Some facts we know about the world today are based on a scientific approach that was established centuries ago. For example, most people know about gravity, the unseen force of nature which pulls things to the ground. If I drop my coffee cup, it will fall to the floor and break (if glass, porcelain, or ceramic). Or the cup will bounce and possibly roll (if Styrofoam, plastic, or aluminum). Regardless of what type of cup I drop or how far it falls (from a standing or sitting position), I will have a mess to clean up, with spilled coffee and possibly coffee grounds splattered at the site of impact. I *know* this from personal experience, having dropped containers with liquid in them over the years. I also know it from direct observation, having watched others do the same thing and experience the same result. There is no doubt about it: cups fall to the floor when dropped or knocked over owing to a phenomenon of nature called gravity. A mess then follows that someone should clean up.

Thanks to personal experience, this is a fact I know about the world: *gravity happens every time*. Thanks to Galileo's early ideas about gravitational resistance and Sir Isaac Newton's observation of an apple falling from a tree (plus an Earth Science teacher I had in high school), I am aware that gravity was discovered in the sixteenth century and described mathematically in Newton's theory of gravitation, which still applies today. Coming forward in time, Albert Einstein's 1915 theory of relativity adds precision to Newton's earlier mathematical work, explaining in part why gravity happens, which has something to do with matter and mass, although very seldom do I think about why gravity happens. I just know that it does: gravity is a scientifically based, indisputable fact about the world in which we live.

Science is one way—but certainly not the only way—to know about the world around us. Ancient scholars of rhetoric, like the classical Greek (e.g., Plato and Aristotle) and Roman scholars (e.g., Cicero and Quintilian), as well as modern-day philosophers, have shown us that we can know about the world in which we live through the application of reason, persuasion, and rational thought. In other words, "truths" are derived and validated through the application of systems of logic. Like a "scientific fact" (e.g., gravity), a "truth" can be meaningful and valid for everyday life, even if it was never tested using the scientific method. From this point of view, one can appreciate the humanities and liberal arts, along with different world religions, as alternate ways of knowing about the world apart from science.

From ancient texts and historic documents, we know that world religions have been in existence for thousands of years. To appreciate religion as a valid approach to understanding the world in which we live, the realization that religious "truths" are inherently *non-logically falsifiable* is key. This means that most religious "truths" do not conform to the tenets of modern science: they cannot be shown through experimentation to be probably true or probably false. For example, *faith* is held as a "truth," and its validity is not in question for many theologians, evangelicals, and religiously minded laypersons. Based on faith, one "knows" things about the world to be true. By biblical definition, "Faith is the assurance of things hoped for, the conviction of things unseen" (New Revised Standard Version [NRSV], Hebrews 11:1). Whether or not religious "truths" can stand up to scientific scrutiny is a non-issue for many believers.

Knowing about the world through the application of "truths" through faith (and nothing but faith) seemingly relegates modern science to the back seat—not necessary, not applicable, not relevant. In the extreme, a scientist and a theologian may have different ideas about the world based on vastly different approaches and assumptions. They may vehemently disagree on which principles should be upheld as valid and which should be dismissed as fantasy, folklore, or fiction in the grander scheme of things.

For our purposes, fundamental doctrinal differences of opinion concerning ways of knowing are recognized, certainly, yet set aside now as grist for someone else's epistemological mill. Setting aside distractions (including personal beliefs and prejudices) is a necessary first step to sharpen the focus on what is important: namely, a strict focus on variables that matter for long-term disaster recovery in the years after these events.

Across the next three chapters, I suggest that faith, humor, respect, gratitude, acceptance, and silver linings are variables that matter and are central to long-term disaster recovery. These variables, presented as principles of healing, are grounded in a scientific approach (for a summary of published research, see Appendix A); yet they also arguably reflect a rational approach to knowing. That is, the authentic voices of Katrina survivors from the coastal parishes of south Louisiana are uniquely persuasive—and may also appeal to our sense of logic, reason, and the human quest for building (or, in the cases of surviving disasters) *rebuilding* a good life. An academic foundation, with participants' narratives interwoven throughout, brings to life this set of principles with the expressed intent of promoting hope and healing after tragedy.

CHAPTER 5

༄

Faith and Humor

INTRODUCTION

Stressful events happen and coping responses follow as individuals and families manage stress's impact on daily life. There are different ways to cope, and these can lead to positive or negative outcomes. These different approaches to coping have been a topic of interest to psychologists and health and wellness professionals for decades. Two major distinctions in the research literature on stress and coping warrant brief discussion for background. First is the distinction between problem-focused and emotion-focused coping strategies.[1,2] Generally speaking, *problem-focused* strategies integrate a human tendency to pursue a rational approach to a stressor or situation using step-by-step logic, which may include getting advice from others regarding possible solutions, a very linear strategy. Similarly, *emotion-focused* strategies involve another human tendency to release emotions through seeking social support, shedding tears, having angry outbursts, and other impassioned responses. Emotion-focused approaches to coping are arguably less linear than problem-focused approaches.

A second distinction among coping approaches is that between approach and avoidance strategies.[3,4] With *approach* strategies, individuals metaphorically roll up their sleeves and tackle a problematic situation or stressor directly, whereas *avoidance* refers to a tendency to turn away from, delay active response to, or ignore a stressor altogether.

Academically speaking, my personal preference is a more recent formulation where these two earlier distinctions are blended,[5] resulting in three categories of coping style.[6] In broad strokes, these coping styles are characterized as follows:

1. *Problem-focused* strategies in which a person enacts active planning and specific behaviors to overcome the problem he or she is facing (i.e., through employing active coping, planning, instrumental support, and/ or healthy forms of religion-based coping)
2. *Active emotional* strategies in which a person reframes the problem to think about it in a new or different way (i.e., positive reframing, humor, acceptance, emotional support, and/or venting)
3. *Avoidant emotional* strategies in which a person may back off or pull away completely from a problem to disengage from the stressor. In the extreme, an individual may even deny that a problem exists (i.e., denial, and self-distraction, behavioral disengagement, self-blame, substance use, and/or unhealthy forms of religion-based coping)[7]

Ample scientific evidence supports the takeaway message that problem-focused and active emotional coping styles are preferable. Both have been linked to positive outcomes and are considered more effective for adjustment and healing compared to strategies in which a person downplays or avoids the stressor.[8] In contrast, avoidant emotional coping strategies are more often associated with psychological distress and are generally considered maladaptive. A note of caution is in order, however: overgeneralizations based on this brief conceptual tour of the research literature on stress and coping should be avoided. The type of stressor and its duration are also likely to affect coping responses, psychological health, and long-term outcomes.[9]

To summarize, faith and humor, the respective sacred and secular coping strategies of central interest here, are presented next as principles of healing. Just as a coin has two sides, both valid, faith and humor are examined as two very different styles of coping with stressors in a post-disaster context.[10] As two sides of the same "stress and coping" coin, faith and humor are illuminated through research findings and narrative text as two different principles of healing in operation after a natural disaster.

FAITH

I have a flame of faith that I got from my grandmother.
—Manuella Perez

For many, faith is relevant in a post-disaster environment. When a sweeping, panoramic glance from the left to the right yields nothing but catastrophic destruction and miles of storm debris, one may have no other recourse than to look upward for inspiration or hope. At an individual level, faith covers one's personal beliefs, practices, and convictions (e.g., a faith in God/higher spiritual power), which may or may not align with the views of family and friends (or anyone else's views, for that matter). At a denominational level, faith may include social factors and group dynamics in connection with a church, synagogue, temple, or other institutionally bounded place of worship.

Academically speaking, faith, as an element of religion, falls under a *problem-focused* coping style. Many participants cited faith as a salient factor that kept them going throughout Katrina's destructive aftermath. For these individuals, faith played a central role in coping with challenges, obstacles, and setbacks after Katrina, discussed more fully elsewhere.[11] The presence of faith-based communities trained in disaster relief and church groups with volunteers from all over the country working side by side was also mentioned by participants, as will be discussed more fully in Chapter 6. Note, however, that the absence of visible disaster relief efforts associated with certain denominations in the hardest hit areas was a painful realization and great disappointment for some survivors as well.[12]

Most would agree that faith is an intellectually and temporally expansive concept, attracting the interest of scholars and theologians for centuries. Indeed, research findings within a disaster context constitute a very small part of a voluminous scientific literature. Interested readers are referred elsewhere for excellent summaries on religion in relation to health outcomes and well-being.[13,14,15] Here the focus is narrow and confined to participants' spoken responses and stories prompted by three research questions: (1) how they coped with challenges, obstacles, and setbacks in the aftermath of the 2005 Hurricanes Katrina and Rita; (2) whether a church or faith-based community helped them cope with challenges faced after the storms; and (3) whether their own religious beliefs and practices helped them cope with challenges after the storms.

Many participants talked about faith in God as fundamental to coping and post-disaster recovery, critical for moving forward in the face of uncertainty and indispensable for adjustment to new circumstances. On a fearsome note, some participants who did not evacuate before the storm and nearly lost their lives battling Katrina's fury cited faith as a key to survival. Many Katrina survivors embraced a faith that provided guidance and reassurance for meeting the challenges ahead, whatever they might be. Two illustrations that reveal faith as integral to survival and long-term recovery are given next. These illustrations (and all that follow throughout this volume) are presented in context, meaning that they include my thoughts and observations as a university researcher doing what we do—collecting data through a structured interview to test hypotheses and to delve into the realm of the unknown. In each of these research visits, I walked into a natural classroom of sorts. That is, the participants were the instructors and I was the student ready to learn about the Katrina experience from those who lived through it directly. *Stepping onto sacred ground* is how this process has been described in the literature, when a researcher is entrusted with stories from people's lives.[16] In this spirit, I offer some observations on faith as a variable that matters for disaster recovery from the voices of people who know.

Illustration: The Flame of Faith

Manuella Perez's dining room was elegant. I sat in a regal and stately captain's chair, comfortably cushioned and positioned at the head of a large mahogany table. My research materials—survey forms and pens, two clipboards, and a digital voice recorder—were laid out on the table in front of me. It was August of 2010. The bright summer sunshine streamed through a side window behind where Manuella sat, filling the room with a diffuse light that was tranquil and serene. I knew that this beautiful home, radiating grace, warmth, and elegance, had suffered a terrible blow—powerful forces of wind and water had brought a swath of destruction through here just five years before, crushing timbers, destroying a household, and disrupting precious lives.

We visited briefly and then the interview began. I anticipated that Manuella would speak of displacement, destruction, and loss and that she would document the details of her Katrina experience as we worked through the interview protocol. I asked her how she coped with the obstacles she faced after the storm. She looked at me and said, "I have a flame of faith that I got from my grandmother." I marveled at this visual—*flame of faith*—which struck me as paradoxical at first. When she said flame, I thought, "Hmm, flames mean fire. Fires consume and destroy, bringing death, destruction, and horrors unimaginable." But as she spoke, I realized that "flame" in this context did not mean death and destruction. Rather, just the opposite—flame as a symbol of hope, denoting an eternal element, something that is never extinguished. A flame of faith—eternal and unending, our *faith* carries us through the hard times and tragedies that befall us. This was a profoundly important life lesson her grandmother had given her. This intergenerational transmission of knowledge and faith was comforting and inspiring to me as well. She gave me far more to think about than I had anticipated that afternoon.

Manuella's phrase, "a flame of faith," reflects an artistic soul. Others spoke of the Katrina experience as a dynamic that tested their faith. For instance, Stephen Wilson-Oakley (whose friends call him "Oates") shared his thoughts on Katrina as God "testing your mettle," meaning an experience that reveals one's true character and determines whether he or she is ready for larger tasks ahead. In his own words, Oates said,

> I felt, [even] . . . before Katrina came along, that God tests your mettle. . . . He wants to make sure you're worthy for the next task. And so I felt like he gave us Katrina because he knew the people of St. Bernard . . . would be able to come through it and end up being an example for a lot of other folks how do you deal with a natural disaster . . . and come through it on the other side. You can look around you today, five years later, and see the recovery that has taken place.

On a broader note, the despicable acts of brutality, looting, and chaos in New Orleans during Katrina's immediate aftermath stood in stark contrast to selfless acts of generosity and grace by countless others during the Katrina era, consistent with Oates's point about Katrina revealing "your mettle" or one's true nature.[17]

In the next illustration, the Katrina experience illuminates faith in relation to the unfolding of a larger "plan"—a plan with purpose. Many participants reported a belief in a Divine plan—that although one may not understand the larger purpose or the reason for misfortune at the time it happens, all events, good and bad, are part of a larger plan with a greater good for humanity, as revealed next.

Illustration: Faith and "The Plan"

She greeted me with a friendly and an engaging smile. I felt instantly at ease as Catherine Serpas welcomed me into her home on a June day in 2010. With a twinkle in her eye, she talked briefly about her husband and family. As we walked toward the kitchen, she pointed to certain features of her house, showing me what had been rebuilt after the storm and explaining how it was different now than before. Her husband, who had died suddenly and unexpectedly a year after the storm, would have loved the expansive kitchen window which now stretched halfway across the room, much farther than before. I could imagine her enjoying the view of her backyard from this new kitchen window—watching birds, squirrels, and other wild-life scampering about, frolicking among the glorious live oak trees. We sat at her kitchen table, and she spoke of her Katrina experience.

Like many seasoned storm veterans, Cathy and her family "rode out" Hurricane Katrina at home. On August 29, 2005, a Monday morning after the worst of the storm had passed, her son was outside surveying the damage. Suddenly, he saw the monstrous wall of water pushing furiously toward them—the levees surrounding St. Bernard Parish had failed! He raced inside the house, frantically ushering everyone into the attic. As she scrambled up the ladder into the attic, she looked behind and saw the floodwaters swirling perilously below, filling her home with great speed and treachery. Safely in the attic, they watched the scene from a window. They were in the attic for days. When she came down from the attic, she had a flash of insight. This is what she said:

> When I walked down from the attic, the Lord spoke to me like I am speaking to you, and He said, "I have a plan." . . . But when he spoke that to me, I knew he wasn't just speaking it to me. I knew he was speaking it broadly, you know? He said, "Don't walk before me and don't walk behind me, but be in the middle of the plan with me." And from that moment on, I knew . . . no matter what I [had] seen, I knew that we were going to get through it.

And they did get through it. In the immediate aftermath, she hung a sign outside of the window which read "The Serpas Family Survived." She gathered her friends who were also homeless after the storm, welcoming them openly as she and her husband transformed their front room into a neighborhood base camp. She talked about those long days where everyone worked tirelessly from sunup to sundown, clearing their properties and recovering what they could, although cleaning was difficult under the circumstances without electricity and running water. Her husband siphoned gasoline from their ruined vehicles to power a generator, providing precious light and a portable A/C unit in the front room where everyone slept at night. One neighbor had a portable music player and a Fats Domino recording that they danced to in the evenings. She described those long and difficult days simply: "We worked, we ate, and we danced."

In time, her neighbors set up a nondenominational Sunday worship service in their carport. By October of 2005, running water was restored to this segment of the parish. An official from the Federal Emergency Management Agency (FEMA) passed through her area, and she flagged him down. With his administrative assistance, she was able to secure FEMA trailers for her extended family and neighbors. Having her children and grandchildren together in trailers on their property was a comfort that helped her cope with storm-related challenges and obstacles. During cleanup, she injured her hand, a serious wound that would eventually require surgery and therapy, although there was no medical facility available for immediate assistance. Despite this painful setback, among other hardships endured, Cathy's central message concerning "The Plan" was unwavering, unmistakable, and clear. In her own words, here is what else she had to say that afternoon:

> And ever since that day I walked down from that attic and the Lord laid that on my heart, anybody I talked to that I think they need that message, I tell them, "The Lord has a plan." And I tell them [they] ought to be in the middle of that plan. Even though I have some questions about it [laughs] . . . I still, I still have to believe it. . . . And actually, somebody gave me this. It's just a token for what I [believe]. . . It's Jeremiah twenty-nine . . . [verse] eleven. . . . I believe this is what the Lord was saying to me.

She showed me the prayer card and I read the verse: "For I know the plans I have for you," says the Lord, "They are plans for good and not for disaster, to give you a future and a hope" (New Living Translation [NLT] Jeremiah 29:11). For Cathy, post-disaster recovery and long-term healing from this ordeal was inextricably linked to her faith. Through faith, she knew her home would be restored in time, along with her family's business and the community: her faith was *the assurance of things hoped for, the conviction of things unseen*—a lifeline for navigating otherwise dark and uncertain times.

Summary

Faith emerges as a key principle of healing from those who have faced and lived through a life-threatening natural disaster. Other participants who looked death in the eye during the Katrina tragedy told us that faith provided direction—a pathway to safety—offering a glimpse of hope that extends beyond one's current and precarious circumstances. From a *flame of faith* through *The Plan*, Katrina survivors' faith is revealed as a principle of healing that can overcome even the most desperate of situations.

By embracing faith, one can see that disaster-related suffering is finite, having a beginning, middle, and resolution or ending, which may be part of a larger plan that we do not yet understand or even perceive. This notion, that suffering is time-limited (not endless) and perhaps part of a larger design, is illustrated beautifully in Rosalind White's poem, *My House*. Written in 2006, her poem illustrates the totality of loss in the aftermath of Katrina. Yet her poem also brings forward the healing principle of faith as a lamp unto her feet, lighting a pathway to a new future that will unfold in time.

My House 2006

It wasn't a beautiful mansion set upon a green hilltop.
The house had years of memories, it knew about my life.
It saw me through motherhood and striving to be a good wife.
So many treasures it held that never could I replace
Now looking at the empty space it's very hard to face.
Katrina took my house and tossed it in the air.
My treasures were pieces in a kaleidoscope—spread out everywhere.
Journals, which told about my life, what I did from day to day,
Katrina took the pages of my life and washed them away.
Could I ever recall those moments that were important enough
   to write?
They have vanished and are now completely out of sight.
Treasures like a tiny silver toothbrush kept in a silk lined blue box.
Or mementos of first haircuts—inside a see through bag were little
   curly locks.
I sit in despair and have chosen this day to say good-bye.
I have cried my last cry.
In faith I open my arms and embrace whatever tomorrow brings.
For I am only a puppet—Jesus controls the strings.
My life is not mine to predict, now this I understand.
The one who guides our life, is far much more grand.
I have learned a valuable lesson about what life is all about.
I will be okay; of this I have no doubt.
It wasn't a beautiful mansion set upon a green hilltop

—Rosiland White
Reprinted with permission

Rosiland's poem is noteworthy as a lasting memorial to her coastal parish home which was completely destroyed by Hurricane Katrina in 2005. Importantly, her poem also reflects an inner peace that may go along with acceptance of events that cannot be undone or reversed, as will be discussed more fully in Chapter 7. As Rosiland so aptly notes in her poem, life goes on despite painful circumstances after a natural disaster, as will be discussed in Chapter 9. While contentment and inner peace in daily living may be interrupted by disaster, positive emotions such as joy and happiness will return, as survivors who embrace faith as a principle of healing will tell you.

HUMOR

"Laugh and the whole world laughs with you. Cry and you cry alone."
—Doogie Robin

Compared to faith, *humor* has received far less systematic research attention, possibly due to the complexity of this variable: humor has been conceptualized as a social behavior (i.e., one tells a joke to others) having a cognitive component (i.e., a joke teller has to remember the punch line, an audience must understand the joke or "get it" to laugh). Humor may also be linked to personality traits, namely, a dispositional tendency to crack jokes regardless of circumstances, like a standup comedian or class clown. For more on the psychology of humor, interested readers are referred elsewhere.[18] For our purposes, humor has been conceptualized as an *active emotional* coping strategy that has a role in coping with adversity.

Some participants made good use of humor in coping with precarious circumstances in the hours and days after Katrina made landfall on Monday, August 29, 2005. For example, Roxanne Bentley had sheltered in place on the second floor of a two-story home near the Orleans' Parish line. Her family had stockpiled two weeks' worth of food and water in preparation, so they helped neighbors who were stranded without provisions. When it was safe, Rox's brother went out in his boat to search for medical supplies and other necessities. In his travels he found a plastic rooster, a seasonal fall decoration that had been swept away in Katrina's floodwaters. He pulled the rooster aboard and secured it to the bow of his boat, mimicking a carnival float. When he returned from his foraging adventure, he tossed supplies to neighbors on second-story roof tops along their street—diapers, medicine, cigarettes—among other treasures he had found. Rox laughed as she described the incredulous scene. There was her brother in his boat, adorned with a rooster on the bow, floating down the flooded street and tossing supplies upward to their neighbors who were reaching and grabbing for the airborne treasures. "It looked like a weird New Orleans Mardi Gras parade!" she laughed as she explained. As natives will tell you, Mardi Gras (literally translated, "Fat Tuesday") refers to the carnival season, that time of year when parties and spirited celebrations organized by Mardi Gras clubs ("Krewes") abound. Parades with lavishly decorated floats roll through the cities and towns of Louisiana in the days and weeks that precede Ash Wednesday, a day of religious observance marking the start of the Lenten season. Revelers riding on Mardi Gras floats toss colorful plastic bead necklaces and other trinkets to the cheering, arm-waving crowds along the parade route. Everyone hollers the signature phrase, "Throw me something, Mister!" as the floats pass by. Back in the two-story home, Rox and her family waited for three days until the floodwaters had subsided to where they could walk safely to the levee. They were airlifted by helicopter to a staging area in a nearby town.

Reliance on humor to overcome adversity is not a new idea. In the words of Viktor Frankl, a Viennese psychiatrist who suffered as a prisoner in four Nazi concentration camps, "The attempt to develop a sense of humor and to see things in a humorous light is some kind of a trick learned while mastering the art of living."[19] In this section, I suggest that the healing power of humor can be realized simply by seeing things differently. When we notice improbable objects, events, and happenings around us that spontaneously spur laughter, like Rox's weird Mardi Gras parade rolling through Katrina's floodwaters on August 29, 2005, we are taking a step in the direction of healing. We are inching closer to recovery and the experience of joy in everyday living.

On Seeing Funny Things

"From there to here, from here to there. Funny things are everywhere." I have often thought of this line from Dr. Seuss's beloved children's book, *One Fish, Two Fish, Red Fish, Blue Fish*. Thinking about Dr. Seuss makes me smile, bringing to mind images of his children's books with their colorful drawings of fantastic creatures doing improbable, amazing things. For instance, there is Horton the Elephant sitting in a bird's nest, taking care of a tiny, delicate egg through stormy weather, tolerating a variety of discomforts because he had promised the whimsical and absent mother duck, Maisy, "I meant what I said and I said what I meant—an elephant is faithful, one-hundred percent."

Or perhaps we think of Sam I Am, the energetic and persistent little fellow who goes to such great lengths while carrying a plate of Green Eggs and Ham, never giving up in his efforts to get his grumpy friend to try this new food. In the end, we see a broad smile sweeping across the face of this former curmudgeon as he finally takes a bite—and discovers that yes, indeed, he does like Green Eggs and Ham! He thanks his friend not once, but twice—"thank you, thank you, Sam I am"—as will be discussed more fully in the context of Gratitude as a healing principle in Chapter 6. Last, our Dr. Seuss musings lead us to fond memories of the dour Grinch—the green, furry creature who stole Christmas, but then gave it back and, in doing so, discovered the deeper meaning of this holiday.

The more I think about Dr. Seuss, the more I realize that he was probably right: funny things are all around us, everywhere we look. Perhaps the key to realizing the healing power of humor is just that: simply to look. Look around, look outside of ourselves and our situations, look beyond our cares and worries. Notice the oddities and unexpected happenings in our everyday surroundings that may prompt laughter, which lifts our spirits for a while, if only briefly. Most people enjoy a chuckle or good guffaw from time to time. Not hard to do and often spontaneous, but what does this require? Perhaps only awareness and an ability to look at things differently are all that we need to see the humor in improbable situations and happenings all around us. After all, funny things *are* everywhere.

Illustration: Funny Things Are Everywhere

Doogie Robin was an older gentleman sitting comfortably in a brown recliner with the air conditioner window unit humming on that sunny afternoon in August of 2011. On the opposite wall from where he sat was a flat screen television. A news channel was playing softly in the background. Framed photographs hung from the same wall, displaying several generations of smiling faces. Like a formal introduction, he pointed to his grandchildren in the pictures on the wall, naming each one and explaining who their parents were among his eight sons and daughters. Beside the family pictures were clusters of fishing rods and reels equipped with bright and colorful lures. There were shiny metal spinners, neon yellow tassels, and round red and white floats that bob up and down when a fish bites. Hung vertically—this collection was grand—more rods than I had ever seen in a private home.

As I learned, Doogie's father was among the first Isleño settlers in this area. He spoke of fishing for oysters before the days of mechanized equipment, using wooden tongs to rake oyster beds and shoveling piles of oysters on a flat boat in the hot sun. Today, Doogie leaves the oyster harvesting to his sons, he said, but he still takes friends and business associates out for fishing excursions on his boat. In fact, he had been out on the water that morning at 5:00 A.M., long before I arrived for the interview. Another individual for whom water is a way of life, the world of fishing seemed as close to his heart as his family, with both prominently displayed on the living room wall of his mobile home.

Sitting on his right side with my clipboards and pens, we worked through the interview. I asked him a few questions that concerned the use of humor to cope with difficult situations. Doogie looked at me and said, "Laugh and the whole world laughs with you. Cry and you cry alone." He went on to explain, "That's what my Daddy used to say and it's true." Months later, back at the university, I looked into the origin of this phrase, which I learned is a variation of the first line of the poem, *Solitude*, by Ella Wheeler Wilcox.[20] The first part, "Laugh and the whole world laughs with you" made sense to me insofar as humor is a social behavior: we often enjoy a good chuckle with others. Or something funny happens to us, and we tell other people who laugh along with us. I'm not sure that I concur with "Cry and you cry alone." Thinking about those poor souls who drowned in St. Bernard on August 29, 2005, still makes me weep, although I never knew any of these storm victims personally. Sometimes, peripheral people—strangers we do not know—can feel our sorrow over a tragic or heart-rending event. Sometimes there is a whole world of compassionate strangers who are moved to tears in the wake of a tragedy.

When we had finished the interview, Doogie asked me if I wanted to see his friend. "Yes, of course," I said, as I watched him reach over the left side of his recliner. I thought there was a small dog on the other side, man's best friend, waiting faithfully on the floor until his master was finished with the interview. I heard a very strange swishing sound, then the thump, thump of a brief struggle, and behold! There in his tanned and muscular hands was an adorable baby alligator! Not more than twelve inches or so long, the little creature with bright eyes flashing and a rounded snout snapped, wiggled, and thrashed until Doogie flipped it over on its back. Gently stroking its long, yellowish white belly, the baby gator settled down under his hands. The bright little eyes slowly closed. In this flipped position of bliss, it looked like the little guy was smiling as he drifted off to sleep. I couldn't contain my laughter over this incongruous sight—and I had thought his friend was a dog!

He told me there was a turtle, too, so I walked over to the left side of his recliner where I found the little mud turtle in a plastic tub, hiding beneath the ramp where the alligator lounges. Thinking about food chain issues—alligators eat turtles—I thought this little turtle had devised an excellent hideout, safely tucked below and away from the treachery of those pearly white, pointy little baby alligator teeth. What a complete surprise that Doogie's four-footed friend turned out to be an aquatic reptile that could be flipped on his back and lulled to sleep with a gentle rub of its soft and scaled belly. Again, I had to chuckle. A research interview in the company of swamp critters—a gator on top with a turtle below deck—that was a first for me! Hilarious and heartwarming, it was a sight to behold. Such great affection between man and his best friend—in this case, a little, baby alligator.

Illustration: Seeing Funny Things in Unlikely Places

Before the first research appointment, I knew that Dave Brubaker was among the essential personnel who had stayed in St. Bernard through Hurricane Katrina. Dave's family had evacuated safely to another state but he remained behind for months afterward, working long days under dire circumstances to restore the devastated parish. Not knowing very much about just who comprised the essential personnel, I had mistakenly thought that Dave Brubaker was a police officer or with the sheriff's office. As we worked through the interview on that June day in 2010, I realized that he was not in law enforcement. Rather, Dave worked for the Water Board, a state governmental agency responsible for water service, supplying running water to homes and other public places across the parish (see Chapter 4).

In the weeks after the storm, Water Board crews fanned out, covering every part of the parish on foot. Systematically working through flooded neighborhoods and homes, they turned off each and every individual water main so that ruined homes would not reflood when water service was restored. As he explained, refrigerators float—in flooded homes, they pull away from the wall. For refrigerators with automatic ice makers, the water hose is detached. Consequently, a continuous flow of water from the broken hose would reflood homes from the inside out if the water mains were left open when water service was restored. In his travels through the ruined neighborhoods of St. Bernard, there were many gruesome and ghastly sites. One day, Dave was approached by a pack of feral dogs—growling menacingly, there was a moment when he was concerned for his safety. The dogs were hungry and had been without food for days—would they attack? He braced himself and stood his ground—mercifully, the dogs turned away and he went back to work.

Homes swept off of their foundations by the forces of wind and water were a frequent sight among the ruined neighborhoods. He came across one house, otherwise intact, but sitting squarely in the middle of a street, as if the wind had picked up this home, spun it around its axis a few times, and dropped it in the middle of the street. Upon closer examination, there was an incredible, but unmistakable sight—a pair of legs sticking out from under the house! Fake legs, complete with dark stockings and silver high-heeled shoes that someone had set up to mimic the scene from the original *Wizard of Oz* movie when a Kansas tornado dropped Dorothy's house on the Wicked Witch of the East! We laughed together as he spoke of other examples of dark humor he came across while working his way through Katrina's swath of death and destruction.

Summary

Humor is an active emotional coping strategy that may help us navigate through times of trouble or difficult circumstances. Two illustrations support the view that humor can be an antidote for stress, where laughter may loosen a stronghold that keeps us locked in a place of pain during sorrowful times. Cultivating a light heart with laughter while working through painful circumstances may be easier said than done for some people, however. Thus, I suggest that humor can be effective despite tragedy—for some, but not all people.

In her book, *Laugh Your Way to Grace*, Reverend Susan Sparks argues that humor can serve as a spiritual exercise, where laughter allows people to realize an inherent human capacity to experience joy in everyday living despite painful circumstances. In her own words, "When we can laugh in a place of pain, we are reminded of our capacity to feel joy amid suffering. We can remember who we are."[21] From this point of view, humor may help with perspective, allowing people to recover and reconnect in spite of adversity. For survivors of natural disasters, remembering who we are may be trying and exceptionally difficult. The physical trappings of a former existence— belongings, homes, neighborhoods, daily routines, social networks, and lifestyles—have been completely erased by the forces of wind and water. An emerging adult told me, "I don't know what I looked like as a kid. There are no baby pictures of me anymore." For this young man, a stable sense of self seemed out of reach, possibly driven by a childhood that could not be so easily recalled without pictures and belongings to prompt memories of his early years.

Yet, despite the losses, somehow people do find traction to move ahead in the face of adversity. For those people blessed (or perhaps cursed) with a strong-willed and self-sufficient nature, the time comes when a resourceful disposition compels them to take matters into their own hands. Firefighters, among other trained first responders, catapulted into action immediately after the storm, rescuing people trapped in attics and clinging to rooftops. Essential personnel (among others) who stayed for the storm didn't wait for outside assistance: they pulled storm victims from the water to safety right away (see Chapter 4). For Rockey Vaccarella, who lost his St. Bernard home and all that he owned in the floodwaters of Katrina, the time to act on his community's behalf came in August of 2006, a year after the storm.

With a "can do" attitude and unsinkable spirit, Rockey Vaccarella took it upon himself to draw national attention to the slow pace of recovery in the first year after the storm. His mission began as an exercise in humor. "If Forrest Gump can meet the President," referring to the 1990s fictional movie character, "so can Rockey Vaccarella," he quipped. He considered his options. Reflecting the hospitable nature of the community of St. Bernard (see Chapter 3), he decided to pull a FEMA trailer to Washington, DC. He served then US President, George W. Bush a south Louisiana delicacy, a steamy plateful of red beans and rice. Over a home-cooked meal, Rockey shared his concerns with the President. He sent a clear message that, one year after the storm, his community was still suffering and the government should not forget about them.

Rockey's remarkable adventure was chronicled in an award-winning documentary film, *Forgotten on the Bayou.*[22] In the end, we learn that Rockey's mission was hugely successful. He did meet with President George W. Bush in the Oval Office and also appeared with him on national television. What had begun as a joke, a ridiculous idea that made people laugh under trying times, evolved into a mission with a serious message. Rockey made the long trek across the southeastern US pulling a FEMA trailer and picking up signatures, encouragement, and momentum along the way. Eventually, a window of opportunity was opened for him in Washington, DC. He delivered his message to the President, simply and politely. And he found that his message was received with executive-level respect. From humor to mutual respect, we can see a step in the direction of healing and long-term recovery for a seemingly forgotten, storm-ravaged community.

Solitude

Laugh, and the world laughs with you;
Weep, and you weep alone.
For the sad old earth must borrow it's mirth,
But has trouble enough of its own.
Sing, and the hills will answer;
Sigh, it is lost on the air.
The echoes bound to a joyful sound,
But shrink from voicing care.
Rejoice, and men will seek you;

Grieve, and they turn and go.
They want full measure of all your pleasure,
But they do not need your woe.
Be glad, and your friends are many;
Be sad, and you lose them all.
There are none to decline your nectared wine,
But alone you must drink life's gall.
Feast, and your halls are crowded;
Fast, and the world goes by.
Succeed and give, and it helps you live,
But no man can help you die.
There is room in the halls of pleasure
For a long and lordly train,
But one by one we must all file on
Through the narrow aisles of pain.

—Ella Wheeler Wilcox

NOTES

1. Charles S. Carver and Michael F. Scheier, "Situational Coping and Coping Dispositions in a Stressful Transaction," *Journal of Personality and Social Psychology* 66 (1994): 184–195.
2. Susan Folkman, and Richard S. Lazarus, "If It Changes It Must Be a Process: Study of Emotion and Coping During Three Stages of a College Examination," *Journal of Personality and Social Psychology* 48 (1985): 150–170.
3. Susan Roth and Lawrence J. Cohen, "Approach, Avoidance, and Coping with Stress," *American Psychologist* 41 (1986): 813–819.
4. Charles R. Snyder and Kimberley M. Pulvers, "Dr. Seuss, the Coping Machine, and 'Oh, the Places You'll Go,'" in *Coping with Stress: Effective People and Processes,* ed. C. R. Snyder (New York: Oxford University Press, 2001), 3–29.
5. Kimberly R. Schnider, Jon D. Elhai, and Matt J. Gray, "Coping Style Use Predicts Posttraumatic Stress and Complicated Grief Symptom Severity Among College Students Reporting a Traumatic Loss," *Journal of Counseling Psychology* 54, no. 3 (2007): 344–350.
6. Katie E. Cherry, Laura Sampson, Pamela F. Nezat, Sandro Galea, Loren D. Marks, and Bethany A. Lyon, "Prior Hurricane and Other Lifetime Trauma Predict Coping Style in Older Commercial Fishers After the BP Deepwater Horizon Oil Spill," *Journal of Applied Biobehavioral Research* 2 (June 22, 2017), 1–18, https://doi.org/10.1111/jabr.12076
7. Katie E. Stanko, Laura Sampson, Katie E. Cherry, Sandro Galea, and Loren D. Marks, "When Reliance on Religion Falters: Religious Coping and Post-Traumatic Stress Symptoms in Older Adults After Multiple Disasters," *Journal of Religion, Spirituality, and Aging* 30 (2018): 292–313.

8. Heather Littleton, Samantha Horsley, Siji John, and David V. Nelson, "Trauma Coping Strategies and Psychological Distress: A Meta-Analysis," *Journal of Traumatic Stress* 20, no. 6 (2007): 977–988.

9. Julie A. Penley, Joe Tomaka, and John S. Wiebe, "The Association of Coping to Physical and Psychological Health Outcomes. A Meta-Analytic Review," *Journal of Behavioral Medicine* 25 (2002): 551–603.

10. Katie E. Cherry, Laura Sampson, Sandro Galea, Loren D. Marks, Katie E. Stanko, Pamela F. Nezat, and Kayla H. Baudoin, "Spiritual Support and Humor Are Associated with Resilience After Multiple Disasters," *Journal of Nursing Scholarship* (2018): 1–22.

11. Loren D. Marks, Yaxin Lu, Katie E. Cherry, and Trevan G. Hatch, "Faith and Coping: Spiritual Beliefs and Religious Practices After Hurricanes Katrina and Rita," in *Traumatic Stress and Long-Term Recovery: Coping with Disasters and Other Negative Life Events,* ed. Katie E. Cherry (New York: Springer International Publishing Switzerland, 2015), 369–387.

12. Loren D. Marks, Trevan G. Hatch, Yaxin Lu, and Katie E. Cherry, "Families and Faith-Based Communities After a Disaster: Successes and Failures in the Wakes of Hurricanes Katrina and Rita," in *Traumatic Stress and Long-Term Recovery: Coping with Disasters and Other Negative Life Events,* ed. Katie E. Cherry (New York: Springer International Publishing Switzerland, 2015), 247–270.

13. Anna R. Harper and Kenneth I. Pargament, "Trauma, Religion, and Spirituality: Pathways to Healing," in *Traumatic Stress and Long-Term Recovery: Coping with Disasters and Other Negative Life Events,* ed. Katie E. Cherry (New York: Springer International Publishing Switzerland, 2015), 349–367.

14. Harold G. Koenig, Dana King, and Verna B. Carson, eds., *Handbook of Religion and Health* (2nd ed.) (New York: Oxford, 2012).

15. Kenneth I. Pargament, *The Psychology of Religion and Coping: Theory, Research, and Practice* (New York: Guilford, 1997).

16. Loren D. Marks, "Sacred Practices in Highly Religious Families: Christian, Jewish, Mormon, and Muslim Perspectives," *Family Process* 43 (2004): 217–231.

17. Katie E. Cherry, Loren D. Marks, Rachel Adamek, and Bethany A. Lyon, "Younger and Older Coastal Fishers Face Catastrophic Loss After Hurricane Katrina," in *Traumatic Stress and Long-Term Recovery: Coping with Disasters and Other Negative Life Events,* ed. Katie E. Cherry (New York: Springer International Publishing Switzerland, 2015), 327–348.

18. Rod A. Martin, *The Psychology of Humor: An Integrative Approach* (Burlington, VT: Elsevier Academic Press, 2007).

19. Viktor E. Frankl, *Man's Search for Meaning* (Boston: Beacon Press, 2006), 44.

20. Ella Wheeler Wilcox, *Poems of Passion* (Chicago: Albert, Whitman & Co., 1883), 131–132.

21. Susan Sparks, *Laugh Your Way to Grace: Reclaiming the Spiritual Power of Humor* (Woodstock: Skylight Paths, 2010), 106.

22. Ghost Rider Pictures, *Forgotten on the Bayou,* last modified 2008, http://www.ghostriderpictures.com/RockeyTrailer.html

CHAPTER 6

⌀

Respect and Gratitude

INTRODUCTION

The term "respect" is likely to conjure up a variety of different images. Respect, what it means and its significance in everyday life, may vary across generations, too. That is, younger and older people may have vastly different ideas about what respect is and how to model it in everyday life.

Arguably, respect goes beyond the simple deferential behaviors for parents and authority figures taught in childhood (i.e., "yes ma'am, yes sir"). For elderly people, thinking about respect may prompt recollections from their own childhood: a broken rule, naughty act, or smart remark to a teacher at school. Back in the day, such misdeeds often had unfortunate but predictable consequences: disciplinary actions imposed at the school, at home, or in both places. Perhaps a trip to the timeout chair in the corner, a close encounter with a wooden spoon, a switch cut from a bush, or an old-fashioned, single-handed spanking on the backside, *respect is a lesson learned* for some folks through corrective punishment that reflects the cultural norms and childrearing practices of the times.

For younger and middle-aged people navigating the working world of adult responsibilities, *respect is a given* that goes along with position or territory. Naturally, one should respect professionals whose career path required years of training, hard work, sacrifice, and dedication. Aren't doctors, lawyers, professors, commanding officers in the military, elected officials, and many other leaders in society entitled to respect by virtue of their position or, as a sociologist might say, "achieved status"? An alternative view is that *respect is earned* based on a history of high-integrity choices and honorable actions (and reactions) that speak of impeccable moral character. Yet respect may also be quite a fragile thing that could erode or be forfeited completely through lapses of good judgment or a betrayal of trust—even a single indiscretion may be sufficient to turn the tide of personal or public opinion.

So what, then, is respect? A lesson learned? A given that goes with a position? Something that must be earned, but could be lost through a single misstep or series of missteps if one is not careful to maintain one's footing on a moral high road? When in doubt, a good practice is to consult the dictionary. According to the *American Heritage Dictionary*, "respect" has several different forms. Depending on usage, respect can be a noun: "a feeling of deferential regard, honor, esteem; the state of being regarded with honor or esteem; willingness to show consideration or appreciation." Respect can also be a verb: "to feel or show esteem for, to honor; to show consideration for; avoid violation of; treat with deference; to relate or refer to; to concern." Last, respect has a plural usage: "polite expressions of consideration or deference," as in *paying one's respects*. In the vernacular, "paying one's respects" is what people say they are doing when they attend a wake, a visitation, or funeral—honoring the person who has recently died. Given the semantic complexity of respect, a term rich with meaning and interpretation that can go off in many directions, a narrower focus is not only desirable, but may be a necessity.

As an academic, I reach for the dictionary to gain clarity or when I simply don't know the meaning of a word or concept. A "top-down" approach to defining respect and clarifying its role in the healing process after tragedy based on a dictionary alone, however, may be limited at best or wholly inadequate. In fact, a dictionary approach may not work at all for people struggling with real losses in everyday life. A "bottom-up" approach, based on a research-driven collection of real-life stories of survival and hope, is arguably better. Real-life stories may be inspiring and easier to relate to than dictionary definitions and certainly more authentic. By listening to survivors in their natural setting who have lived through disaster and their personal accounts of what happened, how they coped, what helped, and what was not helpful, a particular principle begins to take shape: *disaster respect*. After severe weather events, entire neighborhoods may be gone and lifestyles are severely disrupted. Even worse, precious lives may be lost, those unfortunate souls who did not survive the severe weather event. For people who have witnessed death and destruction, respect for the experience of having lost everything suddenly—all material goods plus a way of life—is a step in the direction of healing that may come eventually (or perhaps not at all). Sadly, persistent grief and sorrow imply that some survivors may never overcome disaster, at least not quickly or completely (see Chapter 8).

No discussion of respect would be complete without addressing its flip side: *disrespect*. If respect strengthens well-being, disrespect weakens it. Whether intentional or unintentional, disrespect is hurtful and insulting. Even worse, disrespect may negate healing by prolonging painful experiences. For instance, a disrespectful or insensitive remark may fan the flames of pain in the present or rekindle painful memories from the past.

As a researcher who interviewed Katrina survivors, I recall a conversation I had with Rox Bentley in July of 2012. She had endured a lengthy, four-year displacement before making the decision to return home to St. Bernard Parish. Rox described these years succinctly: "I wandered around the desert of 'I don't know what the hell I want to do' for four years." She and her husband had lived in at least eleven different temporary locations for weeks and months at a time, as far north as Shreveport, Louisiana, and as far east as Picayune, Mississippi. She spoke about the disparaging remarks she heard from indirectly affected people in the receiving cities where displaced Gulf Coast residents stayed in the aftermath of Katrina. The term "indirectly affected" is used in scientific parlance to characterize individuals who did not personally experience loss of property, yet whose daily lives (including work and home life) may have changed as a result of circumstances brought about by disaster (see Chapter 4). These people are affected by the severe weather event, but in an indirect way: hence the term. Rox spoke of harsh and insensitive comments she overheard or received from indirectly affected people in the wake of Katrina. In her own words, here is how Rox described it:

> Now some people got a little crappy after a year or so. Some people would get a little ugly, you know, like you were kind of invading their area [in receiving cities]. And I would say, "Yeah, I felt like waking up on August 29 and losing my whole world just [so I could come here] to aggravate you and [disrupt] your world."
>
> I mean they had some ugly people like . . . you're a foreigner coming out of someplace else or illegal aliens invading your space. Because people still wound up being human beings even after a tragedy, you know? You still have ugly people and that [disasters] don't stop that. And that was very hurtful. I'm going to tell you that was very hurtful sometimes when you'd hear comments, maybe like a year down the road when they thought everybody should be back home. Well, it wasn't always possible to come back home. And then you'd hear rude comments, like, "Oh, those people from Chalmette, or those people from so and so. . . . "

As our conversation on this topic of "ugly people" began to wind down, Rox also pointed out that other strangers had been helpful and good to her. In her own words:

> [There were] more people that helped you and were good to you than were these ugly people and they were ugly before Katrina so . . . people. You know, tragedy doesn't stop people from being ugly. If you're that kind of person, you're that kind of person all the time anyway.

Sadly, many survivors who struggled with the hardships of homelessness and displacement to unfamiliar, geographic locations after Katrina could likely relate to Rox's experience of "ugly people" and insensitive remarks. What Rox has termed "ugly" captures the essence of what I mean by disrespect—the flip side of the disaster respect. I will return to the topic of disrespect and its role in the post-disaster recovery process later in this chapter.

To an outsider unfamiliar with severe weather and its calamitous effects, disaster respect calls for humility and an openness to see, listen to, and consider what survivors may have to say about their experiences. Without prior life experience to draw on, many people may not know what it is like to be suddenly homeless due to a disaster. But we can learn from survivors who will tell us about this experience from a position of authority that comes from having gone down this road of evacuation, displacement, and weather-related losses. From this point of view, one may think of disaster respect as a lesson to be learned from someone who has personal knowledge and life experience. Furthermore, disaster respect may be operationalized as *an awareness to cultivate* based on others' stories of survival and loss, one that begins with an "Aha, now I get it" realization. This insight may be achieved in a moment of solitude and quiet reflection or through conversations with people who have experienced severe weather and profound losses.

As for me, disaster respect has been shaped through years of observation and data collection after the 2005 Atlantic Hurricanes Katrina and Rita (see Appendix A for a research summary). In fact, I can tell you the very day and hour that the concept of "disaster respect" became quite real for me: on a sunny afternoon in April of 2010, while sitting in the principal's office of Chalmette High School in the coastal parish of St. Bernard, Louisiana (see Preface and illustrations presented next). This high school principal, Mr. Wayne Warner, was himself a Katrina hero, although I did not know this at that time. His briefing on the events of August 29, 2005—the day Katrina made landfall—and the horrendous days that followed brought this concept of disaster respect to life in a very real and meaningful way. I will always be grateful to Mr. Warner for his crystal-clear instruction and rich personal insights into the Katrina experience as a leader in the community,[1] with his school serving as a shelter of last resort in August of 2005, and as a survivor who also lost his home in Katrina's floodwaters.

To summarize, disaster respect begins with an awareness that deepens as one grows in knowledge and understanding of calamitous events and their consequences. For survivors, a feeling of appreciation or thankfulness may be realized when they sense respect for their disaster experience(s). Gratitude, despite one's circumstances, is another variable that matters in a post-disaster context. Like respect, a formal approach to defining gratitude could go off in several directions depending on one's background and preferred ways of knowing. A dictionary definition of gratitude may be a bit stiff and narrow, while a scholarly approach may be too frothy and expansive for individuals without formal training in academic psychology. Consequently, the focus in this chapter is confined to respect and gratitude as complementary principles of healing observed among those who have suffered great losses in the years after catastrophic events of nature. In the next two sections, respect and gratitude are presented in turn. Through illustration and reference to the scientific literature, respect and gratitude are conceptualized as unique but complementary principles that are foundational for healing in the years after tragedy.

RESPECT

Katrina took away my past, disrupted my future, and dropped me into a hell of a present.
—Neta Valen

Some people, academics and laypersons alike, might find it odd or perhaps unconventional to conceptualize respect as a healing principle. A purist who is well-versed in linguistics might point out that adding the descriptor "disaster" to "respect," as in "disaster respect," does not really answer the question of just how respect may promote healing and long-term disaster recovery. A more familiar approach may be to think of respect as an attitude, character strength, or virtue. Respect as an attitude makes sense conceptually, and it works based on a dictionary approach, too. Recall that respect has been defined as a "willingness to show consideration or appreciation" (a noun) and also "avoid violation of" (a verb). Laying semantics aside, just how does respect translate to well-being in the present and support recovery in the long run?

In response, I believe that the answer to the question "How does disaster respect promote healing?" has at least two parts. The first part has to do with a release of frustration driven by the thought that "no one understands (or cares) what I am going through or have been through." When survivors sense respect for their experiences from others—even if only fleeting or momentary—they may realize that others do care despite their limited personal knowledge of the disaster experience. In this manner, disaster respect may loosen the grip of frustration or discouragement, among other unpleasant feelings based on the assumption that no one understands or cares, in the aftermath of disaster.

The second part of the answer has to do with a ground-swell of positive emotions that may be felt when one senses respect for lived experiences from other people. For instance, survivors may find it comforting to be around or to talk to individuals with "a willingness to show consideration or appreciation for" their disaster experiences. The experience of positive emotions, in turn, may boost resilience after adversity. Furthermore, disaster relief personnel and other good-natured volunteers who model respect for the disaster experience will "avoid violation of" survivors struggling to move forward in daily life after disaster. A release of frustration, together with positive emotions that bring comfort, may or may not happen quickly. Rather, both are part of the recovery process. Recovery, a process that unfolds over time, calls for patience and endurance, as will be considered in greater detail later in this chapter.

To summarize, respect for an unforeseen event and the totality of its influence, together with respect for the healing process, provides direction for recovery in the wake of a life-changing tragedy. The illustrations presented next cast a spotlight on the key role that respect for the past plays in post-disaster well-being. Respect for the past refers broadly to that which had existed before the storm but is now severely damaged. Some damaged things, like landscapes and the look of the community, may be recovered, restored either partially or completely, in time. Other damage may be better classified as a "storm casualty"—irretrievably gone and not to be recovered.

In addition to physical features of the environment, respect for the past may also include time-honored traditions that contribute to survivors' well-being. This section concludes by drawing attention to respect for the process of disaster recovery, which may vary in scope and duration depending on the individual and his or her life circumstances.

Illustration: Respect the Past—Landscapes and Community Restoration

"Hey! That's my front yard!" Gina Buchanan exclaimed with great angst as she watched a construction worker throw his trash down in what had once been her carefully manicured yard. I listened carefully as Gina related the story of a fall afternoon in 2005. Gray skies and thick, dark mud—devastation as far as the eye could see. Her Colonial Louisiana home, on the National Register of Historic Places with title work to 1805 (before statehood), had withstood many previous storms. This beautiful home was still standing in the wake of Katrina; it had minimum wind damage, yet the rushing water from two different directions had left a swath of storm debris across her three-acre front yard.

On that particular autumn day in 2005, construction crews were hauling away fallen power lines and downed power poles. Military vehicles and utility trucks parked in the mud had left deep grooves in what had been her front lawn. As Gina explained, the National Guard trucks had driven off her street into the mud, possibly seeking shade from the double row of live oak trees and a quiet place to eat as they kept watch over the military checkpoint established along the stretch of highway on the west side of her property. Regardless, the trucks left approximately five-hundred feet of ugly ruts which also threatened the root systems of these beautiful and historic trees. The Katrina experience was painful enough. Did the National Guard have to park in her front yard? Did the power company have to leave coiled cable pieces and assorted trimmings littered about the place? And did the work crews have to throw their trash down on the ground, adding insult to injury?

As an outsider, I could see both sides of this dilemma. To the military personnel and the construction workers, there was no difference between the mud that was her historic property and the rest of the mud that covered the parish. To Gina, mud or no mud, it was still her front yard. Five years later, as I sat at her dining room table, I looked beyond the long, drawn-back drapes and through the thick, antique glass of the tall French doors. I could see the magnificent live oak trees, a double alley of fourteen trees. The thin veils of Spanish moss were reminiscent of an earlier era. There was a beautiful path of flowers—twin lines of bright yellow daylilies leading to the river, reaching skyward and surrounded by well-kept green grass. The property was bordered by a white picket fence.

Without question, this was an inspiring place—a historic home surrounded by picturesque landscape. I marveled at the daylilies, although Gina said they had not fully recovered from the salt marsh water which had nearly destroyed them five years earlier. Never having seen the property before Katrina, I couldn't imagine a more glorious patch of tall yellow flowers than what I was seeing on that May afternoon in 2010. It was peaceful here, quiet and serene. I noticed a bright green anole lizard making his way across the porch in short and sudden bursts. In time, the colors of nature return, I thought. On later reflection, I realized that this participant sensed the brilliance of her property in her mind's eye, even though the long months of drab and dreary surroundings seemed endless in that first year after the horrendous 2005 storm.

Returning to Gina's recollection of that autumn day in 2005, the construction crews toiled under gloomy gray skies, slowly working their way through the endless expanse of mud. After Gina spoke to them, they found a new place to park their vehicles along the street. At that time, St. Bernard Parish had not yet opened to the public. Gina and her husband were among the few essential personnel in the parish, working by day and spending nights at the courthouse, with generators providing power to this building. Their historic home was among the first to be cleaned out, as Gina spent many hours in the hot sun picking up and bagging storm debris from their property after the floodwaters had receded. Despite the circumstances, Gina knew what her property was like before Katrina. She also had hope for what it would look like again someday, once the cleanup and restoration work was completed. She knew that beauty and tranquility would return in time. She saw promise. The construction workers who threw their trash to the ground saw only the mud, with apparently no regard for the tremendous effort that had already been made to clean up this private property.

Many people have spoken of the emotions aroused while watching work crews plow through the layers of debris removal necessary to restore the community. One home owner, Dave Brubaker, talked about the beautiful live oak trees that had lined his street. Before the storm, an arborist from Louisiana State University in Baton Rouge was brought in once a year to tend to these historic trees, meticulously trimming the lengthy, sideways branches with the utmost care, Dave said. During the cleanup phase after Katrina, Dave cringed as he watched the telephone company indiscriminately hacking at these majestic branches with their power saws. The once carefully manicured limbs came crashing to the ground as the chainsaws buzzed mercilessly, taking apart one after the other, after the other. Necessary work, of course, with no guile or malice intended, but nonetheless painful to watch and sad to see.

Five years later, as Dave and I walked across his front yard, he pointed to the stumps of severed limbs and still gaping holes in the canopy of leaves that arced above where we were standing. I could see for myself the permanent scars in the trunks of these magnificent trees and the patch-work of empty spaces which once had been filled with dark green foliage. Looking skyward, I began to grasp the totality of Katrina's destruction. Even the live oak trees, which have flourished for decades (some for more than a century), show noticeable and lasting wounds from this storm. Looking to the left and to the right in a panoramic sweep, one can also see that the neighborhoods reflect the long-term effects of the storm, too. Empty lots where houses used to be can be seen on nearly every street in this commu-nity. Now covered with green grass, these empty lots are flanked by houses that were renovated or rebuilt completely.

The look of the community is certainly very different today—streets winding through incomplete neighborhoods with noticeable gaps in the scenery. In fact, one street has no homes at all now, owing to the Murphy oil spill in late August of 2005 which happened during the intense flooding that followed the levee breaches (see Chapter 4). Respect for what was lost and will not be coming back may be realized quickly for some people, but it may take longer for others to catch on. And still there will be some who may never understand or possess even the slightest awareness of a tragedy's comprehensive impact on the lives of the survivors who experienced it directly.

Illustration: Respect the Past—A School Year and Rites of Passage

Routines and traditions can be readily observed in different life contexts. Sometimes they are defined by the season of the year. As an example, con-sider the tradition of "Back to School" which happens in late summer. Local retail stores with "Back to School" advertisements and sales are a common sight, much to the dismay of those who are not yet ready to bid farewell to summer's slow and leisurely pace. Whether shopping for school supplies or preparing lesson plans, students, teachers, administrators, and others who work in a school system anticipate the beginning of new academic year.

A new school year normally begins in August and is completed in mid to late spring, often in May or June. For a high school senior, that last year of school can be filled with many traditional events, such as receiving a high school ring, attending a dance, and participating in a graduation ceremony. Wearing a cap and gown with school colors, the graduate walks proudly across a stage and receives his or her diploma along with a congratulatory handshake and a smile from the school administrator who officiates at graduation. High school graduations invite sociological contemplation as a *rite of passage* which signifies the end of secondary education and the beginning of a new phase of life in the adult world of responsibility.

*   *   *

Looking back to April of 2010, I remember my visit with Wayne Warner, the principal of Chalmette High School, and Carole Mundt, the assistant principal, as though it were yesterday. Mr. Warner spoke of numerous hardships, obstacles, and setbacks in the weeks and months after the storm. A new school year had just begun, with classes in session for only a few weeks when Hurricane Katrina crashed into the US Gulf Coast in late August of 2005. Facing a Herculean task—transforming what was left of the school, a shelter of last resort where people faced death (see Chapter 4) into a functional place of learning—was a major challenge. Opening the school meant that families with school-age children could return to rebuild their homes and reestablish their lives, a critical piece of the community recovery puzzle.

With unwavering determination, the parish Superintendent of Education, Doris Voitier, successfully leveraged financial support and secured resources needed for the principal, assistant principal, and a handful of dedicated teachers to open the school in November of 2005, just a few short months after the storm. A truly remarkable feat, given how thoroughly overwhelmed the infrastructure, including local and state government, was at the time.[2]

During the course of our conversation five years after Katrina, Principal Warner said, "We gave them a year." At first, I found his remark a bit puzzling. The thought of a school year as a gift would never have occurred to me. I wondered how many students would come back to say, "Thank you for giving me a year?" Or how many parents would compel their school-age children to pen a note of thanks for this gift? Laying social conventions and common courtesies aside, I knew that he was talking about the students who had lost everything in 2005 and had returned with their families to rebuild their storm-ravaged homes. Until that day, I had not realized how fundamentally important the daily routines of a typical school year are for the well-being of students and their families. As I was mulling over the implications of giving students a year, the principal pushed back from his desk. He walked across the room to retrieve a copy of the 2005–2006 year book. As he flipped through the pages, I was amazed at what I saw. The St. Bernard Unified School (SBUS), as it was called that year, had students ranging in age from pre-kindergarten through to adults enrolled in GED classes to earn the equivalent of a high school diploma. The SBUS was the only school in the parish at that time, so students had come from different districts, as reflected in the variety of uniforms seen in the pages of the year book. He spoke of the importance of giving these students a full school year, complete with sporting activities that following spring and, for seniors, a formal graduation ceremony. On graduation day, seniors wore caps and gowns that matched their home district school colors. A diverse array of different-colored regalia, but one unified group of students who stood together at graduation, a time of celebration and joy marking the end of a painful and stress-filled school year.

As my meeting with the principal drew to a close, he gave me a copy of the 2005–2006 year book to keep, along with two illustrative CDs. "Be prepared to shed a few tears," he said. Looking behind his desk, I noticed three black numbers painted on a white ceramic tile plate. Outlined with a delicate blue and yellow floral boarder, this quaint but curious tile plate on his bookshelf seemed oddly out of place among the assortment of books. He explained that this was his house number, salvaged from the wreckage of his home that was sixteen feet under water after Katrina. Clearly a meaningful storm memento for him (see Chapter 9), the house number also served as a valuable teaching tool. He spoke only briefly about what had happened to his house. In that moment, it suddenly dawned on me that, during the fall of 2005 while he was struggling so valiantly to open the school under the most desperate of circumstances with heroic resolve and unwavering focus on the welfare of his students and recovery of his community, he, too, was homeless.

I had come to my meeting with the principal on that sunny afternoon in April of 2010 to learn about Hurricane Katrina's impact from an educator with an insider's perspective on the coastal community of St. Bernard, the catchment area I had selected for a research project (see Preface). What I took away from that meeting was far more extensive than I could have ever imagined. For one thing, I became aware of the persistence of pain and the longevity of suffering associated with the Katrina tragedy, which today seems so obvious but was not so at the time. Grief lies just beneath the surface for some people, it seems, where lingering sorrow and painful memories ebb and flow like the tide rolling across the seashore. The persistence of grief in the years after disaster is a topic unto itself that will be discussed in greater detail in Chapter 8.

Another realization that crossed my mind that sunny afternoon in the principal's office was how deeply school officials could care about their students and the community as a whole. In retrospect, the many sides of respect that complete the long-term recovery puzzle began to come into focus: respect for the positive effect of a "normal" school year on the lives of students and the community, respect for upholding time-honored traditions despite the prevailing circumstances, and respect for the comprehensive and long-lasting impact of Hurricane Katrina on those coastal residents who experienced it directly.

Respect the Process of Recovery: Comfort While Moving On

Undeniably important to well-being is the *process of recovery*, an ongoing reality that plays out over time after a disaster. Recovery, in the literal sense of rebuilding one's home and community, may be painfully slow, but measurable signs of progress can be encouraging. In the summer of 2010, it had been nearly five years since the floodwaters of Katrina had demolished the city of New Orleans and its coastal suburbs. In Chalmette, just five miles south of New Orleans, it was a delight to witness the anticipation and excitement of local residents talking about the movie theater reopening in July of that year. I also had the good fortune of attending a ground-breaking ceremony for the St. Bernard Parish Hospital, whose construction would be completed two years later, opening to the public in August of 2012.[3] Watching the gradual return of a community and the excitement among its lifelong residents is inspiring, bringing hope for better days ahead. With urban reconstruction projects well under way—new buildings, streets, and sidewalks—progress is visible. The gray skies, thick mud, and mountains of storm debris which had once lined the roadways are fading into the recesses of people's minds— perhaps a distant memory, but perhaps not.

In contrast to the observable signs of urban renewal and growth, the process of disaster recovery in the psychological sense of overcoming this life-changing event is a different matter. Stress reactions to loss vary widely. Tracking peoples' psychological recovery is more difficult, too, as signs of progress may not be as readily noticeable as a reopened movie theater or newly constructed hospital building. Reestablishing daily routines and getting on with one's life (colloquially referred to as "the new normal") after a personal tragedy or disaster will be discussed more fully in Chapter 8. For some disaster survivors, the process of recovery may be rushed or overlooked completely if they are in a hurry to heal. There are many reasons that survivors may want to "bend time," as one participant put it to me. By "bending time," she was referring to a feeling of being stuck in place, wistfully wishing for a cosmic fast-forward that could move her quickly ahead to a different place, a different point in time. Being in a hurry to resolve the uncertainty and disruption that disasters bring is certainly understandable. Survivors miss their homes. Tired of living in temporary housing, such as someone else's house, a trailer provided by the Federal Emergency Management Agency (FEMA), or in an RV parked out front while struggling with contractors to repair or rebuild a storm-damaged house behind it, survivors want to get back into a home—*their home.* They want their life back.

Furthermore, it may be other people who are in a hurry for disaster survivors to complete the recovery process and resume daily life as usual. Perhaps survivors' pain makes us uncomfortable. We, the less affected, don't know what to do or say. Thinking more about this social etiquette dilemma, just what does one say to those made recently homeless through disaster? "Sorry for your loss" seems hollow and possibly insincere, yet "I know exactly how you feel" could be taken as an insult, especially coming from someone who has never experienced a catastrophic loss of property or witnessed the death of friends or family who did not make it out in time. For compassionate, well-meaning people who have a heart and want to support survivors through the disaster recovery process, there is no cell phone app or book of etiquette to consult for proper guidance on what to say to a survivor that would be helpful and make a difference or have a positive impact on recovery.

Such musings about what to say or what not to say, coupled with a genuine desire to avoid insult or offense, prompted me to ask Lucy Collins and Ashley Bowen to share their thoughts on what would be the right thing to say to a survivor in the wake of disaster. Lucy Collins, a nurse who had been on shift at Chalmette Medical Center over the Katrina weekend, sheltered in place on August 29, 2005. She had survived the storm and its horrendous aftermath there in the hospital, a building that sustained irreparable damage and would eventually be torn down as yet another Katrina casualty. Lucy looked me in the eye with a deep and penetrating stare when I asked her this question. She said slowly, "It was really bad." She spoke of patients dying in the hospital in the insufferable heat and the chaos and mayhem outside of the hospital, with thieves trying to break in to steal controlled medicines.[4] When she finally left the hospital, Lucy's home down the road was ruined. There were snakes lurking about the property— some poisonous—among other oddities that had washed up in the yard. Given the natural and social context of chaos, she carried a gun for protection anytime she worked outside. After this brief but grisly description, Lucy answered my question simply and succinctly. She told me, "You can say to people who were here, 'It must have been really bad.'" In that moment, I realized that Lucy's experiences in the immediate aftermath of the Katrina disaster were outside the realm of anything I could have imagined. If I found myself speechless, not knowing what to say, "It must have been really bad" was just right, allowing Katrina survivors the freedom to fill in with illustrative, personal stories or simply nod quietly in agreement.

Ashley Bowen had a very different answer to my question of "what does one say to a disaster survivor?" Ashley had survived the intense flooding on August 29, 2005, and she endured days on a rooftop waiting for rescue with her husband, Mike, and teenage son, Brandon. In Ashley's opinion, the appropriate response to a disaster survivor would be: "I'll be there for you when you are ready to talk about it." I was particularly struck by the "when you are ready to talk about it" part of her answer. In this single phrase, Ashley brought light to a great truth. That is, disaster survivors may each have their own timetables for the recovery process and coming to terms with their experiences. Moreover, they may also have different thresholds of readiness for opening up and talking to others about their losses. Last, when a survivor is ready to talk, whenever that may be, someone should be ready to listen patiently and supportively, without judgment. Such an approach models respect. For people who have never suffered catastrophic losses, relating to someone else's disaster experience may be difficult. Yet a simple show of respect, regardless of professional training or personal knowledge, is important, even vital, to a survivor. One may wonder why this is so. The answer seems to be that leading with respect, whether or not one can personally relate, is a courtesy. Showing disaster respect is also a kindness that may help by sending a message of support and validation. That is, disaster respect may remind survivors of how far they have come in the recovery process, while offering the assurance that they are important and their experiences are worthy of consideration. One takeaway message: disaster respect is a variable that matters, a key piece of the post-disaster recovery puzzle.

If disaster respect is comforting, disrespect, then, in whatever form it may take, is painful, as noted earlier in this chapter. Moreover, disrespect may be counterproductive to the recovery process. During the course of conducting research interviews, many participants voiced their feelings of frustration and angst on receipt of a dismissive comment like "It's been so many years since Katrina, you really should get over it." There is a fundamental problem with this instruction and its many variations ("Let it go, get on with your life," "Don't dwell on the past," etc.). That is, the logic behind such a statement presumes that the process of healing is linear, meaning that as time moves forward by one unit, so does healing. The recovery process does often move forward, but it sometimes moves two or more steps backward. Recovery is not a smooth linear progression. This realization is discouraging enough, yet coupled with a terse and insensitive remark ("Get over it!") implies that survivors are choosing to wallow in their misery. Such an insult can surely dampen one's spirits. Or worse, insensitive remarks may derail the recovery process with an unwelcomed reminder of how much the disaster experience may still hurt.

When a person suffers a bodily injury, there is often physical evidence of the hurt that captures our attention, like a cast on a broken arm or bandages covering a wound. Such physical cues remind us, particularly strangers, that bodily damage was sustained and the person may be in pain or experiencing discomfort. In response, we hold the door open for someone using crutches to ambulate. Or we reach for a desired item on the top shelf in a grocery store for the wheelchair-bound shopper, happy to assist. Such courtesies are usually extended automatically, with little thought or hesitation. For people with prior trauma exposure or tragedy in their developmental history, there may be no physical signs to indicate that this person is burdened by soul-crushing pain. Their tragedy, along with their recovery, may not be obvious to other people. For survivors, healing associated with a traumatic experience may not be observed outwardly, felt inwardly, or realized quickly. In fact, it may take years, decades, or possibly a lifetime before a survivor feels the wholeness of spirit that accompanies authentic healing from a painful experience. Disaster respect can shine light in an otherwise dark place, bringing hope and inspiring survivors' next steps on the long road to recovery after disaster.

Summary

A case is made for respect as a principle of healing. For disaster survivors, respect may lessen the frustration fueled by the feeling that "no one understands what I have been through." Regardless of a survivor's age or season in life, the feeling that other people, even strangers, have respect for their experience with severe weather events is important. With respect comes validation, a positive emotion which is comforting and may renew survivors' sense of the authenticity of their experiences. For everyone— first responders, disaster relief personnel, indirectly affected family and friends—respect can be thought of as an *awareness to cultivate*, one that may enhance survivors' well-being and post-disaster resilience.

Respect for the past and what was lost, as well as respect for the process of recovery, may work in tandem as survivors pick up the pieces after disaster. Whether literally picking up the pieces, as in cleaning out what had been one's home and tossing ruined possessions to the street for storm debris pickup later, or figuratively, as in reestablishing routines (or forming new routines), respect for the disaster experience helps.

To my way of thinking, a deeper awareness of the role of respect in everyday life after disaster is needed. Disaster respect—for people and their experiences—may bring value and human compassion to survivors. In the light of disaster respect, a survivor may come to the realization that he or she matters as a person and is worthy of consideration and care. For survivors, then, respect for their disaster experience as a finite event that happened at a particular point in time is an important step in the direction of healing. Respect for the process of recovery may protect well-being and promote a feeling of wholeness that can lead to inner peace for some individuals.

GRATITUDE

I don't know what to do. . . . I just want to tell you thank you. Thank you for taking your time out of your life to come down here and help people you don't even know.
—Patsy Shapiro

We all know what gratitude is. A thoughtful person does something nice for our benefit. Maybe this person has extended a courtesy or a kindness. A feeling of appreciation follows, one that we label "gratitude." Upon receiving an act of generosity from another person, the socially proper response is a simple, two-word utterance: "Thank you!" These two words are likely to prompt a smile from the benefactor who has done something nice, perhaps accompanied by a light-hearted and equally snappy, two-word reply: "You're welcome!"

At this general level of analysis, gratitude is simply a reaction that follows a kindness shown by others, a well-practiced exercise in good manners. Upon further reflection, however, one may come to realize that gratitude might be something more than just a simple response packaged neatly into the words "thank you." Rather, gratitude can become a perspective, a way of looking at the circumstances of one's life, good or bad.[5]

As an example of looking at events (good or bad) from the vantage point of gratitude, consider the end-of-life circumstances of physician and author Oliver Sacks. Dr. Sacks died of cancer in 2015. At the end of his life, here is what he had to say (emphasis added):

I cannot pretend I am without fear. *But my predominant feeling is one of gratitude.* I have loved and been loved; I have been given much and I have given something in return; I have read and traveled and thought and written. . . . Above all, I have been a sentient being, a thinking animal, on this beautiful planet, and that in itself has been an enormous privilege and adventure.[6]

At the thought of terminal cancer, I find myself recoiling just a bit. Nonetheless, I am drawn to Oliver Sacks's quote, finding his intellectual honesty to be quite remarkable. He begins with "I cannot pretend I am without fear." But I wonder just how long it took after his terminal cancer diagnosis to reach a predominant feeling of gratitude? Did he pass through all five of Elisabeth Kübler-Ross's stages first? Did he go through the stages in order, or did he skip a stage or two? Does that really matter? We will revisit the topic of cancer and Kübler-Ross's framework briefly in the context of acceptance as a principle of healing in Chapter 7. Setting questions about Oliver Sacks' personal journey with cancer aside, it would appear that his earthly life ended on a high note of gratitude.

For disaster survivors, gratitude may not be among the top ten emotions experienced, at least not at first. In the aftermath of a categorically destructive hurricane, flood, or other severe weather event, the healing potential of gratitude may not be realized quickly or discovered easily. Gratitude may require time and effort to cultivate. At the very least, gratitude requires a willingness to look at the circumstances of one's life differently. In short, gratitude after disaster might require some thought.

A skeptical reader might also wonder why respect and gratitude are presented here, side by side, as principles of healing after disaster. In response, consider the common features that bring these two concepts into alignment. There are at least two if not more striking similarities between *respect* and *gratitude* that invite contemplation.

The first similarity pertains to the early developmental origins of these two concepts. Both are likely to have been taught in childhood, which implies that respect and gratitude are foundational for navigating complex social relations encountered later in life. If asked directly, most parents would probably state that they want their children to know how to get along with others and how to function effectively in society when they are grown. So parents, extended family, even daycare providers may try to teach young children how to respond to the world around them with respect and gratitude. By doing so, adults hope to impart "people skills" which will allow children to excel on the playground and in school. By including respect and gratitude as core elements of home training, parents may be positioning children for success in future social and academic contexts.

Taking the long view, there are other contexts of life beyond the world of secondary education in which children will need to know how to operate.[7] For instance, parents who model respect and gratitude at home may be preparing the next generation of survivors who will lose homes and property in future natural disasters that have not happened yet. Another equally plausible scenario is that parents may be preparing the next generation of first responders and disaster relief personnel whose skill sets will be pressed into action to meet the challenges of future disasters when they occur. Whether or not parents can adequately prepare children for the severe weather events they will face several decades or more in the future is an academic question for which there may be no satisfying answer. Nonetheless, gratitude, together with respect, would appear to matter in a disaster context.

Thus, arguing from a strictly developmental point of view, gratitude loosely resembles respect in that it may be counted among the *lessons learned* in childhood whose origin can be traced to parental instruction (e.g., "Say thank you to the nice lady/man" or "You should be thankful for what you have"). Thinking about childhood lessons on the importance of saying "thank you" reminds me of Dr. Seuss' classic children's book, *Green Eggs and Ham* (see also Chapter 5). The plot, briefly: the protagonist, Sam, is an energetic little fellow who makes his entrance in the story by dashing across the first few pages carrying a sign which reads "I am Sam" on one side. On the flip side, his sign reads "Sam I am." After several annoying passes in front of a bystander, Sam stops to proffer this standoffish character a plate of food. This food, green eggs and ham, looks and sounds singularly unappealing. The snooty bystander declines Sam's offer to try green eggs and ham. Fast forward through the story: Sam refuses to take no for an answer. He goes to great lengths to get the close-minded character to taste this new food. Exasperation builds as the disgruntled character declines again and again, repeating his mantra emphatically; "I do not like green eggs and ham, I will not eat them Sam I am." In the end, the grouch finally takes a tiny, delicate bite to appease Sam . . . and to his amazement he discovers that yes, indeed, he likes green eggs and ham! "Thank you, thank you, Sam I am!" is his heartfelt reply, punctuated visually with a broad smile of appreciation.

Gratitude, not once but twice, leaves an impression on young readers about the value of embracing new culinary experiences, however unappealing at first glance. It's also a lesson in saying "thank you," a socially appropriate response to an act of kindness or generosity bestowed by another person. To my way of thinking, gratitude expressed twice ("thank you, thank you, Sam I am!") closes the social etiquette loop while at the same time opening up new possibilities. For instance, we can imagine that the once grumpy bystander and Sam I Am become friends, enjoying each other's company. Maybe Sam I Am and his new friend meet for lunch from time to time? Maybe they reminisce about the good old days over a steamy plate of green eggs and ham at a restaurant? Or maybe the former curmudgeon can laugh at himself, now chuckling over his stubborn streak and silly reluctance to try something new, while Sam I Am admits that sometimes he does go just a little bit too far pushing his agenda? Speculatively, the possibilities seem endless for a meaningful new friendship between these two storybook characters. Real-life situations can unfold this way, too. When life circumstances bring people from different worlds together, sometimes what began as an unpleasant encounter can be transformed into something positive and meaningful, like a new friendship.[8] Gratitude would appear to be an important catalyst for this transformation from irritant to benefit to happen. *Benefit finding*, a coping strategy where people look for something good that can come from bad situations or unpleasant experiences, will be discussed more fully in Chapter 7.

Setting children's literature and the two-dimensional world of Dr. Seuss's fantastic drawings aside, there are many real-life stories of disaster survivors who formed lasting friendships with their benefactors, those good-natured people who stepped up to meet the challenge of providing disaster relief in response to Katrina's devastating impact. New social relationships formed for the benefactors who voluntarily contributed to the disaster relief effort, too. Regardless of which category a person falls into (survivor or benefactor), people who respond to challenging and difficult circumstances with a grateful outlook may discover a deeper appreciation of life experiences, both good and bad.

Let's return to the comparison of respect and gratitude as complementary principles that support healing after disaster. In addition to lessons learned in childhood, another striking similarity between these two concepts centers on peoples' presumptions about the ground rules of social behavior. Gratitude, like respect, may be considered *a given* by some. For instance, good manners based on rules of social etiquette dictate that a thank-you note should be sent in recognition and appreciation of a gift received within approximately three weeks of the receipt of the gift. Surely all of us have (or can imagine having) an elderly Aunt Eloise, that family member from a different generation who taps her toe impatiently while she waits in expectation for her thank-you note to arrive by regular post. After all, based on social convention alone, a personally handwritten note of thanks should arrive within three weeks of gift receipt.

Who among us hasn't been compelled at least once in life to write that obligatory thank-you note? Or send a commercially prepared thank-you card with added words (handwritten) to acknowledge the unwanted gift or thank someone for performing some action that really wasn't wanted in the first place? As an example, I am reminded of the participant who told me about the scores of volunteers who came through St. Bernard Parish during the cleanup phase of the disaster. One day, they came through his neighborhood, distributing cleaning supplies and handing out free bottles of bleach, a valuable commodity after a disaster. Bleach is a necessity after disaster to stop the growth of black mold, an environmental hazard connected with gutting a flooded house. He greeted the visitors but politely declined the gift of bleach, stating that he already had more than enough bleach to complete his house. The volunteers had a different opinion, though. They would not take "No thank you" for an answer. Sensing the futility of refusing this gift, he accepted his obligatory bleach and the volunteers moved on. Five years later, in the context of a research interview, he thought I might like to see his stash of obligatory bleach. So we took a break from the interview and went outside to his garage to take a look at it. There, in a straight line against the outer edge of the garage, stood at least a dozen or more white plastic bottles of bleach.

To summarize, saying thanks on command, either verbally or in a written format, based on strict observance of social etiquette or a well-ingrained sense of protocol or duty, may be labeled "gratitude" by its outward appearance. Yet gratitude on command arguably lacks the authenticity and the inward healing potential of heartfelt appreciation. Like respect "from the depths of your soul," gratitude can also be thought of as an *awareness to cultivate.* This awareness is important. That is, heartfelt gratitude may enhance survivors' well-being and further the process of recovery in a post-disaster environment.

Disasters, Gratitude, and Transformative Life Experiences

Most people can relate to a sense of gratitude after having been given something—a gift, a kindness, a new opportunity. But what about gratitude when everything is taken away? When all of the trappings of life—home furnishings, family photographs, cherished heirlooms—everything a person has spent a lifetime working to acquire is now in a debris pile at the end of the driveway; who can feel thankful? The sad truth is that material possessions and the lifetime of memories associated with them are sitting at curbside waiting for pickup. From one neighborhood to the next, a community lies in ruin after disaster strikes. For people who live in disaster-impacted neighborhoods, sorting through what is left and making a conscious determination over what is salvageable and what is not is a long and painful process. Most would agree that debris piles waiting for pick up are a disheartening sight. Mountainous piles of rubbish standing tall in the hot sun, day after day for weeks at a time and sometimes months after a disaster, are an eyesore. One could also make the point that debris piles are more than just an eyesore; rather, they are a monument to the destructive forces of nature.

Against this backdrop of devastation and loss, is it reasonable to expect a grateful outlook from survivors? After a severe weather event has destroyed homes and lifestyles, bringing piercing pain and sometimes endless despair, who would consider voicing the words "thank you"? Even if one could or should be thankful, a new social etiquette quandary arises: To whom should thanks be directed? Do we thank Mother Nature for her generosity in providing an abundance of wind and rain?

As tempting as it may be to poke fun at the rules of social etiquette in a disaster context, carrying the logical argument of whom to thank to the outer fringes of sarcasm is just not helpful. As discussed in Chapter 5, dark humor may offer a temporary reprieve to some survivors after disaster. However, it is worth noting that how people choose to respond to disasters or how they may think about their disaster experiences in the years after these events can either support the healing process or delay its resolution, possibly creating new problems. As will be discussed at the end of Chapter 8, negative musings and dark thoughts can act as roadblocks to healing after disaster that may complicate the grief resolution process or derail it completely.

Let's return to a simple and reasonable question. Can gratitude be counted among the emotions experienced after disaster? Consider what is left after a deadly storm has ripped through a community: catastrophic destruction of homes and properties, chaos, and upheaval. And loss! People and places are gone. In fact, certain south Louisiana towns were eliminated by the 2005 hurricanes, simply wiped off the map. Under such difficult post-disaster circumstances, the notion of gratitude does seem unlikely. In fact, gratitude might be the last thought to cross the mind of disaster survivors whose lives have changed and who have lost everything in a severe weather event. For a typical American teenager, the very thought of *gratitude* after a life-changing, painful event like Katrina might be met with a sour look—that quintessential adolescent grimace, a slight and defiant upturn of the chin—possibly coupled with a pronounced eye roll and audible sigh of exasperation. A terse remark might follow: "Gratitude . . . seriously?" The truth is, most people who have been through Katrina or a comparable experience might share the very same sentiment, although without the attitude and drama characteristic of adolescence.

Nonetheless, for some people, a very different take on gratitude in connection with the Katrina experience may be emerging in the years after the disaster. As counterintuitive as it may seem, the answer to the question of whether gratitude can be counted among the emotions experienced after disaster is a resounding "yes," as will be revealed in primary interview data presented later in this chapter. In the years after severe weather events, gratitude may even be a "predominant feeling," as Oliver Sacks, the physician who died of cancer, might say. As revealed in the examples presented next, gratitude may seed new thinking. Gratitude may also illuminate directions for interpersonal growth, opening up new pathways to healing after disaster.

In the spring of 2011, I listened as a college student spoke of his Katrina experience. Looking back, Darren Davis was a fifteen-year-old in August of 2005, a high school sophomore who evacuated with family to Texas. Like so many people who lost their homes in the storm, this teenager endured a lengthy displacement and was stuffed into a hotel room with too many people and too few personal belongings in an unfamiliar city. After several weeks of this, Darren was sent to Louisiana to live with extended family so he could attend a large city high school, one very different from the small-town feel of home. In January of 2006, his immediate family was reunited, returned to their flooded home and lived in a FEMA trailer on their property. Darren was glad to be back in his hometown. He attended the St. Bernard Unified School (SBUS) among friends who had experienced similar losses in Katrina and were living through the aftermath in step. This young man spoke of gutting his family's ruined house, tearing away sheet rock and pulling nails from the wood, one nail at a time, in the spring and summer of 2006. In his own words, here is what Darren had to say about this experience five years later (emphasis added):

> I definitely believe that I can do . . . whatever I want, and I attribute all of it to the experience I had . . . the experiences that I went through during Katrina.
>
> I mean, I would even say, it's safe to say that *I feel thankful for all of it.* I don't know where I would be without all of that happening. And it kind of scares me to think how crappy of a person I might be without all of those things happening to me. You know, I feel like now I'm growing up to be a functional contributor to society with my personal goals and my career goals.
>
> I had the attitude of wanting to give back everything that I can to society and be, the best citizen and the best patriot and the best scholar and athlete and everything. And I don't know that I would have that same attitude had all of those things not come along.

From the eyes of a young man looking back on his Katrina experience, a sympathetic reader could imagine the disruption of the lengthy displacement and slow process of rebuilding his coastal parish home while holing up in a FEMA trailer in the yard. Yet, five years later, Darren spoke of being thankful for this experience. Gratitude for Katrina as a life-changing, transformative event might be unexpected. Yet this participant spoke of a desire to give back to society as a result of having lived through the Katrina experience.

This young man's positive outlook and desire to give back can be contextualized against a backdrop of the Katrina disaster relief and cleanup phase which was still evident five years later. As discussed in Chapter 4, trained professionals and volunteer groups alike from across the nation came to help meet the needs of storm-ravaged communities in south Louisiana. Through the efforts of countless organizations, individual and community-wide restoration projects were undertaken in the months and years after Katrina's devastation. People of all ages and religious denominations helped restore devastated communities after the 2005 hurricanes. From gutting peoples' flooded homes to cleaning and restoring community properties, the multitudes of workers who came to lend a helping hand had a lasting impact on the survivors whose homes and property were destroyed in 2005.

Many of the coastal residents whom I talked to expressed heartfelt appreciation for the volunteers whose actions made a tremendous difference for survivors made suddenly homeless after Katrina. Some organizations and volunteer groups traveled great distances to contribute to the recovery effort. For instance, I watched an organized youth group in their matching neon chartreuse tee-shirts planting trees along Colonial Boulevard in front of Our Lady of Lourdes Catholic Church in Violet, Louisiana, in the summer of 2010. Watching these young people busily working along the border of the church property was an inspiring sight to see. Youth from the same organization were also working farther down the road at the quaint St. Bernard Catholic Church that had withstood Katrina's fury (see Chapter 4). On a Sunday afternoon in 2010, I chatted briefly with an adult chaperone from Milwaukee, Wisconsin, who explained that these young people, ranging in age from 14 to 20, were part of the National Youth Gathering (NYG). As I learned, the NYG is affiliated with the Lutheran Church. An estimated 25,000–30,000 youth were in the greater New Orleans area assisting with the recovery effort that summer.

On that particular Sunday afternoon while I was there, the NYG volunteers were working behind the church. Youth were receiving instructions and preparing to paint a shed out back. Looking away from the shed, I could see for myself the fresh coat of black paint on the historic iron fence that stood in front of the church. Five years earlier, this same fence had been used to secure an unearthed coffin that had floated free of its resting place in the Terre-Aux-Boeufs cemetery on the other side of the road (see Chapter 4). The iron fence in front of St. Bernard Catholic Church glistened brightly in the summer sunshine on that Sunday afternoon. What had been an anchor for death was now restored and returned to its stately and sanctified appearance thanks to the chartreuse-clad youth with paint brushes in hand.

I was not the only one who appreciated and admired the NYG volunteers' work at this little church down the road in southeastern St. Bernard. In conversation with local residents, I learned that the youth had also been involved in restoring the historic cemetery across the road from St. Bernard Church. Here is what Patsy Shapiro had to say about this effort:

> A bunch of kids painted the wrought iron fence in front of [the] St. Bernard church, the black wrought iron fence . . . the black iron fence. . . Some kids. They, well they're probably sending a bunch down there, too. They cleaned out the cemetery down there . . . pulled weeds. I mean, after the storm they had all kinds of stuff in that cemetery. Those kids came down, helped clean it out. I mean it was just amazing. You would not have been able to do all of that without people like this. Because you . . . were trying to get a house done to get back into.
>
> So you weren't even thinking about going [to] clean the cemetery. I mean, you might have did your own little brave thing, but I mean, when you have grass this high . . . and all we ask for was, "You got a shovel or a rake? A garbage bag?" That's just goodness of the people coming out, like all the people that went to Haiti and the big disasters, you know? People just go and they give [of themselves]. That's the best thing to give us.

Thinking about the NYG in the greater New Orleans area in 2010, these teenagers worked diligently to restore the physical environment in the hot summer sun. These "kids" were doing their part to advance disaster recovery in south Louisiana. They left an indelible impression on the coastal residents whom I talked to and noticeable improvements in the outdoor environment.

As for me, thinking like a developmental psychologist, I know that adolescence can be a phase of the life course that some middle-aged and older adults disparage. In particular, prejudicial thinking based on an age group stereotype may portray teenagers as self-centered, impetuous, and moody. Such ageist presumptions could be countered and dispelled with one glimpse of the youth toiling in the heat of summer to restore coastal communities devastated by Katrina and the horrendous flooding that followed. One might hope that ageist musings of any sort, especially unkind thoughts directed toward teenagers, would lessen when the contribution of these "kids" and their chaperones from distant cities across the nation are considered.

In summary, disasters happen worldwide, sometimes with little advance warning, as discussed in Chapter 1. A disaster response follows, which includes coordinated relief efforts from faith-based organizations, governmental agencies, and international humanitarian groups. In the case of Katrina, unspeakable evacuation dilemmas and tragic miscalculations cost precious lives. Yet there were also heroic responses to this disaster by individuals and faith-based and humanitarian organizations.[9] Either by choice (as a family member) or necessity (one's job required it), volunteers and professionals alike made a tremendous contribution to the Katrina disaster relief effort, as discussed in Chapter 4. In light of survivors' heartfelt appreciation for the widespread assistance and kindness shown by strangers, the Katrina disaster response invites further consideration in the context of gratitude as a healing principle, as discussed more fully next.

Gratitude in a Disaster Context

In the fall of 2005, displaced south Louisianans, among other Gulf Coast residents, showed up in record numbers in towns and cities across the nation. In turn, faith-based and humanitarian organizations were catapulted into action. To characterize this process, we asked participants if a church or faith-based community had helped them cope with Hurricanes Katrina and Rita and, if so, in what way? Content analyses of these narrative data[10] provide a unique window into survivors' coping responses during the immediate aftermath of the Katrina disaster (see Appendix A for a summary). Countless churches provided shelters and coordination of services, including helping survivors register with the Red Cross. The next quotes illustrate the disaster relief effort and participants' gratitude for their assistance while far away from home. Vicki Brubaker, a woman who had evacuated to Georgia, told us (emphasis added) that

> They were [a] big, big, big help. Especially when you're away from home. You don't know where to turn, where to go, you know? And then we went to Georgia, one of the things one of the churches helped us with was . . . they got . . . one of those little bitty transport [buses]. . . . And they took everybody [who had evacuated and needed to go to] Atlanta. . . . And they brought us and we registered for Red Cross and whatever we needed. Other churches had brought school supplies, and they had different stations [with] clothes. . . . They made sure all of those things were taken care of for you so that while you were waiting

to be handled by the Red Cross or whatever that you were being taken care of [by the churches]. . . . I'll tell you . . . [I made it] a point to go to the table and say, *"We thank you that you're here. You don't know how much difference you make by being here."*

James Bradley had evacuated to North Carolina. James, a Catholic, described his experience with the Baptist churches who participated in the relief effort. He spoke of their kindness and generosity. In his own words:

When we got airlifted out of here, we went to North Carolina. And the Baptist churches got together and they gave us, they collected food and they collected clothing and all, and toiletry items. The churches got out, and they asked them to fill up a gallon bag with the things that we need. We went over there, the Red Cross gave us a gallon Ziploc bag. They had soap, toothbrush in there, toothpaste, a washcloth, and nail clippers and a comb and things like that, that people donated. And it was the Baptist churches that did all of that.

James also told us about attending a worship service and forming an impromptu band for an appreciation concert, to thank the Baptists for their efforts and assistance. Here is what he said:

People brought me to a Baptist church, and I guess I was never before in a Baptist church, but we sang hymns and we read out the Bible in North Carolina. And I didn't have my glasses, I lost my glasses [in Katrina], the lady gave me her glasses and says, "Here, you can read the Bible with this." I said, "Wow." People really cared, you know? And things like that, yeah. So the churches, basically the Baptist church, helped out tremendously. The Baptist churches were there, I'll always hold that up. I'll never forget as long as I live, no matter where we went, the Baptists were there to help the people [with] food, clothing, whatever. We even gave a concert to them. They gave us food, and I formed a band in North Carolina, and I got VHS pictures of all of that, and we played for them over there.

His benefactors helped him organize the concert by contacting locals who brought in instruments so they could play music to thank the Baptists for their assistance and hospitality. James spoke of the congregants forming a "Second Line" in response to the music, a New Orleans' jazz funeral tradition. In his own words:

Yeah, they helped find the people or contacted people that . . . went to the Baptist church and all, and they came back with the band instruments and all. And I called the band "Gumbo." And we went to the Baptist church on a Sunday morning, they fed us, I introduced the band, and we played "When the Saints Go Marching In." I don't think that church will ever be the same because people came out of the pews and were doing the Second Line, which they've never done before. Up and down the aisles with their handkerchief dance, you know? They enjoyed it. They really did. Now we brought a little New Orleans to them.

Five years after the Katrina disaster, participants spoke of volunteers who put forth the effort to make a difference for coastal residents who were suddenly homeless, most for the first time in their lives. After Katrina, there were despicable acts and criminal activities, not only in New Orleans, but in receiving cities across the nation, too. Yet there were also acts of grace, where volunteers used their time, talent, and resources to advance the disaster relief effort, possibly bringing a sense of normalcy to survivors whose lives had been shattered by disaster and its aftermath.

Illustration: Gratitude for Help from Strangers—"I Just Want to Say Thank You"

The last open-ended question that we asked research participants was, "What would you like others to know about your experience with Hurricane Katrina?" In response to this question, participants frequently voiced gratitude for the volunteers who came to rebuild homes and communities in the aftermath of the 2005 hurricanes and for the people who welcomed them in distant cities and towns while they were displaced. Kim Nunez told us:

> I guess one of the first things that I'd want them to know is how much we appreciate all of the volunteers and the total strangers who were willing to put their lives on hold for a week, or one week every year, for five years, or every spring break . . . that they came down here and volunteered for total strangers, for people that didn't have any idea of, that they could, how they could be helping.

In fact, Kim made the effort to personally thank those people who came to help whenever she could. In her own words:

> . . . those volunteers and those strangers made a tremendous, I mean a *tremendous* difference. To me personally, they didn't do anything. They didn't gut my house and all, but for some people, it was the only way to get things done, so and just the fact of, even though I didn't need anybody to do anything for me, the fact that they would come here and I would see them working [lifted me], you know?

And I would embarrass my daughters to no end because let's say, for instance, we were at Subway, and I would see Americorps was in there and twenty of them were eating at Subway, and I'd go in there . . . when I'd walk by the tables, [I would say] "Thank you all for coming down here . . . Thank you for being here. We appreciate all that you've done."

No matter where I was. Even if they didn't have an Americorps shirt on, you can tell people who were here by the way that they talked . . . for one thing, it's May and they're still white as a sheet of paper, so you know they living in some Northern state somewhere. They haven't seen the sun or anything [laughs], so you could just tell by how red-faced they were and how hot they were, the clothes they had on, that they were gutting [flooded houses] and they were, working and so even though you might not have had a t-shirt on that said, "I'm a volunteer," you still . . . could tell that they were volunteers. So I would never pass up the chance to thank everyone, because we . . . really do [appreciate them] . . . it brightens your day that people would do this, that they would come down and help.

Kim was not the only one who talked about taking the time to say thank you. Patsy Shapiro described her profound sense of gratitude for the strangers who came from far away to help with the relief effort. During a research interview, Patsy told me about the day she stopped on her way to work to thank volunteers who had come from New York. She shared her recollection of the gratitude she felt toward complete strangers on that day. In her own words (emphasis added):

And they would just. . . . It was unbelievable, and it's still happening all over this area. And I remember one more . . . the first time that they came, I'm like, "You know, what could I do?" So they were having breakfast at the Knights of Columbus hall across the street from [Our Lady of Prompt Succor] the church on Paris Road, and I'm like, "I couldn't do anything. I'm on my way to work." Well I went over there and I asked, I forget the guy's name now, if I could just say something to everybody. So he says, "Oh sure—*Ding-ding-ding-ding-ding! He clinked on a glass to get everyone's attention.* This lady wants to say something." And I just thanked them.

I said, "I don't know what to do." You know, I said, "The church is doing the meal." I said, "I don't know what to do. I'm on my way to work. I just want to tell you thank you. Thank you for taking *your* time out of *your* life to come down here and help people you don't even know! Knowing you can't get repaid, but just out of goodness of your heart, taking your vacation time and coming down here to help." I mean it was just so nice.

And they would tell me thank you back. "Thank you for taking your time out to come see us." I said, "Oh, thank you for taking your time out to come see *us*."

Unbelievable . . . these people. And they're all over, and they're still coming. That's the thing—five years later and they're still coming. And they still got a lot to do.

Looking back, Pasty remembered as though it were yesterday that the volunteer from New York *thanked her* for taking the time to express gratitude for their relief work! Truly an inspiring scene: strangers coming together in mutual appreciation for each other's efforts in the aftermath of the Katrina disaster.

Stories of mutual gratitude may be heartwarming for some readers, yet such stories also invite sociological contemplation. We are reminded that people can and do come together in times of tragedy. For instance, candlelight vigils, among other community-based gestures of goodwill, can be interpreted as evidence of the goodness of humanity.

To conclude this section on the exercise of saying "thank you" to volunteers who advanced the Katrina relief effort, I reference "this lady who has something to say" once more. This is what Patsy wanted others to know about the life lessons Katrina taught (emphasis added):

> The generosity of people . . . and not necessarily of things, as much as their time and their talents. It's like everybody had something to bring to the table. *So they appreciated you, too.* And you got to see the good in people because in times of messes, it seems like the goodness of people come[s] about.

On further reflection, how curious it was that the volunteers at the Knights of Columbus hall did not respond to Patsy with a quick "you're welcome" or a dismissive, "it was nothing." Instead, the volunteers who came from New York to help south Louisiana strangers in St. Bernard Parish seemed appreciative of her stopping by on her way to work to thank them. They also seemed grateful for the opportunity to contribute to the Katrina relief effort in some measured way. It would appear that gratitude is an emotion that can go both ways. Benefactors who contributed to the disaster relief effort seemed grateful for the opportunity to do so, as examined more fully next.

Illustration: Gratitude Goes Both Ways—Benefactors Are Grateful, Too

After the 2005 Hurricanes Katrina and Rita, there were many opportunities for concerned citizens and caring people to help displaced coastal residents who had evacuated to distant cities and towns where they lived for weeks, months, and, for some, even years. After having lost everything in Katrina, some evacuees spent as long as two years or more in transit before they were able to return to coastal communities to rebuild homes and reestablish lives. Participants recounted stories of the goodness and generosity of strangers in faraway places who were kind. As an example, Kim Nunez was purchasing clothes for herself and her daughter at a JC Penny department store in Baton Rouge, Louisiana, in the first weeks after the storm. The people in line behind her picked up the tab. This was not an isolated incident. Acts of grace for displaced coastal residents were witnessed across the nation in the months and years after the 2005 storms.

Participants spoke about strangers who warmly welcomed them into their homes and communities, giving them a place to stay and providing necessities including food and clothing. On an autumn afternoon in October of 2011, I listened as Sharon Rollins described her Katrina ordeal. A terrifying experience, Sharon fled with her children and her memory-impaired elderly father and nearly drowned in a van getting out of St. Bernard on August 29, 2005. She spoke with great affection for the Baptist church community in Tennessee who provided for her and her family during their two-year displacement. Sharon told me during the interview, "They said *we were their angels* . . . they called us angels." What a powerful image: displaced coastal residents perceived as angels by the benefactors who cared for them. Counterintuitively, extending one's self and one's family in the service of others—often complete strangers—was considered a blessing by some people who graciously opened their homes to displaced storm survivors.

Other participants who endured lengthy displacements spoke warmly of their benefactors in different cities and states, expressing heartfelt gratitude toward those who opened their homes and provided abundantly for them. As an example, Mrs. Lori, the author of the journal chronicling her Katrina nightmare in Chapters 2, 3, and 4 described her host family in north Louisiana using heavenly terms, "They were our angels." As discussed in Chapter 4, this host family welcomed Lori and her mother into their home in the middle of the night in early September of 2005. Mrs. Annette, the north Louisiana host family matriarch, kept the ragged t-shirt Lori had worn in the long days of her Katrina ordeal. Ironically, this t-shirt had the cartoon image of a favorite Disney character, Grumpy, from Snow White and the Seven Dwarfs, emblazoned on the front side. On the back side of the shirt was also an image of Grumpy from the rear. With sewing scissors in hand, Mrs. Annette, the thoughtful host mother from North Louisiana, carefully excised both images of Grumpy (front and back) from the tattered shirt, discarding the remaining scraps of cotton. After proper cleaning,

Mrs. Annette carefully sewed both t-shirt segments with the front and rear images of Grumpy onto a blanket. On the backside of the blanket she embroidered the Lori's name and the year, 2005.

This thoughtful benefactor transformed Lori's dirty and tattered shirt, an otherwise ugly reminder of a brutal experience, into a piece of delicate handiwork, a treasured keepsake. I've thought about this transformative gesture, wondering whether Lori would want to receive such a gift from Mrs. Annette, considering the trail of memories it must surely evoke. Maybe not a blanket to use in daily life or display on the living room couch; rather, a special keepsake tucked away in the closet of a spare bedroom or some other place for safe keeping—something to look at from time to time and maybe remember that, by the helping hands of a kind stranger, a tragic experience can be transformed into something different from what it was originally. The possibility of something useful and good arising from a bad experience is examined more fully in the context of silver linings as a principle of healing (see Chapter 7).

*   *   *

Many participants described the beneficent acts of strangers in other cities and states, kind-hearted people who stepped up to meet their needs during Katrina's aftermath. Most people appreciate a kindness, the feeling of support, or an act of generosity that others may bestow on them when there is no hidden agenda or selfish motive—in other words, no strings attached. Over the years, I have wondered why benefactors sought out the opportunity to volunteer and why it would be important to them to participate in Katrina relief work. A skeptical and discerning reader might question the underlying reason(s) why a seemingly generous person volunteers, gives, or does for others, asking "What is in it for them?"

As I have learned, sometimes questions that are simple on the surface quickly become increasingly complicated on further reflection. Thinking like a social scientist, I realize right away that there are many possible answers to this question and as many potential reasons why people volunteer after disaster.[11] A series of carefully designed experiments would be necessary to yield an empirical answer to the question of "what's in it for them?" With this disclaimer in mind (and lacking a systematic, scientific answer), I tentatively offer a simple observation: when volunteers provide disaster relief for other people for unselfish reasons, thus improving a survivor's lot in some meaningful or observable way, they may feel valuable or needed. Inwardly, a feeling of being valued may renew a benefactor's sense of self-worth.

Interestingly, such positive emotions can come to the surface for survivors, too. That is, their sense of self-worth may be boosted when they are on the receiving end of a considerate gesture or kindness, which might sound like this: "You cared enough about me to come down to this part of the country to offer your help." In this manner, authentic gratitude underscores a general feeling of being valued that can and does go both ways: as the one who receives and as the one who gives.

To speculate further, consider this possibility: it may be that volunteers associated with faith-based communities or church groups are exercising a literal interpretation of scripture, equating disaster relief work with Hebrews 13:2 (NRSV): "Do not neglect to show hospitality to strangers for by doing that some have entertained angels without knowing it." In a similar vein, it is also possible that a volunteer may sincerely want to meet the needs that he or she can see based on an application of the "Golden Rule" (i.e., "do unto others as you would have them do unto you"). Meeting basic needs (including shelter and material goods) is a necessity for survival in a post-disaster environment. So is compassion and understanding. Conceivably, benefactors may need the blessing that comes from directing kindness toward others with no obvious gains in return.

An alternative viewpoint to consider is that benefactors do what they do simply because they can. That is, they sense an opportunity to close the gap on resource linkage, so they do it and nothing more than that. Simply put and without religious, cultural, moral, or ethical overlays, benefactors step up and give of themselves, making a difference in the lives of those who were devastated, with no strings attached.

There is an important caveat to consider, though. An act of kindness, however genuine or authentic, may not be received as intended if the recipient interprets that there are or could be strings attached. "Strings" might mean a perceived new obligation(s) that comes with a gift. It is also conceivable that gifts or helpful actions by strangers to assist those in need may leave the intended recipient feeling inadequate. Or worse—the recipient might feel insulted, with resentment, not gratitude, rising to the surface. In short, gratitude, like respect, can have a flip side; namely, ingratitude or resentment. An unpleasant and very real emotion, the reality of ingratitude in post-disaster life is addressed next.

Why Gratitude? Why Not Resentment?

Sometimes a feeling of gratitude just isn't quite right. For some people, gratitude may be out of reach or just too much of a stretch. Gratitude after tragedy may be a step beyond the limits of comprehension. When a sense of gratitude after disaster does not resonate, where does that leave us?

In reality, a majority of people may struggle with the idea of gratitude after catastrophic, life-changing events like a natural disaster. For people who fall into this category, gratitude just does not compute—it does not work for them. In fact, some people may be incensed at the thought of gratitude after tragedy. Gratitude, you say? Why gratitude? Why not resentment?

One can think of gratitude as having a flip side. For expository convenience, we will call this opposing feeling *ingratitude*. Perhaps ingratitude reflects ungratefulness or resentment over new life circumstances that were imposed by forces beyond our sphere of influence that cannot be changed. In fact, resentment may be the only feeling that registers with any degree of clarity after profoundly painful negative life events. I'll never forget the day I visited with Arthur Bronson, a first responder who was on the rooftop of a government building in Chalmette, Louisiana, after the levee breaches that flooded the region. When it was safe to venture out, Art spent long hours in the August heat for many days engaged in search-and-rescue efforts with a handful of other first responders and essential personnel.

I had been to Art's home in St. Bernard Parish several times before while working on this research project. The house was new, he said, a modular structure which sat on his property where the old house had been before it was torn down. With water into the attic in 2005, the forces of nature had swept his old house off its foundation, rendering it uninhabitable and beyond repair. When I arrived at his home to complete the research interview in 2011, Art had something he wanted to show me first. We walked into the living room where his television was playing in the background. He had recorded recent news coverage of the 2011 Fukushima nuclear power plant disaster, which happened after the Great East Japan earthquake and tsunami.[12] He wanted me to watch a certain news clip that he had recorded showing aerial coverage of the tsunami, a monstrous, gray wall of water. We watched that wall of water moving across the television screen. He hit replay and showed me again. He told me to watch closely because this visual of the tsunami was as close as he had ever seen to his Katrina experience on August 29, 2005. On that day, he witnessed a gray wall of water consuming Judge Perez Drive from his vantage point in the government building after the levee failures that flooded New Orleans.

We continued to watch the news coverage of the 2011 tsunami, although seeing the footage of this horrendous disaster clearly upset him. With thinly veiled angst Art emphatically stated, "The US was there in two days! Two days! Look at those ships!" He pointed to his television screen, commenting on the alacrity of the worldwide relief effort. "In two days, we had ships and disaster relief over there in Japan!" At first, I did not know what to say. Puzzled, I could not figure out if he was upset over the nuclear power plant disaster, which unleashed a frightening level of radiation contamination. Or maybe it was the tsunami and the hundreds of thousands of people who had drowned that upset him? Inwardly, I thought that such a powerful image of global assistance mobilized so quickly after natural and technological disaster combined was amazing—surely this was a good thing? But to him, amazing or not, it was a bad thing. Quite frankly, I did not understand, nor did I know what to say. So I just stood there in his living room in silence, watching the news coverage as he pointed at the television broadcast.

Art must have sensed that I didn't get it. After a few minutes of watching this news clip together, he explained his reaction. As he spoke, my confusion subsided, and I started to grasp why he was upset. I realized that seeing this tsunami had propelled his thoughts back to August 29, 2005, and the dark days that followed, with sixteen to thirty feet of water covering St. Bernard Parish, his home, and his world.

From earlier research interviews, I knew Art was a well-seasoned first responder in a position of authority. On that day, watching the news coverage of Japan's twin disasters in his living room, he talked about his experience during Katrina's immediate aftermath (see Chapter 4). He described the Black Hawk helicopters zooming above the city of New Orleans. These helicopters approached and hovered (ostensibly for assessment). Then they turned and circled back, flying away from St. Bernard Parish, where thousands of tax-paying, US citizens were stranded on rooftops, he said. For at least five days, the people in St. Bernard were left to await rescue in the stifling August heat. They had to be plucked from rooftops with no drinking water or provisions of any sort. They were dying in attics (or already dead). He, among the other first responders and local citizens, spent days in heroic rescue efforts in commandeered boats while the helicopters hovered and turned away at the St. Bernard Parish line. Yet it only took *two days* to have US boats speeding through the Indian Ocean and providing coordinated disaster relief to Japan, half a world away. Did I get it now? Intellectually, yes, I think so. The word "unfair" doesn't begin to capture the depth of emotion I witnessed that afternoon while watching the news coverage of the tsunami and its aftermath, including the Fukushima nuclear power plant disaster, with a Katrina survivor who saved as many souls as he and his crew possibly could, alone and with only the resources they could scrape together in their flooded parish (see Chapter 4).

So intellectually, yes, I think I can imagine an intense feeling of abandonment and profound dismay harboring on resentment over why strangers in a country half a world away were the focus of immediate global attention, with the US government speeding to their rescue while he had been seemingly forgotten and left to his own devices to figure out how to stay alive and get help for others in his American community. Not only this first responder, but also others who were there during the flooding after Katrina have voiced a similar feeling of abandonment and resentment.

* * *

This section opened with a question, "Why gratitude, why not resentment?" Arguably, gratitude and resentment are both legitimate feelings that can come into play in the months and years after disaster. This is good to know. But acknowledging the legitimacy of opposing feelings does not answer the question, "Why gratitude? Why not resentment?" Thinking from the vantage point of one's gut, resentment may be a better fit. Resentment makes sense, too. Pragmatically, it may also be easier to harbor resentment stoked by a real injustice than to pursue gratitude in light of the unbearable suffering and catastrophic happenings that defined the Katrina experience for so many people.

To my way of thinking, a glance at the scientific literature on gratitude can be informative, providing direction for readers to consider the question, "Why gratitude?" An academic approach may also put gratitude in its proper place in relation to other emotions experienced after a disaster. That is, scholarly research designed to provide evidence about gratitude can provide an objective and dispassionate foundation for interested readers to think about the potential benefits of gratitude.

There is a sizeable research literature on gratitude as a human emotion that is associated with well-being and happiness. To an academic with scholarly depth in emotion, gratitude can be conceptualized as an attitude, a coping strategy, a virtue, or a state of mind. Which way we go with it depends a lot on one's theoretical perspective.[13] As an example, consider the words of Robert Emmons, a noted psychologist and gratitude scholar.

> Gradually, I've come to experience the freedom of gratitude. By appreciating the gifts of the moment, gratitude frees us from past regrets and future anxieties. By cultivating gratefulness, we are freed from envy over what we don't have and who we are not. It doesn't make life perfect, but with gratitude comes the realization that right now, in this moment, we have enough, we are enough.[14]

Freedom from past regrets and future anxieties, even if only momentary, is a comforting thought. From this point of view, gratitude practiced in daily life may lead to surprising and unexpected outcomes, including a pathway to healing. In the wake of disaster, regret over what one no longer has, in terms of material possessions, can be painful, if not excruciating. Furthermore, regret over lost social and/or professional identities or roles (pre-disaster) can be crippling, too. Gratitude in the face of catastrophic losses and uncertainty may seem improbable or unlikely. However, an outlook on life that includes a thankful heart can be liberating for everyone, especially those who have lost so much in the wake of severe weather.

As an example, consider what Stephen Wilson-Oakley had to say about the response of the country in the wake of Katrina. I asked participants what they wanted others to know about their Katrina experience. Here is what "Oates" had to say in response to this question:

> How great it made me feel, to see and personally feel the outpouring of compassion for the refugee. I was one of them . . . Katrina refugees that fellow Americans and countrymen [helped] because we were all over the country. And that just made me feel great to be a part of something. Be in a country where you had people that were willing to . . . make the sacrifices to help you and [I] would like others just to know that was an incredibly awesome part [of my Katrina experience].
>
> Government was a part of that as well. We get frustrated at government because of the slowness. I mean the process just takes so long, and the inefficiencies of it. And you knew it was there. You knew . . . the government was going to have programs out that it [the government] was going to assist you. But the . . . that process being so slow is where . . . it gets a little negative, but they were part of that outpouring of compassion and support that you felt, and that's what I'd like people to know. It touched my heart deeply and reaffirmed my faith in humanity and my country.

Summary

Most people have an implicit sense of gratitude and what it means to be appreciative. From the ups and downs of everyday living, people know about giving and receiving and the social conventions of saying "thank you" and "you're welcome. They may also come to realize that gratitude is an encompassing emotion that can go both ways: the one who receives and the one who gives can both be appreciative at times.

A case was made for gratitude as a principle of healing after disaster. Beginning with gratitude for the disaster experience as a transformative event seen through the eyes of teenager (now an emerging adult), to gratitude for the countless volunteers who contributed to the disaster relief effort. For survivors who lost so much, a sense of gratitude for strangers who came to help was very real. Some survivors, like Patsy Shapiro who stopped to say "thank you" on her way to work, took the initiative and extra steps required to vocally express her heartfelt appreciation to the volunteers from New York whose efforts made such a tremendous difference to post-disaster recovery in her town.

We have also considered those individuals, families, and faith-based communities who provided disaster relief assistance across the US Gulf Coast and the nation. Many people made sacrifices for Katrina survivors, providing time and personal resources to help those struggling with overwhelming losses. Many were deeply moved by the goodness of people in different receiving cities and states rising to meet the challenges after a significant environmental event. As noted earlier, these volunteers sometimes expressed their gratitude for the opportunity to serve Katrina survivors in need. Taken together, the illustrations presented earlier in this chapter strengthen the takeaway message: gratitude matters in a disaster context.

Nonetheless, a feeling of gratitude after disaster may not work for everyone. No matter how hard one may pound, square pegs just don't fit into round holes. Some people do not (or cannot) feel gratitude in response to certain life experiences, including Katrina; feelings of anger or resentment may come more easily. So what do we do? We recognize that gratitude and resentment are both legitimate emotional responses to disaster. In the words of Fred Rogers, the beloved star of the children's television show, "Mr. Rogers' Neighborhood" and author of the book, *The World According to Mr. Rogers: Important Things to Remember*:

> There's no should or should not when it comes to having feelings. They're part of who we are and their origins are beyond our control. When we can believe that, we may find it easier to make constructive choices about what to do with those feelings.[15]

Illustrations from Katrina survivors support the notion that gratitude may act as a principle of healing after disaster. The voices of Katrina survivors from south Louisiana tell us that gratitude can be observed and practiced in spite of desperate circumstances, as improbable as this may seem. Gratitude as a mindset or way of looking at the world is a process that may take time and effort. Cultivating gratitude may be difficult, but we can surely get there, as this quote from Ashley Bowen, a woman who survived Hurricane Katrina shows:

> I wake up every morning, put my feet on the floor, and thank God for another day I get to share with my family. For another day, I get to talk with my son and maybe if his school schedule, work schedule permits, we can have lunch together and he comes and eats dinner with us at home.

The thought of gratitude after disaster may seem unlikely at first, yet gratitude has the potential to emerge as a powerful pathway for overcoming great losses after disaster. Cultivating an attitude of thankfulness for the people and difficult life circumstances endured may put people on a different path to healing after disaster than they had ever imagined or expected.

NOTES

1. Cade Brumley, *Leadership Standards in Action: The School Principal as a Servant-Leader* (New York: Rowman & Littlefield Publishers, 2012).
2. Laura Bush, *Spoken from the Heart* (New York: Scribner, 2010), 346–347.
3. Alison Schroeder, "St. Bernard Parish Hospital Is a Final Piece of Katrina Recovery," *New Orleans Times-Picayune*, accessed on June 24, 2012, http://www.nola.com/health/index.ssf/2012/06/st_bernard_parish_hospital_a_f.html
4. Keri L. Kytola, Katie E. Cherry, Loren D. Marks, and Trevan G. Hatch, "When Neighborhoods Are Destroyed by Disaster: Relocate or Return and Rebuild?," in *Traumatic Stress and Long-Term Recovery: Coping with Disasters and Other Negative Life Events*, ed. Katie E. Cherry (New York: Springer International Publishing Switzerland, 2015), 211–229.
5. Robert A. Emmons, *Thanks! How Practicing Gratitude Can Make You Happier* (New York: Houghton-Mifflin, 2007).
6. Oliver Sacks, *Gratitude* (New York: Alfred A. Knopf, a division of Random House, 2015), 20.
7. Carl F. Weems and Stacy Overstreet, "An Ecological-Needs-Based Perspective of Adolescent and Youth Emotional Development in the Context of Disaster: Lessons from Katrina," in *Lifespan Perspectives on Natural Disasters: Coping with Katrina, Rita and Other Storms*, ed. Katie E. Cherry (New York: Springer Science + Business Media, 2009), 27–44.
8. Trevan G. Hatch, Katie E. Cherry, Yaxin Lu, and Loren D. Marks, "Seeing Silver Linings After Catastrophic Loss: Personal Growth, Positive Adaption, and Relationships That Matter," in *Traumatic Stress and Long-Term Recovery: Coping with Disasters and Other Negative Life Events*, ed. Katie E. Cherry (New York: Springer International Publishing Switzerland, 2015), 389–402.
9. Katie E. Cherry, Priscilla D. Allen, and Sandro Galea, "Older Adults and Natural Disasters: Lessons Learned from Hurricanes Katrina and Rita" in *Crisis and*

Disaster Counseling: Lessons Learned from Hurricane Katrina and Other Disasters, ed. Priscilla Dass-Brailsford (Thousand Oaks, CA: Sage, 2010), 115–130.

10. Loren D. Marks, "A Pragmatic, Step-by-Step Guide for Qualitative Methods: Capturing the Disaster and Long-Term Recovery Stories of Katrina and Rita," *Current Psychology* 34, no. 3 (2015): 494–505, https://doi.org/10.1007/s12144-015-9342-x

11. Jennifer L. Silva, Loren D. Marks, and Katie E. Cherry, "The Psychology Behind Helping and Prosocial Behaviors: An Examination from Intention to Action," in *Lifespan Perspectives on Natural Disasters: Coping with Katrina, Rita and Other Storms,* ed. Katie E. Cherry (New York: Springer Science + Business Media, 2009), 219–240.

12. Masaharu Maeda, and Misari Oe, "The Great East Japan Earthquake: Tsunami and Nuclear Disaster," in *Traumatic Stress and Long-Term Recovery: Coping with Disasters and Other Negative Life Events,* ed. Katie E. Cherry (New York: Springer International Publishing Switzerland, 2015), 71–90.

13. Robert A. Emmons and Michael E. McCullough, *The Psychology of Gratitude* (New York: Oxford University Press, 2004).

14. Emmons, *Thanks,* 209.

15. Fred Rogers, *The World According to Mister Rogers: Important Things to Remember* (New York: Hatchette Books, 2003), 20.

CHAPTER 7

⌒⌒⌒

Acceptance and Silver Linings

INTRODUCTION

In conversations about the 2005 Hurricane Katrina and its devastation, Dr. Claire Landry, a retired high school principal, told me "It is in the past. It happened. You have to accept it and go on with your life." Dr. Landry, affectionately known as Claire to her friends and family, is a former coastal resident. She had lived through Hurricane Betsy in 1965 (which flooded New Orleans) and countless other storms. Her words reflect a depth of wisdom that comes from years of experience with severe weather events. Sadly, I have heard her voice this sentiment on more than one occasion.

The first time Claire spoke of acceptance and moving on was in the context of a research interview five years after the Katrina disaster. The second time I heard her say the words "it happened, accept it" was after the flood of 2016, which impacted a twenty-parish (county) region in Louisiana. Like many displaced US Gulf Coast residents after Katrina, Claire and her husband had permanently relocated inland to Baton Rouge in the fall of 2005, to ostensibly higher and safer ground. There they were flooded again in August of 2016. Holding hands and trudging through water over their knees, this dear lady and her husband left their flooded Baton Rouge home together the morning of August 13, 2016. Wading slowly and stepping carefully into a rescue boat, they were taken to safety. Once again, they were displaced from their home as a result of a natural disaster. This time they were out of their home for nearly a year. In June of 2017, Claire and her husband were able to get back into their newly renovated Baton Rouge home after the flood repairs were completed.

During her displacement in the immediate aftermath of the Great Flood of 2016, I met with Claire on several occasions for research interviews. She and her husband were staying with her sister in Baton Rouge, whose home did not flood. Grateful for the hospitality, she said many times, "I don't know what we would have done without her." Once again, Claire and I worked through paper-and-pencil surveys. This time, the assessment focused on the impact of the 2016 flood. Stoic and resilient, without a trace of "poor me" or audible lamentation of any sort, Claire said, "It happened. Accept it and move on with your life." That was her take on the 2016 flood. That had been her take on Hurricane Katrina, too, as will be discussed more fully later. I am not sure if she remembered our prior conversations about Katrina, in August of 2010, when we met in the spring of 2017 for the flood study, but I did. I also had the benefit of Claire's 2010 transcript to verify her statements about acceptance and "moving on" after Katrina, as documented in greater detail later in this chapter. According to Claire, acceptance is something you have to do, and then you move on with your life. To my way of thinking, she is right.

I believe that there is great wisdom born of real-world experience in Dr. Claire Landry's seven words: "It happened, accept it, and move on." So how do I know this to be true? How can I be so certain that this octogenarian, a retired high school principal and former coastal resident, is absolutely and unequivocally right about acceptance and moving on with life? In response, I believe that she is right based on evidence derived from at least three different sources. First, taking a personal approach, I know she is right based on my own life experience. Second, from a rational approach, she is also right based on the strength of argument and application of logic (i.e., one can't turn back time to undo events in the past). Third, from a scientific perspective, I conclude that she is right about acceptance and moving on because her thinking lines up with at least three decades of scientific research on successful aging.[1-7]

To elaborate briefly, the concept of acceptance has theoretical underpinnings that can be traced to the research literature on successful aging.[8,9] Acceptance also figures prominently among the findings from studies on psychological well-being in late adulthood. As an example, Carol Ryff found that middle-age and older adults' views of psychological well-being in adulthood included enjoying life and having a sense of humor, positive relations with friends and family, and *accepting* changes related to aging (both role and physical) as well as *accepting* changes in the world around them.[10] Other scholars have made the point that successful aging involves developing alternative activities to compensate for losses. *Compensation* as a way of coping with changes in later life can take many forms. For instance, modifying the environment to adapt to physical changes with aging is a form of compensation. Older persons can also compensate for aging-related losses by drawing strength from family and friends and cultivating optimism, a positive outlook, and hope.[11] From an academic point of view, successful aging means adapting to changes within one's control while accepting changes that are beyond one's control.[12,13]

Most would agree that acceptance can be quite difficult, especially when life is hard. When painful events occur, denial may come first (i.e., "I cannot believe this has happened"). Resistance to life-changing events may also be in the forefront of peoples' initial psychological reactions (i.e., "I refuse to accept this situation"). The notion of *resistance* is curious, inviting further thought. Conceivably, resistance may indicate that a person has become stuck, unable to see potential meaning in their experience of suffering. Yet pushing through initial resistance and other negative emotions (anger, bitterness, or hatred) may be necessary to reach a point where acceptance becomes a possibility. In turn, reliance on acceptance as coping strategy, where survivors work through calamitous events one small step at a time, can be helpful.

Academically speaking, acceptance of circumstances that cannot be altered or reversed is a step in the direction of successful aging. In addition, it is conceivable that something good can be realized after a painful experience, a "silver lining," for those who are willing to look at their life circumstances differently, as discussed later in this chapter.

Prior research with Katrina survivors has shown that acceptance and "benefit finding" were among the coping strategies participants described to manage post-disaster stressors.[14-16] Like acceptance, searching for benefits or silver linings in connection with difficult life experiences has been conceptualized as an emotion-focused coping strategy for dealing with outcomes that cannot be changed. Emotion-focused and problem-focused coping strategies were introduced in Chapter 5. Academically speaking, both acceptance and silver linings are styles of emotion-focused coping that may lessen stress and improve post-disaster adjustment. In the next two sections, participants' stories and direct quotes provide illustrations of acceptance and silver linings as principles of healing after the Katrina disaster.

ACCEPTANCE

This, too, shall pass.

—Grace McCarthy

"Acceptance" is a familiar term. In everyday parlance, acceptance means taking situations or circumstances as they are. When one has reached a point of acceptance, he or she is no longer expending time, effort, or material resources in a perhaps vain attempt to change or alter an unalterable situation. People can accept situations as they are as well as accept the feelings they may have in connection with these situations. For some people, acceptance may mean closure. Acceptance also implies release. Most people will never forget painful, life-changing events, but they can choose to accept these events. A step in the direction of acceptance happens when people realize they are no longer dwelling on or mulling over unalterable events.

As discussed earlier, acceptance as a construct can be found in the scientific research literatures on adult development (i.e., successful aging) and the psychology of adjustment (i.e., stress and coping). Acceptance also appears in the popular press (i.e., magazines, inspirational material, or written works on newsstands and in bookstores). Acceptance has a mainstream presence in the context of death and dying, too. Consequently, acceptance may be a familiar term to those who have lost loved ones to terminal illnesses like cancer.

Continuing this line of thinking, acceptance may call to mind Elisabeth Kübler-Ross's framework, where acceptance is the fifth and final stage of dying for patients with incurable illnesses.[17,18] For the dying, acceptance is characterized by quiet and peaceful moments with little interest in outside activity, conversation, or television. All that is required for meaningful communication at this time is the gentle touch of a loved one at bedside. The patient has fought the good fight. He or she is no longer fighting. Death is coming. The last breath in this world will be drawn soon. The next breath will be taken in eternity, a comforting thought for people who embrace a Christian perspective on life after death.

Based on Kübler-Ross's theoretical framework, acceptance signals a final step in preparation for death. A cancer patient who has reached the acceptance stage has relinquished hope for a longer life. From this clinical point of view, the takeaway message could be that acceptance is antithetical to hope. With cancer or other terminal conditions, acceptance and hope may stand in opposition to each other. For instance, a cancer patient who has not yet accepted his or her terminal diagnosis might say something hopeful like this: "I can beat it! I haven't given up hope for remission or a cure." Or this: "I'm still hoping this situation will get better." Evidence that acceptance and hope are opposites can also come from cancer patients who have moved beyond denial. Conversations with patients who are farther along in the disease process might sound more like this: "I have accepted my fate."

"I know there is no hope for a cure, a change in status, or longer life." This later example shows the presence of acceptance signaling the absence of hope for a different outcome in the context of death and dying.

In contrast to the clinical world of healthcare and terminal illness, acceptance and hope may coexist harmoniously for survivors of a natural disaster. To illustrate, consider Jeremy Fortenberry's remarks when asked about the challenges he faced after Katrina and how he coped with these challenges. Jeremy told us (emphasis added)

> It was a big adjustment living up here [in town], compared to living down there [near the water] because of the amount of people around and the traffic. I was always raised with a lot of land around me. . . . And, you know, now I live in a subdivision where there is not that much room, so I guess that was another adjustment that I had to get used to, you know, that took me actually awhile to actually get used to.
>
> I guess it took me around two years to actually sit and say, "Okay this is where I am now," and *I guess to accept it* and say, "Okay, I'm not moving back home. And this is where I'm going to be." So that was, I guess, considered part of coping with being affected by it.

For clarification, I asked Jeremy if that was a conscious decision he made—to accept his new living situation—or did acceptance just come gradually over time? Here is what he had to say in response to my question:

> It gradually came over time. We actually had hopes to . . . move back home, and [my wife] started her business. Well, we started the photography business that we run, and it just didn't make sense to move back home, so even though, if you said right now, "Let's go back home" . . I would go in a heartbeat.

While Jeremy has accepted the realities of a forced relocation inland as Katrina dictated for so many people in 2005, one can also sense the presence of hope moving in the same direction as acceptance. That is, he and his wife may yet return home without delay or hesitation—"in a heartbeat"— if given the opportunity. In this example, acceptance of a new life in a different town with new constraints and new opportunities is intertwined with the hope of someday returning to his childhood home near the water. For this man, acceptance and hope would appear to be balanced. In fact, one could say that acceptance and hope are complementary, interwoven in equal measure and moving in the same direction.

When I think about acceptance and hope lining up side by side—in harmony, instead of pitted against each other—the image of a particular tapestry portrait comes to mind. Framed and hanging on the wall in a friend's home, the front side of this picture shows the face of a man who is wearing a floppy black hat. His look and clothing reflect a different era. Sitting on a wooden chair, he is turned slightly at the waist. His right elbow, bent sharply, rests haphazardly over the chair's back. As I have learned, the tapestry is a needlepoint version of a masterpiece painted by the Dutch artist Frans Hals, entitled *Portrait of a Man in a Slouch Hat* (c. 1660–1666).[19] Painstakingly stitched by hand, the crisscrossed wool threads in this tapestry bring colors together. Side by side, in a balanced and complementary way, the colors form a man's face with cropped brownish hair and a stiff white collar. An image from the seventeenth century, the beauty of this framed tapestry portrait arises from the artistic blending of many different shades of color. Black threads form his floppy hat, tilted slightly to the left side of his head. The fair colors of his face are framed by browns with streaks of yellow accenting his hair. Maroons and dark reds convey a cloak draped over his shoulders. Lovely, serene, and peaceful, the different-colored wool threads align harmoniously in this portrait of a man with a floppy hat.

In stark contrast, the backside of the needlepoint picture is a loose and textured jumble of color, with multiple strands of various lengths going in many different directions. Yet these very same threads yield a crisp and unmistakable image of a man with a black floppy hat when viewed from the front side. It is the same picture. What a person sees depends on which side of the picture he or she chooses to view. Life circumstances can be this way, too, sometimes. That is, people with hope for a brighter tomorrow may come to the realization that a jumbled and disorderly mass of colored thread is a recognizable and meaningful picture when accepted as is but turned and viewed from the other side.

Illustration: Acceptance in the Years After a Natural Disaster

Earlier in this chapter, I referenced a conversation that I had with Dr. Claire Landry, a retired high school principal, who had permanently relocated to Baton Rouge with her husband after losing their coastal parish home in Katrina. A 2016 flood caused significant damage to their Baton Rouge home. Twice flooded within an eleven-year period, Claire did not complain to me. She spoke of the Flood of 2016 in the same way that she had described her take on Katrina in an earlier research interview. In her words, "It happened. You have to accept it and go on with your life." Looking back, I remember the first time Claire and I talked at length about the human impact of Katrina's devastation. Let me now return to that first visit so many years ago.

On an August afternoon in 2010, I was sitting at a kitchen table in the lovely home of a retired couple who had permanently relocated inland to a new community after experiencing catastrophic losses in Katrina. Like so many people, the Landrys were displaced through the fall of 2005, living with family in a different state at first, then staying with other family in Louisiana, and finally purchasing a new home in Baton Rouge, Louisiana. Choosing to relocate rather than return to their coastal community to rebuild meant establishing a new life in a different and unfamiliar city. Relocating is stressful and challenging under ordinary circumstances. After having lost one's home and community, material possessions, social network of family and friends, and a lifestyle passed down from one generation to the next, a move to a new city filled with strangers would certainly be difficult.[20] Unless one has experienced such upheaval, the magnitude of loss for newly displaced persons is almost beyond comprehension. So many challenges, obstacles, and setbacks, I thought, but maybe new opportunities, too.

As we worked through the interview, I glanced around the kitchen. I noticed a flyer announcing an event at a local Catholic school that hung prominently on the refrigerator. We chatted briefly about this school. As I learned, Claire and her sister volunteer at this school on a regular basis; they help out in the front office on Tuesdays and Fridays.

I knew that Claire had been a high school principal in the years before the 2005 storm, so volunteering at a local school was certainly a natural fit. She talked about her volunteer duties, pitching in wherever an extra set of hands was needed. She specifically recalled one day when she took on the task of copying materials in the office. She spoke of how deeply grateful the teachers were for her assistance, calling her "their angel." Listening to this story, I could imagine Claire perfectly comfortable and at home in this school, stepping up and solving problems with grace and a quiet confidence born of years of experience in academic settings. In her own words, here is what Claire said:

> Now I just wish I had more time, especially now that school has started again. But the teachers and the administration and staff over there have been more than helpful. . . . We save the teachers a lot of trouble, even the administration, if they have things to run off [duplicate to make multiple copies]. Sometimes they were books . . . we do all of that.
>
> We have adult company because even while we are doing it [office work, making copies] the teachers on their off period will stop in and we'll talk and

that has been, I think, a real savior for us. They've made us feel welcome and wanted and appreciated. I think we all need to feel needed. And they make us feel like we're their angels. . . . Most of them are very appreciative.

Five years after Katrina's devastation, she seemed settled and content in a new community, making the best of her situation, forming connections in this new social environment, and lending her expertise in a local school. I asked Claire what she wanted others to know about her experiences with Hurricanes Katrina and Rita in 2005. Here is what she said:

> Well, I tried to think about that. The only thing that I could think of was, don't look back and wish that it hadn't happened. It did happen . . . accept it and know that you're starting a new phase of your life and look forward to what wonderful things could be happening to your life in the future. But don't dwell on what you had or what you lost. It's gone. It's a fact and try to accept it. Make new memories. I guess I didn't even realize everything can change, like we said before, in an instant.

I asked Claire if she had anything else to add concerning her experiences with Katrina, and she offered the following:

> No, I really tried to think and that's all I could think of was, don't say, "Oh poor me, poor me." Don't have pity on me. Take things as they are. Know that you're blessed and that you have your life, that things could be a lot worse. [You] could have lost your life. Life is precious.

Claire brings up an interesting point. In her opinion, one should not play the Katrina sympathy card because things could have been worse, as they were for the people who drowned in St. Bernard Parish on August 29, 2005. These souls, among the estimated 1,800 who perished in the hurricane and horrendous flooding that followed, were not so fortunate (see Appendix B for a list of names of those who drowned in St. Bernard Parish). From Claire's perspective, it would appear that acceptance falls into place, in step with the spiritual exercise of counting blessings for what one *does* have after a natural disaster, starting with one's life.

"Counting blessings" implies a thankful heart with a focus on the present—what one does have and can look forward to, as opposed to the past and what no longer exists. For some people, counting blessings is an effective strategy for coping with stressful, life-changing experiences. Other participants also reported that they felt immense gratitude for life after Katrina, as revealed in the next two quotes.

At the time of her interview, Susan Franklin was a college student in her twenties. Looking back at Katrina's devastation and its disruptive impact on her life as a high school student at the time, Sue told us (emphasis added):

> The majority of how you deal with stuff is attitude. You know, my mother is one of those who, she'll say about all the stuff she lost. She lost her clothes, but it's like, *but you're alive.* You have people who didn't make it out, [like the people] at that nursing home [where] thirty-something people died [the St. Rita's nursing home tragedy]. . . . So, when you look back . . . our family was all together, our family was all alive. To me, it's just, . . . [there] was much more positive [that] came out of it.

After having lived through Katrina, Ray Lynn Routledge, a middle-aged woman in her forties, had this observation to offer:

> So, as far as the positive outcomes of this, every day is a positive outcome. That God allows me to wake up. That's as positive as it gets. I woke up on the right side of the dirt [today I am alive].

Taken together, Sue's and Ray Lynn's quotes reflect not only gratitude for having survived the Katrina disaster (see Chapter 6) but also for positive outcomes that have emerged from this experience. Silver linings, referring to potential positives that can emerge from dire situations, will be considered in greater detail later in this chapter.

In contrast, other people may be of the opinion that emphasizing the present and future comes at the expense of the past, somehow diminishing the centrality or importance of prior painful experiences. From this point of view, counting blessings for what one has might mean turning a blind eye to what was lost. Moreover, exclusive reliance on the takeaway that *things could be worse* might minimize or somehow trivialize the very real pain that disaster survivors have experienced. Suffering can be a defining event for some people who may not want to let go of their pain or dismiss it casually as a relic of the past. For these individuals, suffering may mean courage, an interpersonal virtue that should be noticed and admired. A legacy of courage implies strength of character. From this alternate vantage point, a disaster survivor might see value in suffering which they might not to want to release or relegate to a mental file drawer with other items of historical interest only.

Coming full circle, it is important to recognize that people process major losses differently. The interpretation or meaning one assigns to an experience will be addressed more fully in the context of silver linings presented later in this chapter. Remembering the "one size doesn't fit all" rule of post-disaster recovery, strategies that are effective for some people may be ill-suited or ineffective for others (see Chapter 1). Cultivating awareness or sensitivity toward different responses and interpretations of the same event is certainly a critical consideration for survivors and disaster relief personnel alike.

Illustration: "This, Too, Shall Pass"

Thinking about acceptance in the years after Katrina, I am reminded of a conversation I had with Grace McCarthy, a coastal parish resident who returned to her coastal community to rebuild a home and recover a life-style in St. Bernard Parish. While answering questions during a research interview, Grace revealed an alternate route to acceptance that did not involve a complicated cerebral analysis of past versus present and future. For Grace, acceptance was reflected simply in four words, "This, too, shall pass." During our conversation, I asked her a question concerning whether a church or faith community had helped her cope with the challenges she faced after the storm. In her response, a depth of wisdom is revealed that pertains to the finite nature of pain and suffering, while the promise of healing and hope for better times ahead is eternal. Here is what Grace said:

> Yes, they have. I consider a faith community just a group of people believing, trusting, and praying with you. I consider a church as a church family wherever you serve and choose to dwell among others. The church is inside of you. You carry the church with you. The church is in your heart. The building is there for us to gather as one great body and support each other. I found that in churches I visited during the time of Katrina, not only because I walked in the door expecting something, but I went in with something on my mind and in my heart and that was to recover from what I know was only for a season.

I was struck by her answer that the Katrina tragedy was *only for a season*. By this time, I was well aware of the persistence of pain related to this disaster. Additionally, there is abundant evidence to document Katrina's lingering effects, which for many people seem to reach forward in time, but not for her. Grace McCarthy's take on the storm and its aftermath as finite, something that she knew would pass in time, was novel to me. In her own words:

> And this, too, will pass, and that's what happened. At that time I felt like, in my heart, this, too, shall pass.

For clarification, I asked Grace if she knew that storm-related suffering was only for a season when she was in the middle of the chaos, uncertainty, and pain that defined the Katrina experience for so many coastal residents. Here is what she said:

> Yes. In the middle of all of it, I knew. Because as we go through the tunnel Jesus is watching us, and he's saying, "C'mon my daughter, you can make it." Because on the other side he will say, "Well done, my daughter. You made it through that. Look at my child." And that's what I believe.

Grace's metaphor of the Katrina experience as a tunnel is compelling. As an engineer or construction worker will tell you, tunnels are cut deep into the ground. Tunnels are dark, possibly frightening, and may seem endless while traveling through them. However, tunnels are finite, having a clearly defined entrance. Perhaps more importantly, there is an equally well-defined exit as the traveler emerges from this darkened passageway below the ground into the light of day.

For Grace McCarthy, emergence on the other side of a tunnel of suffering was guaranteed, known in advance, and inextricably linked to her Christian perspective (see Chapter 5). "This, too, shall pass" is a powerful belief statement which exemplifies the healing principle of acceptance. It may be that survivors can come to accept devastating events and the unpleasant circumstances that follow when they realize that "this, too, shall pass." Driven by faith or possibly lessons learned from prior sorrows (or both), Grace's tunnel metaphor offers a new way to look at current or past painful experiences. To my way of thinking, her notion of a tunnel through dark experiences lends a unique image to the process of acceptance. The tunnel imagery also conveys a fundamental message: painful experiences, though dark and treacherous at the time, are finite. Acceptance of difficult life experiences, then, may be easier to reach when conceptualized as a tunnel with a well-defined beginning, middle, and exit on the other side.

Summary

The notion of acceptance has a long and varied history. Psychologists have conceptualized acceptance as an emotion-focused coping strategy that can be associated with positive outcomes.[21,22] Health and wellness professionals who come into contact with death and dying may think about acceptance as a final stage for patients with terminal illnesses and their loved ones, following on Elisabeth Kübler-Ross's clinical framework. Here,

I have suggested that acceptance can be put into practice as a healing principle that supports the process of recovery after disaster based on primary data from research interviews after the Katrina tragedy.

Survivors' styles of coping, though different on the surface, seemed to converge at a deeper level of analysis to reveal the healing potential of acceptance. From acceptance voiced in uncertain terms, like Jeremy Fortenberry's "I accepted it, I guess," to acceptance as more of a directive, with Dr. Claire Landry's "It happened, accept it, and move on," and, last, to Grace McCarthy's acceptance as a time-limited awareness: "This, too, shall pass," the illustrations presented here characterize acceptance as a powerful principle for healing in the years after a natural disaster.

At least five years had elapsed since Katrina's devastating wind and water had destroyed peoples' coastal homes and communities for the illustrations presented in this chapter. What about survivors' immediate psychological reaction(s) to a sudden, devastating loss? Can acceptance promote hope and healing in the days following a catastrophic event? In response, consider the life and times of American businessman Horatio G. Spafford who lived in Chicago, Illinois, in the 1800s. While he may not have made it into many American history books, his life warrants a closer look as a model of acceptance after disaster. Moreover, Horatio's response to his personal tragedy also provides an example of a silver lining realized by generations of strangers in the century that followed his losses, as discussed more fully next.

In brief, Horatio Spafford was a lawyer and successful businessman working in real estate in the 1860s. He was no stranger to natural disaster, having lost his business and everything he owned in the great Chicago Fire of 1871.[23] Two years later, he was scheduled to attend a meeting in Europe. He planned this trip to include a vacation with his family and booked passage to Europe on the *S.S. Ville de Havre*. When it was time to leave, he remained behind to attend to a business matter. His wife, Anna, and their four daughters went on ahead of him. While at sea, their boat collided with another vessel, sinking swiftly in the Atlantic and claiming the lives of most of the passengers on board. Anna was found alive among the wreckage. She was pulled from the water and taken to Wales. At home in Chicago, Horatio received a cryptic telegram from his wife that said, "Saved alone." Reading between the lines, he realized suddenly that his four daughters had drowned when the boat sank.

Horatio Spafford provides a spectacular example of acceptance as a pathway to healing in the face of soul-crushing pain. Here is an individual who was well acquainted with grief: suffering multiple tragedies with excruciating losses yet he found his way to the other side of suffering. And how do we know? After receiving the cryptic, fate-filled telegram, he raced to Wales to get to his grief-stricken wife, crossing the Atlantic Ocean by boat. When they neared the area where the shipwreck happened, the captain notified Horatio that here was the spot where his daughters had drowned. Taking note of the precise location, he jotted down the words, "It is well with my soul."[24] *Acceptance* in the face of tragedy would appear to be how he reacted at that moment in time many years ago.

In the wake of his personal tragedies, Horatio Spafford later developed the concept that flashed in his mind when he passed the location where his daughters had drowned, penning the verses of the well-known church hymn, "It Is Well with My Soul." These lyrics were later set to music by Philip P. Bliss.[25] For well over a century, this exquisite hymn has been sung in churches and played at funerals across the nation. I'm not sure whether Horatio Spafford or his wife, Anna, ever knew the silver lining of their personal tragedy—a hymn which to this day still offers comfort to the bereaved and others shouldering burdens that may seem insurmountable. The lyrics of his somber hymn reflect *acceptance* and *faith*, offering a glimpse of peace after tragedy for the ages and the promise of healing and deliverance despite excruciatingly painful circumstances.

SILVER LININGS

My father . . . finding out that he had cancer . . . Katrina did have a silver lining because I was able to be with him for his entire last year. If Katrina never would've happened . . . I wouldn't have been able to be with him just on a day-to-day basis, because I'd have been at work.

—Skip Lagarde

"Every cloud has a silver lining." Or so the saying goes. When life has become hard, a well-intentioned friend or family member may say something about dark clouds and silver linings for encouragement. But what does it mean?

Turning to Webster's *New Compact Office Dictionary*,[26] "silver lining" is defined as "some basis for hope or comfort in the midst of despair." During difficult and challenging times, "looking for a silver lining" means searching for something good that can come out of a bad situation or experience.

Interestingly, the expression, "Every cloud has a silver lining" is based on a real phenomenon of nature. Any person can see a silver lining—just look at storm clouds or gray skies after bad weather. Notice that dark clouds occlude the sun; they will have a lighter side that is silver in appearance. The silver lining that storm clouds have is the result of rays of sunshine streaming through the clouds' outer edges. Literally speaking, searching for silver linings makes sense after a severe weather event. Metaphorically speaking, coping with negative life events might be somewhat easier when people are able to perceive a positive outcome associated with these events. Thus, a current or future benefit would be the silver lining, something good that can come out of a bad situation.

In everyday life, looking for a silver lining is one way of coping with negative life events. If every cloud has a silver lining, then people can have a reason to go on: there is hope. Silver linings mean that bad situations will eventually improve and become meaningful and positive, somehow, despite the present suffering and pain. Thinking like a teenager for just a moment, I found myself questioning the authority of this phrase. Specifically, I wondered just who came up with such an idyllic notion? Surely it wasn't someone who lost their home in a hurricane or flood!

Even people who have not lived through a natural disaster can watch news coverage of catastrophic environmental events on television. Given the widespread media attention directed toward the devastation of homes and communities in the immediate aftermath of a disaster, could positives really emerge from such dire circumstances? Wouldn't a person who has just experienced a heart-breaking, major loss of any sort balk at the idea of a positive, of something good coming out of it? Yet happy endings are implied by the saying, "every cloud has a silver lining" so is there some "truth" to this idiom?

Setting such musings aside, a scholarly approach is necessary to evaluate the relevance of this concept for survivors in the wake of a deadly hurricane. Accordingly, the concept of silver linings is discussed a bit more objectively next.

Philosophical Antecedents and the Psychology of Silver Linings

So who came up with the phrase "every cloud has a silver lining"? John Milton is considered the first to use the term "silver lining" in a poem published in 1634, in his book, *Comus: A Mask Presented at Ludlow Castle,* excerpted here.[27]

> Was I deceiv'd, or did a sable cloud
> Turn forth her silver lining on the night?

Two hundred and more years later, the silver lining idea as we know it today is found packaged in a phrase that appeared in an 1840 literary review published in *The Dublin Magazine, Volume 1*: "there is a silver lining to every cloud that sails about the heavens if we could only see it."

The evolution of this phrase, courtesy of the nineteenth-century literary world of England, is striking. In particular, we move from what had seemed naïve and idealistic at first (*"every* cloud has a silver lining . . . *yeah, right, if you say so"*) to a conceptually richer notion, reflecting deeper wisdom and truth (*"every* cloud has a silver lining . . . *if we could only see it"*). From a rational point of view, then, silver linings are available to all but realized only by those who can see or perceive them.

Taking this line of reasoning one step further, a key question comes to the surface: Just who can see or perceive the benefits? Is it a matter of patience? Maybe the benefits associated with tragic outcomes are realized by those who wait for the silver lining to eventually materialize, even if it takes a lifetime. Alternatively, maybe patience is not the important factor, but faith. That is, the positives that can arise from a bad situation are perceived by all who reach out in faith, exercising a deeply personal conviction concerning the "knowledge of things unseen and hope of things to come," as discussed in Chapter 5.

To speculate further, some individuals may be constitutionally equipped to see silver linings everywhere they look, every time. For people with an optimistic personality, seeing the bright side of a dark situation might come easily. For such people, there is no doubt that positives can arise from difficult and painful negative life events eventually. Others may struggle, being less able or possibly less inclined to find a silver lining after disaster, while people with the personality trait or characteristic of optimism may look at situations differently. Perhaps genes or dispositional tendencies matter, when we consider whether or not potential benefits associated with dire situations are perceived.

Or maybe anyone can realize a benefit associated with a distressing situation, but it doesn't happen without assistance. Maybe all that it takes is a supportive environment to get there. Maybe by having the ear of a trusted friend with whom one can talk things through, a survivor can come to a new understanding of post-disaster life. Or perhaps with the guidance of a trained therapist with reflective listening skills and expertise in post-disaster recovery, a survivor can come to realize a silver lining that he or she had not been able to see before.

Given that many variables could be important for seeing a silver lining(s) in connection with a tragic happening, it is clear that the intersection of individual differences and coping with disaster stressors is a rich topic that calls for systematic research. Having research-based answers to replace unbridled speculation is desirable and practical, too, providing direction for translational work to mitigate adversity and assist survivors with the ups and downs of long-term disaster recovery. In this spirit, I turn briefly to the extant literature on stress and coping in a disaster context.

Academically speaking, seeking silver linings associated with catastrophic events is an example of emotion-focused coping to alleviate distress associated with calamity.[28] There is scientific evidence to confirm the notion that looking for a silver lining or the bright side of an otherwise desperate situation provides some relief to survivors coping with great losses.[29,30] For example, Tammy Henderson and her colleagues[31] found that older adults who were displaced by Katrina coped with their situations using strategies that included relying on their religious beliefs, cultivating positive attitudes of hope and gratitude (for surviving), and reappraising situations in a positive light. Furthermore, in a meta-analysis by Prati and Pietrantoni,[32] positive reappraisal was highly correlated with posttraumatic growth. Thus, it can be beneficial to a person's overall well-being to be able to look for the "silver lining" after a disaster or other calamity.

Practically speaking, knowing that storm clouds have silver linings implies hope. Looking for silver linings, then, should help people work their way through painful experiences without losing hope for better days ahead. The focus of the remainder of this chapter is centered on silver linings as a way of looking at life after disaster. Several illustrations are presented next to illuminate the concept of silver linings as a principle of healing in the context of the Katrina disaster.

Seeing Silver Linings After Disaster

Traumatic events which happened in the past cannot be changed or undone. That is obvious, as most people already know. What people may not realize, though, is that how they react to such events may be more dynamic by comparison. People can choose how they think about events from long ago and the consequences of these events for daily life in the present. To illustrate, consider this quote from Darren Davis, a young man who was a 15-year-old high school student when he lost his home in the floodwaters of Katrina:

> At the time [of Hurricane Katrina], I couldn't see the big picture at all. I really couldn't see how any of this would have benefitted me. . . . It's a tough thing to go through at the time. . . . It's really, really a time of personal darkness to do some of the things that we did. Like, gutting my house and, and dealing with

my parents having their problems and all of those things. It was a very, very rough time. But, it's shaping. . . . It's a molding experience. It molds you into who you are.

And if you were to ever tell a fifteen-year-old, if they had the choice of having a storm come wipe out their house, I don't think they would say, "Oh, that would be a great character building exercise". . . I think I'll opt out on that one. But, we don't really have a choice of what we get to go through.

As Darren so aptly points out, "we don't really have a choice of what we get to go though." But we do have a choice on how we respond to such experiences when they happen and in the years after these events.

To learn more about possible silver linings after the 2005 Atlantic Hurricane Katrina, we used a mixed-method approach that included an open-ended question that invited participants talk about potential positives they may have experienced after Katrina. Open-ended questions are desirable as a research tool insofar as they allow greater insight into how adults of different ages cope with natural disaster. The narrative prompt given to all participants was "They say every cloud has a silver lining and even the most awful events can have positive outcomes. Do you think there are any positive outcomes that can come from Hurricanes Katrina and Rita? If so, what are they?"

Qualitative analyses of participants' narrative responses yielded three principle themes: (1) personal growth and change in perspective, (2) appreciation for a new positive social environment, and (3) relationships with friends and family are what matter most. These themes are documented in Appendix A. They are also discussed in greater detail elsewhere, along with supportive primary data.[33] One gentleman's response to the "silver lining" question stands out in memory for me, being the quintessential example of the third theme, *relationships with friends and family are what matter most.* Briefly, Skip Lagarde was a former coastal parish resident. Skip had permanently relocated to Baton Rouge, Louisiana, with his family after having lost his job and his home in Katrina. I asked him about possible silver linings that may have come out of the Katrina experience. Skip spoke of his elderly father. In his own words:

And my father becoming sick, finding out that he had cancer. . . . Katrina, actually I looked at it as a silver lining. It did have a silver lining, because I was able to be with him for his entire last year. . . . Whereas, if Katrina never would've happened, and if I would have had a full time job someplace else, I wouldn't have been able to be with him just on a day-to-day basis, because I'd have been at work some place.

Maybe something good can come out of a disaster for those who are willing to look at the circumstances of their post-disaster life differently. For Skip Lagarde, Katrina's silver lining was the gift of time and being able to spend each day with his terminally ill father in the last year of his life.

*   *   *

Another example of a silver lining in connection with the Katrina disaster does not align with the three research-based themes just mentioned. This silver lining concerns the gift of a new life, which began with the rescue of a dog named Pearl. Left behind by owners who evacuated before Katrina, Pearl was saved by a then seventeen-year-old boy and his family. Some readers may wonder why the plight of a dog is important or worthy of consideration. To my way of thinking, Pearl's story is not only important, but also significant at several levels of abstraction.

At a general level of analysis, Pearl's ordeal casts a spotlight on the plight of an estimated quarter of a million cats and dogs who were left behind on August 29, 2005.[34] Many people thought they would only be gone for a few days and reasoned that their pets would be fine for a short period of time. Not necessarily a heartless decision, but rather one of necessity as dogs and cats were not permitted in disaster shelters at that time. Sadly, a percentage of those who perished in Katrina's intense flooding were pet owners who had refused to evacuate because they did not want to leave their animal companions behind.

I have often thought that the world can be divided into two camps: those people who have a love for animals and those who, for whatever reason, do not share this sentiment. Thinking this way reminds me of Martha Hart, an elderly participant who reflected on her experience during Hurricane Betsy in 1965. Looking back, Martha told me about the intense flooding and severe winds that she had experienced nearly a half century earlier. She spoke of scrambling to the roof of her home as Betsy raged through lower Plaquemines Parish. Martha had her little dog under one arm and her purse under the other arm. As the wind threatened her precarious perch on the roof, she crawled toward the chimney for shelter. In that split second, she needed to free an arm to grab onto the chimney, but what would she drop: her beloved little dog or her purse with what money she had and her important papers? Martha dropped the purse, grabbed the chimney, and saved herself and her little dog on that day. Had I been in her shoes, I believe that I would have done the very same thing.

Today, the rules have changed. There is now a federal law for companion animals to be evacuated and stay with their owners at disaster shelters. Specifically, the Pets Evacuation and Transportation Standards (PETS) Act of 2006 is a legal provision which allows state and local governments to create and implement a protocol for the humane treatment and evacuation of service animals and personal pets threatened by disaster. Today, the PETS act comes into play when a federal disaster declaration has been made.[35] As an example, many pets were saved after Hurricane Harvey, which struck Texas and portions of Louisiana in September of 2017.[36]

Setting politics and more recent severe weather events aside, readers who have a heart for animals might nod in agreement that the solitary life of one dog matters. At a personal level of analysis, Pearl the dog is significant. She is worthy of consideration. Pearl's story is one of a life that was saved, and, in return, she brought nearly a decade of joy to the Bowens, her new family. In short, Pearl's story illustrates the unconditional love that only a pet can provide, bringing hope and healing to the Bowen family who endured unspeakable suffering during the Katrina disaster.

Illustration: Pearl the Dog, a Silver Lining After the Katrina Disaster

Thinking about silver linings brings back fond memories of Brandon Bowen, a college student, and his parents, Ashley and Michael, who permanently relocated to Baton Rouge, Louisiana, after having lost their home in Katrina. In March of 2010, Brandon took time out of his busy schedule of classes to meet with me for the study. As I learned during the course of his research interview, Brandon and his parents were trapped on the top of a building in St. Bernard Parish for nearly a week during Katrina's horrendous flooding. An unimaginable nightmare, I learned later that Brandon had witnessed death at least twice during the Katrina disaster as a seventeen-year-old high school student at the beginning of his senior year.

During his interview, Brandon spoke openly about his Katrina experience, dutifully checking boxes on the paper-and-pencil surveys and answering the open-ended questions thoughtfully and completely. When I asked him about potential silver linings associated with the Katrina disaster, he did not hesitate for an instant. With a twinkle in his eye, Brandon talked about Pearl, the dog his family rescued during their ordeal. In his own words:

> I think the positive outcomes in my life . . . obviously we gained Pearl, our dog. That made us really happy because seriously a month before the hurricane, our bull dog died. We were still hurting from that. He [Max the bulldog] had been with me since I was growing up . . . since I was in first grade. He was lucky,

though, because otherwise if we would have stayed, he would have died up there with us, you know, in the heat. He was just unhealthy. But I think that really helped my family out . . . getting Pearl.

We talked briefly about Max the bulldog, a family pet throughout his childhood. The fact that Max had died in July of 2005 was probably a blessing, he said. Max wouldn't have survived the August heat on the rooftop where they were stranded for five days after Katrina. The conversation shifted from Max the bulldog to Pearl the boxer and how his family acquired this dog in the immediate aftermath of Katrina.

As I learned, Pearl was the neighbor's dog who was going to be left behind. Instead, the Bowens graciously took Pearl into their care. In Brandon's own words:

> My neighbor, he was evacuating to Chalmette High School and they said "No pets," or anything, so he was going to leave her in the second story of the house, and it was right down the block from ours, so before he left, we offered to take her. So we got her food, you know, her big buckets [for drinking water], everything for her and moved it up into Village Square [the building where they were stranded].
>
> And just after that, she stayed with us throughout the hurricane and whenever we left, you know, she got nervous. She knew we were leaving, and really we had to leave her because they said "No dogs in the helicopters" or anything like that . . . so we left her. My uncle came back the next day though, looking for us ironically . . . [but they had left by that time].

As Brandon explained, they were airlifted from the rooftop by a Black Hawk helicopter but forced to leave Pearl behind. They were flown to a staging area on the bridge in New Orleans. Eventually, they were able to get transportation to Baton Rouge. From there, they headed to Abbeville, in Vermillion Parish, to stay with family. Abbeville is approximately 150 miles west of New Orleans and sixty miles southwest of Baton Rouge. "It was not easy getting out of the city" Brandon said. In all, their evacuation took approximately thirty-two hours. Sadly, Abbeville would soon be pummeled by Hurricane Rita, a second Category 3 storm that hit on September 24, 2005, just four weeks after Katrina, forcing the family to relocate again.

Returning to Pearl's story, Brandon told us more about the sequence of events during those first weeks after Katrina made landfall.

> And once we got to Abbeville, we called him [my uncle], and we got in touch with him, and he said that he went looking for us, [but] Pearl wasn't there. So we were

like, "No you have to go back. Go get Pearl." So he went back the next day again, paddled out there [in his boat], got Pearl, brought her back, and they rescued a lot of animals actually.

It was my uncle and his wife's ex-husband, because he was a police officer down in New Orleans. So they rescued a bunch of animals and a funny thing, he said that they put them all in the back of the truck on the way to Baton Rouge, but Pearl wouldn't get in the back of the truck. She had to sit up front with them [in the cab of the truck].

And the whole way [laughing], he said she would just turn and look at both of them, you know, like look at one and turn and look at the other person and just, you know, licking them at all times . . . so friendly . . . just so happy [to be rescued].

Brandon concluded with this thought:

I don't know what our life would be like without that dog right now. . . . It sounds stupid . . . but she's an integral part of the family now. She really is. Because my dad loves the dog . . . they spoil it like another child. Every time I go back home [to visit] there's a new toy . . . every time! Guaranteed. And all she does is just rip it up as soon as she gets it. Rips the stuffing out . . . right away! Destroy, destroy, destroy! [laughs]

As we wrapped up the research interview, Brandon and I chuckled together over the thought of Pearl having fun with her chew toys and doing what boxers do. To this day, it still makes me smile to think about this dear family and their beloved dog, Pearl. Luckily, I had the unique opportunity to meet Pearl in their Baton Rouge home in June of 2010. Pearl was every bit as lively and vivacious as I had been told. She sat patiently by the table as I petted her head. A beautiful animal, she had a light brown coat of very short hair, large white paws, and soulful brown eyes. I was told that Pearl and her rescuer, Brandon, were inseparable. Pearl enjoyed her family time and would roll over to have her tummy rubbed on a daily basis.

Sadly, I recently learned that Pearl passed away in 2014. A new life after Katrina with a new family in a new home for nearly a decade, Pearl is the silver lining that remains in the hearts of this dear family. The mother, Ashley, recently told me that others who know them talk about their having rescued Pearl from Katrina. In her own words, Ashley said, "People say we rescued her, but truthfully, she was our saving grace! The unconditional love she gave us was such an enormous blessing!"

Where Is the Silver Lining?

Participants' answers to the silver lining question covered a wide range of responses, which varied tremendously. From new opportunities for personal growth and professional development, to new home renovations, to new friendships and social relationships, there were positives in the years after Katrina for some people. Other evidence has shown that silver linings after Katrina included lessons learned and better preparedness for future disasters (see Appendix A). Nonetheless, for some participants, there were no silver linings to be found, not then and not now. The following quote from Julie Hanover is illustrative:

> But I don't know about any silver linings, I looked at that question and asked myself that many times. I don't know where the silver lining is? . . . [Katrina] certainly destroyed a lot of people . . .
>
>   And I might add we had a Father [Catholic Priest] over at church [who] remarked about a year after Katrina, that he had more funerals that year after Katrina than any other year. Not from the effects of people and flooding, from the emotional and the stressful [happenings]. Especially the elderly, because they weren't able to come back home, most of them, there was nothing. . . . So then they went with their children or went into nursing homes or you know, just very sad way to wind down their lives before. Their little homes and their everyday routine, and that was gone. So their purpose was gone.

It pained my heart to listen to her talk about such suffering, especially among older adults. As the conversation continued about older adults dying after the storm, Julie went on to say

> You could read the paper . . . in the obituaries and you could just see, because all over, people were spread all over, not only just the metro area, but Mississippi and you could read [about the people who had died]. In fact, my Dad came back to stay with me. [He and his friends] at the Council on Aging . . . he would go every day . . . and that would be the topic of conversation. "Who died? Oh, so and so died in Picayune. You remember them, they lived in Arabi." It was a topic of conversation, because we were losing so many of them, they were [dying] from broken hearts. Despair is a terrible thing.

For people suffering and in prolonged despair, coming to terms with painful experiences or seeing them in a different light may be too difficult to handle alone. Guided by the wisdom of a trained professional with a state board certified license to heal, therapeutic intervention may be necessary for overcoming painful experiences, including disasters or other tragedies. Therapists with experience treating disaster survivors can offer hope and a way out of an otherwise dark and seemingly hopeless situation for those burdened with grief and loss. A skilled therapist will foster healthy coping skills and conflict resolution strategies in a supportive manner, helping survivors manage the pain of loss and get on with the task of daily living. Therapeutic intervention can be remarkably liberating, too. In other words, the right therapist will support the healing process gently and without judgment, resulting in a noticeable improvement in one's quality of life. Note, too, that the benefits of therapy may spill over into other life domains, including relationships with family, friends, and coworkers. In short, counseling resources can be quite helpful and may be vital to the success and completeness of long-term recovery.

Summary

The saying "Every cloud has a silver lining" has a long history that can be traced to the seventeenth century. Looking for silver linings after catastrophic events like the Katrina disaster is one way that survivors may cope with their experiences. In principle, there are many different ways to look at a disaster's impact and the changed life circumstances associated with catastrophic events. How one chooses to interpret these events is important and has an impact that may shape the course and direction of long-term recovery.

It is also possible that survivors reassess and reevaluate their circumstances, possibly seeing the disaster experience in a different light later on. The words of Pam Mones, a wife, mother, and grandmother from a coastal fishing family come to mind:

> I don't believe God does bad things to people. I think He may allow things to happen in your life and then give you things for you to make your own choices, where you go with it, and how do you learn from it? And . . . even though Katrina's been several years, we're still learning, we're still processing the losses and the blessings.

Pam's quote is noteworthy for several reasons in my opinion. First, she gives voice to a critical assumption: that is, losses and blessings coexist, and both can be realized after a disaster. Second, Pam's quote, which is essentially a belief statement, reflects an overarching faith in a fundamentally beneficent God. Last, faith together with acceptance of losses and looking for positives or "blessings" that can arise even out of the most desperate of situations are styles of coping that would appear to work for her (see Chapter 5).

Readers are reminded that the process of identifying silver linings may involve sacrifice along the way, although celebrating small victories on the long road to recovery can be helpful. In his own words, Oates, a successful businessman, told us:

> Also, don't be afraid to recognize the silver lining, the opportunities, and the good that can occur if you're willing to make the sacrifice. Remember sacrifice is a natural part of our journey. And look at the small successes that occur every day. . . .
>
> You know, as you're going through something like this, remember to look back at the little [successes], it might be something minor but it's a success, and you can build on that as you're going through every day. And that's one of the stories I told you about . . . every morning, I'd wake up and think back about the small success that occur along the way. That can help you with this experience. I think I've told you how I felt about my religion and the things that . . . . the lessons that I learned from that have helped me along the way.
>
> And then, also, the crucial importance of your health and maintaining it along the way. Exercise has more than. . . . It's always been, like I said, it's always been a part of my life, but it's. . . . It goes a lot not just toward the physical, but the mental well-being of who you are and how you feel. You know, it helps you relieve stress and work out different problems you have. And sometimes, if you just go take a little thirty-minute jog, or even if it's a little walk around the park, give yourself a few hours and give your mind a little opportunity to work that situation out. Sometimes you'll come up with the right answer. A good night's sleep, too. That's always important. Make sure you get a good night's sleep and a couple beers along the way each day doesn't hurt at all either.

NOTES

1. Paul B. Baltes and Margret M. Baltes, *Successful Aging: Perspectives from the Behavioral Sciences* (New York: Cambridge University Press, 1990).
2. Theodore D. Cosco, A. Matthew Prina, Jamie Perales, Blossom C. M. Stephan, and Carol Brayne, "Operational Definitions of Successful Aging: A Systematic Review. *International Psychogeriatrics* 26, no. 3 (2014): 373–381.
3. Katie E. Cherry, Sandro Galea, S., and Jennifer L. Silva, "Successful Aging and Natural Disasters: Role of Adaptation and Resiliency in Late Life," in *Handbook of Clinical Psychology: Volume 1* eds. Michel Hersen and Alan M. Gross (New York: John Wiley & Sons: 2008), 810–833.

4. Katie E. Cherry, Loren D. Marks, Tim Benedetto, Marissa Sullivan, and Alyse Barker, "Perceptions of Longevity and Successful Aging in Very Old Adults," *Journal of Religion, Spirituality and Aging* 25 (2013): 288–310, https://doi.org/10.1080/15528030.2013.765368

5. Daniella S. Jopp, Dagmara Wozniak, Amanda K. Damarin, Melissa De Feo, Seojung Jung, and Sheena Jeswani, "How Could Lay Perspectives on Successful Aging Complement Scientific Theory? Findings from a US and a German Life-Span Sample," *The Gerontologist* 55 (2015): 91–106.

6. Rachel Pruchno and Deborah Carr, "Successful Aging 2.0: Resilience and Beyond," *The Journals of Gerontology: Series B* 72, no. 2 (2017): 201–203, https://doi.org/10.1093/geronb/gbw214

7. Maureen Wilson-Genderson, Rachel Pruchno, and Allison R. Heid, "Modeling Successful Aging Over Time in the Context of a Disaster," *The Journals of Gerontology: Series B* 72, no. 2 (2017): 328–39.

8. Jutta Heckhausen and Richard Schultz, "A Life-Span Theory of Control," *Psychological Review* 102, no. 2 (1995): 284–304.

9. Rob Ranzijn and Mary A. Luszcz, "Acceptance: A Key to Well-Being in Older Adults?" *Australian Psychologist* 34 (1999): 94–98.

10. Carol D. Ryff, "In the Eye of the Beholder: Views of Psychological Well-Being Among Middle-Aged and Older Adults," *Psychology and Aging* 4, no. 2 (June 1989): 195–210.

11. Baltes and Baltes, *Successful Aging.*

12. Katie E. Cherry, Bethany A. Lyon, Emily O. Boudreaux, Alyse B. Blanchard, Jason L. Hicks, Emily M. Elliott, Leann Myers, Sangkyu Kim, and S. Michal Jazwinski, "Memory Self-Efficacy and Beliefs About Memory and Aging in Very Old Adults in the Louisiana Healthy Aging Study (LHAS)," *Experimental Aging Research* 45, no. 1 (2019): 28–40.

13. Deborah L. Duay and Valerie C. Bryan, "Senior Adults' Perceptions of Successful Aging," *Educational Gerontology* 32 (2006): 423–445.

14. Trevan G. Hatch, Katie E. Cherry, Yaxin Lu, and Loren D. Marks, "Seeing Silver Linings After Catastrophic Loss: Personal Growth, Positive Adaption, and Relationships That Matter," in *Traumatic Stress and Long-Term Recovery: Coping with Disasters and Other Negative Life Events,* ed. Katie E. Cherry (New York: Springer International Publishing Switzerland, 2015), 389–402.

15. Tammy L. Henderson, Karen A. Roberto, and Yoshinori Kamo, "Older Adults' Responses to Hurricane Katrina: Daily Hassles and Coping Strategies," *Journal of Applied Gerontology* 29 (2010): 48–69. doi: 10.1177/0733464809334287

16. Katie E. Stanko, Katie E. Cherry, Kyle S. Ryker, Farra Mughal, Loren D. Marks, Jennifer Silva Brown, Patricia F. Gendusa, Marisa C., Sullivan, John Bruner, David A. Welsh, L. Joseph Su, and S. Michal Jazwinski, "Looking for the Silver Lining: Benefit Finding After Hurricanes Katrina and Rita in Middle-Aged, Older, and Oldest-Old Adults," *Current Psychology* 34 (2015): 564–575.

17. Elisabeth Kübler-Ross, *On Death and Dying* (New York: Scribner, 1969).

18. Elisabeth Kübler-Ross and David Kessler, *On Grief and Grieving* (New York: Scribner, 2005).

19. Henricus P. Baard, *Frans Hals*, trans. George Stuyck (London: Thames and Hudson Ltd, 1981): 158–161.

20. Keri L. Kytola, Katie E. Cherry, Loren D. Marks, and Trevan G. Hatch, "When Neighborhoods Are Destroyed by Disaster: Relocate or Return and Rebuild?," in *Traumatic Stress and Long-Term Recovery: Coping with Disasters and Other Negative*

Life Events, ed. Katie E. Cherry (New York: Springer International Publishing Switzerland, 2015), 211–229.

21. Kelly Carr and Patricia L. Weir, "A Qualitative Description of Successful Aging Through Different Decades of Older Adulthood," *Aging & Mental Health* 21, no. 12 (2017): 1317–1325.

22. Ryff, "In the Eye of the Beholder," 201.

23. Kenneth W. Osbeck, *Amazing Grace: 366 Inspiring Hymn Stories for Daily Devotions* (2nd ed.) (Grand Rapids, MI: Kregel Publications, 2002), 194.

24. Ira David Sankey, *My Life and the Story of the Gospel Hymns and of Sacred Songs and Solos* (London: Forgotten Books, 2012, originally published 1907), 190–192.

25. Crich Baptist Church, Derbyshire, UK, "It Is Well with My Soul: The Hymn and the Story," accessed June 20, 2019, https://www.crichbaptist.org/articles/christian-poetry-hymns/it-is-well-with-my-soul/

26. *Webster's New Compact Office Dictionary* (Cleveland: Wiley Publishing, Inc., 2003), 599.

27. G. Martin, "The Meaning and Origin of the Expression: Every Cloud Has a Silver Lining," *The Phrase Finder,* accessed June 19, 2019, http://www.phrases.org.uk/meanings/every-cloud-has-a-silver-lining.html

28. Howard Tennen and Glenn Affleck, "Finding Benefits in Adversity," in *Coping: The Psychology of What Works,* ed. Charles. R. Snyder (New York: Oxford University Press, 1999), 279–304.

29. Hatch, "Seeing Silver Linings After Catastrophic Loss."

30. Stanko, "Looking for the Silver Lining."

31. Henderson, "Older Adults' Responses to Hurricane Katrina."

32. Gabriele Prati and Luca Pietrantoni, "Optimism, Social Support, and Coping Strategies as Factors Contributing to Posttraumatic Growth: A Meta-Analysis," *Journal of Loss and Trauma* 14, no. 5 (2009): 364–388.

33. Hatch, "Seeing Silver Linings After Catastrophic Loss."

34. David Grimm, "How Pets of Hurricane Harvey Are Benefitting from the Lessons of Katrina," *Huffington Post,* September 5, 2017, http://actionnews.ca/newstempch.php?article=/entry/how-pets-of-hurricane-harvey-are-benefiting-from-the-lessons-of-katrina_us_59af1f02e4b0b5e53101cf02

35. American Veterinary Medical Association, "PETS Act (FAQ)," *AVMA,* last modified 2018, accessed August 3, 2018, https://www.avma.org/KB/Resources/Reference/disaster/Pages/PETS-Act-FAQ.aspx?PF=1

36. Karin Brulliard, "How the Chaos of Hurricane Katrina Helped Save Pets from Flooding in Texas," *Washington Post,* August 31, 2017, https://www.washingtonpost.com/news/animalia/wp/2017/08/31/how-the-chaos-of-hurricane-katrina-helped-save-pets-from-flooding-in-texas/?noredirect=on&utm_term=.81c39ec73337

PART III

Life After Disaster

The older you are, the more there was of life in the past to have lost.
—Althea Lloyd

CHAPTER 8

✿

Grief and the "New Normal"

"It's not like it used to be." Both former and current residents of St. Bernard and Plaquemines Parishes have offered similar observations about their hometown and way of life in these coastal communities in the years after the 2005 hurricanes. Many of my conversations with lifelong residents have been packaged temporally, organized into "before the storm" versus "now or today" stories, as though Hurricane Katrina and the terrible flooding that followed the 2005 levee breaches etched a permanent dividing line into their personal recollections. More than just a phenomenon of auto-biographical memory, this line etched in the collective conscious also marks the start of significant discontinuity, forever changing lives and the course of the future for so many residents across the US Gulf Coast.

For some people, thinking about or talking about what life was like be-fore the Katrina disaster stirs emotion. While people of all ages may ex-perience distress after a disaster, older people are likely to have the added worry that they will not live long enough to recover a sense of normal living during their lifetimes.[1] To illustrate, consider this quote from Julie Hanover, a sixty-four-year old woman, in response to the question: "When did normal living come back for you?" (emphasis added):

> It will never be normal again. What was normal before is not normal now . . . now [I have] all these people living with me, where before it was just my husband and I. Now we have people living with us because they have no place else to go. They need to fix up their homes, family and friends are gone. Community destroyed. So it's a new normal. Not one that I like because it's really hard to, *it's hard every day to know what was. And you've got to kind of hope it will be. But will you be around*

to see it? Family had moved away. Friends have moved away, neighbors, I was in my home for forty years. Neighbors moved away. Now we don't know who our neighbors are. The closeness . . . that was a real close-knit community. And [now] that part is gone.

Older participants have also said that their grandchildren have no recollection of the community, lifestyles, and traditions "before the storm." From this point of view, one might get the sense that disaster-related sorrow is *retrospective*, meaning that this sadness is fueled by looking back to a world that no longer exists. There is another possibility to consider, though. That is, disaster-related sorrow may not be only retrospective, related to what is now gone or has been lost in the disaster. Rather, disaster-related sorrow may be *prospective* as well, reaching forward in time. For instance, thinking about futures that will not unfold as planned may drive sorrow. Family traditions will not be fulfilled or carried out by children as their parents had at one time thought or expected. Consider the sons and daughters of families who work in the commercial fishing industry for a living. The children of fourth- and fifth-generation shrimpers and oyster farmers may not fall in line beside their fathers and grandfathers on the family boat in the natural waterways of south Louisiana. For this generation and for generations to come, water may not be a way of life anymore, a painful and perhaps frightening realization for their parents who have known nothing else. On the contrary, cutting losses and moving to a new city after Katrina offered a fresh start for some people, an opportunity for new beginnings[2] (see also Chapter 7).

Thinking about disaster sorrow in the years after these events may lead to a question of relevance: Why does it matter? For directly affected individuals and families who have moved on with their life, the Katrina disaster may be nothing more than a distant memory from the past, seldom referenced in daily life. For indirectly affected persons, there were no significant losses to accept or grief to resolve. The question, "Why does this matter?" for people who did not have catastrophic damage and losses in 2005 might sounds something like this: "It's been so many years since Katrina, why are you still talking about it? You really should be over this by now." As discussed previously (see Chapter 6), insensitive remarks of any sort (especially those containing the word, *should*) are not particularly helpful.

Let's get back to the question of relevance. An academic response to the question of relevance has to do with *sampling*. Social scientists who study the psychological and behavioral impacts of disaster know that there will be a certain percentage of the population for whom disaster distress remains.

The reality for this sample is that disaster sorrow may still permeate their everyday lives, sometimes for many years. For those people who have not yet found their way to the other side of suffering, grief after disaster may be as obvious as the nose on their face. This reality is reason enough to prompt continued concern.

Whether disaster sorrow is retrospective or prospective in origin (or a combination of both) is an academic question that probably doesn't matter to most people. What does matter is that sorrow associated with disaster losses and changed life circumstances is real. Authentic and unquestionably painful, sorrow after disaster impacts survivors' lives in ways that the rest of the world may not appreciate or ever fully understand.[3] Both former and current coastal residents who lost homes in 2005 will tell you that their life today is not at all like the one they had before Katrina. To illustrate, consider the next two quotes. The first is from former coastal resident Janice O'Brien, who relocated permanently inland after Katrina. The second quote is from Sherri Lopez, a current resident who came back to take up residence down the road in St. Bernard Parish after a lengthy displacement because Katrina had destroyed the physical structure of her family's house.

Former coastal resident Janice O'Brien spoke of her new life with new furnishings in a new home in a new community after Katrina. Her response to the question, "What would you like others to know about your experiences with Hurricanes Katrina and Rita?" was as follows:

> Life was never, ever going to be the same. Often times people will say to us, "But look at the beautiful home you have. You all have everything you could possibly want." And that's true. But what we don't have is life as we knew it before Katrina. So although you can go out and buy furniture, the loss—it never, ever goes away. When I say loss, what I mean is your life is never the same.

Next, consider Sherri Lopez, a forty-three-year old wife and mother who lost her coastal parish home down the road in southeastern St. Bernard. Sherri and her family eventually returned to St. Bernard Parish and purchased a new modular home. Her response to the question, "What would you like others to know about your experiences with Hurricanes Katrina and Rita?" was remarkable. Her answer seems to capture the same feeling of loss described by so many current and former coastal residents in the years after the Katrina tragedy. Sherri told us (emphasis added):

> I want everyone to know that your home community and way of life could be washed away, but *it was harder to lose the community than it was my home.* You

can rebuild the house, but you cannot rebuild the community. It's very hard. You can lose a home, but if you have nowhere to go when you get home, then it's not a home. If you don't have a school, you don't have groceries, you don't have neighbors, you don't have family, I wouldn't want to live there. So it was much harder to lose my whole way of life more than what it was to see my house gone.

As Janice and Sherri aptly point out, life after Katrina is never the same as it was before this disaster. The challenge for survivors, then, becomes one of awareness: to recognize the presence of disaster sorrow and see it for what it is. Cultivating awareness may, in turn, lead to greater insight regarding the potentially disruptive influence of disaster sorrow on a survivor's daily life. Greater awareness may in turn reveal the futility of expecting others to understand the disaster experience when such people have no prior knowledge to draw on for comparison. In short, disaster-related sorrow may be crippling in a way that friends and family do not comprehend. That said, the question then becomes how to manage sorrow unique to the disaster experience and how to eventually overcome it. Simply put, how do people get to the other side of suffering in the wake of a life changing disaster?

* * *

In Chapter 7, the concept of posttraumatic growth (PTG) was referenced in the context of benefit finding, which is a coping strategy that may be helpful for some people after disaster. Participants' descriptions of *silver linings* realized in the aftermath of the 2005 Katrina tragedy brought to life the idea that sometimes good things can come out of bad circumstances. To my way of thinking, there is a second "PTG" that has generated comparatively less academic and research attention compared to posttraumatic growth: "posttraumatic grief." By posttraumatic grief, I refer simply to the observation of *grief after disaster*, an important but perhaps overlooked or understudied aspect of post-disaster life. The experience of sorrow after disaster examined in this chapter will be referred to as "postdisaster grief" (PDG).

Before I speculate further, recall the different ways of knowing outlined earlier. We can be certain about the existence of something—say, gravity as a force in nature—based on at least three different approaches: personal, rational, and scientific. These approaches essentially provide us with at least three different sources of information: (1) *personal observations*, meaning that which we see with our own eyes or hear with our own ears; (2) *rational arguments*, as in the humanities through the application of systems of logic; or (3) *scientific hypotheses*, as in the enterprise of basic research carried out within the parameters of the scientific method. From this later frame of reference, we also know that a good scientist begins by defining his or her terms. In the parlance of scientific research, this means formulating an operational definition that has measurement implications.

To operationalize a concept such as *postdisaster grief*, one must first state categorically what it is *not*: PDG it is not the same thing as depression, anxiety, or posttraumatic stress, although these comorbidities (prevailing conditions) can happen in the context of disaster.[4] PDG is not the same as *prolonged grief disorder* either, a relatively new clinical term pertaining to situations where the normal processes of grief do not resolve. Last, PDG may resemble an emotional state known as *complicated grief* (CG), which has been studied in a disaster context.[5] However, the clinical presentation and associated features of CG are not confined to a disaster context, as discussed more fully elsewhere.[6,7]

By PDG, I am simply referring to grief after disaster, which can be defined as *the sadness or sorrow that survivors experience in connection with disaster-related losses.* This definition of PDG, though loose scientifically and certainly subject to criticism, does provide a reasonable place to start. Based on a strict adherence to the scientific method of knowing, a good scientist then proceeds with observation, hypothesis testing (which means data collection to generate objective evidence), and drawing conclusions in an effort to formulate new knowledge about PDG. This last step, concerning conclusions based on research outcomes, will be necessarily tentative. That is, a good scientist will also want to replicate a research finding to confirm its reliability and generality before offering firm conclusions to the public. Thus a disclaimer is in order here. Specifically, the discussion of PDG offered in this chapter must remain speculative, confined to personal observations and published scientific findings generated within my own research program (see Appendix A). Replication and extension of these findings by other social scientists, together with eventual translation to therapeutic contexts, are important challenges that await future research and the next generation of scholars.

Setting scientific disclaimers aside, the pain and sorrow of PDG are both obvious and undeniable for directly affected individuals who have lived through a natural disaster. For individuals who have not yet been exposed to disaster, PDG is not part of their developmental history. Such persons would have no direct personal experience to draw upon to illuminate PDG. Yet they may know about its existence through *observation* of others who are suffering in the wake of disaster. So what does PDG look like? To illustrate, I reference a poem written by Rosiland White, a lifelong resident of St. Bernard. She penned these words in late 2005, just a few short months after as much as twenty feet of floodwater from Hurricane Katrina demolished her home and community. Beautiful in its simplicity yet powerful and compelling in the message it conveys, Rosiland's poem succinctly captures the idea of PDG. That is, her poem illustrates both the breadth of the loss and depth of sorrow for those left homeless in the wake of a catastrophic natural disaster.

Silent Winter

The nights are so quiet, so still, so dark . . .
Where are the dogs that used to bark?
Where are the crickets with their chirping sound?
There are no animals to be found.
Frogs no longer croak for rain.
Or hang onto my windowpane.
There are no birds singing in trees.
Even the trees have tattered leaves.
Sadness surrounds me; everything seems dead.
Except for the thoughts, which dance in my head.
Thoughts of what was and what could have been.
Are now lying under crumbled sheetrock and tin.
My life has been deleted from me.
Scattered pictures surround me with faces I do not see.
A neighborhood of people have disappeared from here.
Will I ever see them again, I wonder in fear?
Let this silent winter come to an end.
And let my life begin to mend.

—Rosiland White
Reprinted with permission

This poem is rich in imagery, providing a vision of what post-disaster life looked like to a Katrina survivor in 2005. To my way of thinking, Rosiland's poem is noteworthy for at least three additional reasons, if not more. First, her words convey the breadth and depth of losses after catastrophic natural disaster. She also provides the reader with an insider's perspective on what Katrina's immediate aftermath *felt like*. From the familiar sounds of nature now gone—no birds chirping, dogs barking, frogs croaking, or other sounds of coastal wildlife indigenous to the region—to the neighborhood of friends who had vanished, all things familiar were just not there anymore. Second, the reader can perceive an overwhelming sense of despair that speaks to the totality of hurricane devastation and loss. Third, her poem concludes with an almost audible cry, pleading for the conclusion of disaster-related suffering—in her words, "Let this silent winter come to an end. And let my life begin to mend." As I read these lines, I sense hope (i.e., there is an end at some point) and optimism (i.e., life will mend, with better days ahead).

As I have learned through the process of conducting basic research, hope and optimism are two variables that matter after disaster.[8] As bad as the Katrina tragedy was, the pain, despair, and overwhelming sense of loss can be corralled, contained temporally, have a definite beginning, a middle part, and an end. From this point of view, one can sense parallels between PDG in connection with the loss of material possessions (home, neighborhood, and community) and the natural process of grief over the death of a loved one.

The focus of the remainder of this chapter will be confined to grief associated with disaster-related losses in the years after these events. Grief counselors and bereavement specialists often use the term "the *new normal*" to describe life after the death of a loved one. For disaster survivors who have lost the comfort of the familiar—homes, communities, and routines of daily living—there is a grieving process to work through and "a new normal" to be discovered that in many ways resembles the sequence of events that unfold in the weeks, months, and years after a loved one has passed away.

The takeaway point in this chapter, then, is that *grief*, a natural emotional response to loss, is uniquely part of the disaster experience. PDG may be a subtle yet pervasive aspect of life after disaster that warrants consideration. Grief associated with disaster-related losses likely contributes to difficulties navigating the many unanticipated and unwelcomed adjustments to be made after a disaster. Sometimes grief unfolds in a disruptive manner, with an intensity and persistence that may call for therapeutic intervention. In turn, the process of *grief resolution,* or, in common parlance, the journey which survivors must take to overcome their grief, is also a necessary step for discovering a "new normal" in the wake of a life-changing disaster.

IN SEARCH OF THE "NEW NORMAL:"
SEVERED ATTACHMENTS AND POST-DISASTER GRIEF

When disasters strike, everyday living comes abruptly to a halt. For those who reside in disaster-impacted regions, established routines do not fit the current circumstances. New problems may also arise as survivors struggle to restore order and a sense of balance and coherence to their disaster-shattered world. Their world is no longer the same, as any witness to the 2005 Katrina tragedy can tell you.

Undoubtedly, former and current residents of the US Gulf Coast who lived through the 2005 Atlantic Hurricanes Katrina and Rita can relate to the feeling that "the world changed in the blink of an eye." They know this reality to be true based on direct experience (see Chapters 2–4, where a survivor's daily journal entries provide a window into this disaster). In the immediate aftermath, local and national disaster relief efforts are mobilized. Directly impacted survivors may be swept into a chaotic existence as they move from one temporary shelter or another.[9] In the long days, months, and years ahead, survivors will form a new script for everyday living. A new set of daily routines will come into play, and family traditions will be upheld, although possibly in a new form adapted for post-disaster life, as discussed more fully in Chapter 9. In the paragraphs that follow, I make the point that disruptions in relationships with special people and places after disaster can be challenging to navigate in the years after these events. However, a growing awareness of the impact of numerous changes in survivors' social and physical environments after disaster may be a key to resolving the pain of loss and discovering "the new normal" after disaster.

For greater insight into the post-disaster adjustment process, let's return to primary data that were collected in the post-Katrina study. Recall that we asked participants in this study to respond to a set of open-ended questions. Of special interest are participants' responses to the question: "When did normal living come back for you?" Content analyses of 125 participants' answers to this question yielded five major themes which are documented in the Appendix and discussed in greater detail elsewhere.[10,11] For the purpose of the present discussion, consider the theme, "There's no going back: the 'old normal' is gone forever." Both former and current coastal residents spoke of *the loss of a way of life*. The next two quotes illuminate what was lost and why everyday life would never be the same after Katrina. These quotes are noteworthy in that they illustrate the breadth of disruption, with attachments to important people and places strained, if not severed completely. First, let's hear from Janice Rogers, a sixty-five-year-old woman who relocated permanently inland. Janice told us:

> Well, the loss wasn't a material loss so much as losing our sense of home, family, community, and plans for the future. And we feel that will never be the same. All of our families lived in close together, and we felt even if we went back to St.

Bernard it could never . . . everybody wasn't going back for one reason or another, so that way of life, we'll never have again.

With the loss of a way of life comes the disruption of many relationships
and strained, if not severed, attachments to important people. Christina
Dirksen, a seventy-seven-year old woman who returned to rebuild her
coastal home, shared a similar sentiment that life would never be the same.
Christina's quote is particularly revealing as she enumerates her severed
attachments, naming them one by one. In her own words:

> I lost my neighbors. I lost my neighborhood. I lost my church. I lost my parish
> priest. I lost everything. I lost my way of life. My life today is not the same as it
> was before Katrina. It will never be the same and I know one of your questions,
> I have to look at, it says, "When did your life get back to normal?" My life has
> never been normal. It's not going to be because I can't get my normal life back.
> It's not there anymore. I have made a new life, a new normalcy.

To contextualize the new normal after a natural disaster, it may be helpful
to broaden the discussion to include lifelong attachments to special people
and places that comprised the "old normal." From an academic (construc-
tivist) perspective, it may not be possible to build a new future after disaster without first recognizing and accepting the loss of a network of
attachments.[12] This next quote from Gerald Henderson captures the process of accepting the loss of the pre-Katrina "old normal." At sixty-six years
of age, Gerald has rebuilt his home, essentially creating a new normal in
a world that has changed. Yet he notes this was a process he would never
want to have to do over.

> I don't think it will ever be normal. I think that's just something you have to
> live with and deal with, you know. And try to understand what happened. And
> what could be done about it and just hope it don't happen again. If it did happen
> again I would probably have a negative attitude about coming back, and trying
> to have to re-do it again. Doing it once was hard. I don't regret it, but I wouldn't
> want to do it again.

Attachments formed over a lifetime are foundational for everyday living.
In other words, attachments to special people and places provide a framework within which everyday life can be ordered. Attachments to people
and places can give people a sense of purpose and meaning in life. Thus,
it should not come as a surprise that there may be untoward emotional
consequences for survivors when attachments are strained or severed

completely. To speculate further, severed attachments may contribute to grief after disaster or to other comorbidities, such as depression, anxiety, and posttraumatic stress. To bring the topic of attachments and disaster grief into sharper focus, a brief overview of attachment as a psychological construct with developmental implications is provided next.

*   *   *

The field of developmental psychology provides scholarly insight into what most people may know from personal experience. Humans, like some animal species, are social by nature. People form lasting and meaningful bonds to other people beginning early in life. Attachments are important to who we are and how we live, and they are foundational for psychological health. Broadly defined, "attachment" refers to a strong, affectionate tie to special people in our lives. Their presence brings us pleasure. They are also a source of comfort in times of distress.

The first signs of attachment appear in infancy. That attachments occur so early in life can be interpreted to suggest that there is an evolutionary aspect or survival value associated with having strong emotional bonds to other people.[13] For instance, within the first weeks and months of life, healthy infants become attached to their parents and primary caregivers, among others (e.g., siblings, grandparents, close friends). In time, social networks expand, and attachments are formed that extend beyond the nuclear family. People to whom we are attached are central in our lives. We seek their company and enjoy spending time with them. We miss them when they are not around. They may frustrate and disappoint us at times. Differences of opinion and disagreements may arise, but the underlying emotional bond prevails, holding people together through difficult situations, the good times and the bad times.

People can also form attachments to nonanimate objects like special places, belongings, and even ideas. When an attachment is severed, a painful, emotional reaction follows. When a friendship ends, a marriage fails, a beloved pet dies, or a prized possession (e.g., a wedding ring, a family photo album) is destroyed or lost, people are pained by their loss. These are just a few examples to show the variety of circumstances where some level of sorrow may be experienced. *Grief* is the formal term psychologists, grief counselors, and other professionals use to describe this pain. With grief, people mourn the loss of something that had been important or emotionally meaningful to them. When an attachment to a loved one is severed, as is the case with death, the result can be devastating. Simply put, the emotional reaction that follows the death of a parent, child, spouse, or other important person in our life may be unbearable, keeping us in a painful place for a time—in some cases, indefinitely.

Grief in and of itself is a noteworthy topic for which an expansive literature exists.[14-16] Not surprisingly, grief has also been defined in a number of different ways in the scientific literature as well as in the mainstream popular press. In scholarly pursuit of a definition of grief, I came across this one that I like very much: "Grief is the form love takes when someone we love dies."[17] Although Shear and Delaney's original formulation is specific to the death of a person, it would appear to apply more generally to disaster-related losses. Furthermore, the proximity of these two variables, grief and love, is noteworthy. The underlying assumption contained within this definition is that grief and love are tightly intertwined. Simply put, those who love deeply will grieve deeply. In the context of disaster, survivors who loved their homes, friends, neighborhoods, and way of life will grieve all of these losses when disaster strikes and robs them of one or all of these.

For disaster survivors, as for the newly bereaved after the death of a loved one, authentic grief resolution that leads to healing and long-term recovery calls for patience and effort. The resolution of grief due to a loss or multiple losses is a process that must be worked out over time, sometimes with the assistance of a therapeutic intervention. Academically speaking, we know that people may process major losses incrementally. For example, with death of a loved one, the loss may be recognized intellectually right away ("Yes, he died on this day, May 29, 2003"). It may take longer to accept such a loss emotionally ("I still feel his presence—I can't believe he is really gone"). In time, new routines and adjustments are made as grief-stricken people work through their losses and navigate the life changes that lay ahead of them.

Seeking comfort from trusted others during times of great distress and sorrow can be helpful, promoting grief resolution and the discovery of a new normal after significant loss. Furthermore, there is ample evidence in the disaster science literature to document the beneficial effects of social support on measures of health and well-being after disaster.[18] In fact, our research team has shown that perceived social support is predictive of mental health outcomes five to seven years after the Katrina tragedy.[19] Social support seeking is a proactive strategy of coping that can be comforting during times of distress. Receiving social support from concerned others should not be overlooked as a potentially helpful and sometimes positive source of comfort, too.

To illustrate the potential benefits of social support in the wake of tragedy, let me draw on a favorite example from nineteenth-century

American history. Abraham Lincoln, the sixteenth President of the United States, may be remembered for his part in many historical events of that era including the Civil War, the Emancipation Proclamation (issued January 1, 1863), and his assassination in Ford's Theatre by John Wilkes Booth, an actor and Southern sympathizer. Perhaps a lesser known historical fact is that Abraham Lincoln took the time to pen a letter of condolence to Fanny McCullough. She was the young daughter of his friend, William McCullough, a lieutenant colonel in the Fourth Illinois Cavalry who was killed on December 5, 1862, in Mississippi during the Civil War. His letter of comfort and encouragement to Fanny on the loss of her father appears here (emphasis added):[20]

Executive Mansion, Washington, December 23, 1862

Dear Fanny

It is with deep grief that I learn of the death of your kind and brave Father; and, especially, that it is affecting your young heart beyond what is common in such cases. In this sad world of ours, sorrow comes to all; and, to the young, it comes with bitterest agony, because it takes them unawares. The older have learned to ever expect it. I am anxious to afford some alleviation of your present distress. Perfect relief is not possible, except with time. You can not now realize that you will ever feel better. Is not this so? And yet it is a mistake. You are sure to be happy again. To know this, which is certainly true, will make you some less miserable now. *I have had experience enough to know what I say; and you need only to believe it, to feel better at once.* The memory of your dear Father, instead of an agony, will yet be a sad sweet feeling in your heart, of a purer and holier sort than you have known before.

Please present my kind regards to your afflicted mother.

Your sincere friend,

A. Lincoln

President Lincoln's letter to Fanny McCullough is remarkable for a number of reasons. To my way of thinking, there are at least three features of this letter that invite further contemplation. First, Abraham Lincoln lost his own mother as a nine-year-old child when she died suddenly in 1818. Thus, he knew from his own personal experience the piercing, heart-rending pain of losing a parent during childhood. Perhaps this knowledge compelled him to respond to Fanny McCullough's loss in such a deeply personal and paternal manner. Second, Abraham Lincoln's eleven-year-old son, Willie, died of typhoid fever earlier in that same year, on February 20, 1862. Surely Lincoln was struggling with fresh grief from the loss of his child when he penned his letter of condolence to this grief-stricken daughter. Finally, Lincoln reassures her that relief from the pain of loss will come with time. Knowing that relief comes in time will help her feel less miserable now. Although not explicitly stated, one can also detect an undercurrent of faith, which was defined in Chapter 5 as the knowledge of things unseen ("you are sure to be happy again") and the hope of things to come ("The memory of your dear Father, instead of an agony, will yet be a sad sweet feeling in your heart, of a purer and holier sort than you have known before").

In summary, whether attachments are strained or severed completely, as is the case with disaster or the death of a loved one, respectively, it stands to reason that grief will follow. Realize, too, that grief may be expressed differently among those directly impacted by the loss. Individual differences among survivors are likely to influence the choice of methods to cope with loss and how adjustment unfolds when lives have been disrupted by disaster or death. As discussed later in this chapter, obstacles to grief resolution may block the pathway of healing and long-term recovery. Professional guidance may be desirable or necessary to assist survivors with *grief work*, with sorting out the issues related to a significant loss when circumstances and situations are complicated.

Regardless of the constellation of issues, grief must be addressed and allowed to run its course. Distraught people may attempt to minimize or circumvent grief, but there are no short cuts. The experience of grief after a significant loss is obligatory: this pain cannot be bypassed. Even if people are temporarily successful in their efforts to suppress grief, it will eventually resurface, sometimes when least expected. Grief may also resurface in a form not recognizable to laypersons as grief, per se (e.g., anger, detachment, numbness). In my view, unresolved grief is an unnecessary burden that complicates current and future relationships in ways that may be unrecognizable to everyone except a trained professional with expertise in grief and bereavement. Simply put, grief is a "pay now or pay later with interest" phenomenon. In the next section, an illustration is presented to show the longevity of grief from the past, which may come forward in time to haunt the present circumstances.

Illustration on Prior Negative Life Events: When the Past Resurfaces in the Present

Throughout the course of conducting interviews, I noticed that a number of participants in our study spontaneously referenced other negative life events that had happened at some earlier point in their lives. These events included the tragic death of children, siblings, and parents. Work-related accidents were discussed, too, such as severed fingers, bodily injury from an explosion, and electrocution. For those with prior trauma exposure, talking about the storm seemed to bring painful experiences from the past into sharp focus—as if Hurricane Katrina was a giant magnet, pulling to the surface all manner of tragedies from long ago. Puzzled over this seeming phenomenon of memory, I wondered why some people spoke openly and freely about personal tragedies they had experienced when we had only asked them to tell us about the 2005 storm.

During one interview, Richie Byrd, a seasoned coastal resident, spoke of the force of storms. Hurricane Camille in 1969 was so strong, he said, that it pulled a sunken steel tug boat, engine and all, and a wooden ship from their watery graves in the Gulf of Mexico and threw them ashore. The image of heavy, waterlogged vessels pulled to the surface by the forces of nature from their resting places in the murky water deep below was powerful. I began to sense the parallels between the physical and emotional consequences of storms. Pulling up sunken ships or pulling up sunken memories of past trauma, it seemed to me that hurricanes are remarkably comprehensive in the swath of sorrow they leave behind. During his interview, Richie, who had served his country as a soldier in Korea, spoke of the early days after the storm and the first time he returned to his house in southeastern St. Bernard. In his own words, here is what he said:

> We were watching TV and they give us an aerial photo of Hopedale and I saw the roof of my house. The walls were still up from the ground up. And if I tell you how I built it then it'd take too long. But, from the aerial photo I could see the roof real plain and there wasn't a piece missing off the roof or nothing.

Many residents who had evacuated before the storm learned the fate of their homes and property from aerial photographs shown on national and local news broadcasts. By this time, the National Guard had been activated to secure the region, and access to storm-devastated areas was restricted. Coastal residents familiar with the natural waterways accessed their property by boat. Richie spoke of borrowing a boat, searching for gasoline cans, the long trek by water to his home in southeastern St. Bernard, and being stopped by the National Guard.

> They saw us coming in the boat and, whoever they are, comes and stops us, "Halt, where you going?" So, we was going to see my house. "You can't go there." Well, I says, "We are going there." And, he put the gun on me. . . . The kid with a rifle in the National Guard. Some kid with a rifle. . . . And I thought, son, have

you ever squeezed off a round? "No sir." It will stay with you for the rest of your life if you have to put a bullet in somebody's chest. . . . Don't point that rifle unless you're going to use it.

Listening to Richie recount this story, it seemed to me that his prior military service and combat training had resurfaced, along with the singleness of purpose and courage of a soldier intent on carrying out a mission—getting a job done—no matter what barriers or obstacles arose along the way. His steely determination was met with an equivalent singleness of purpose by the National Guard on that day.

So, we started getting along and he [the National Guardsman] said, "You have any weapons on you folks?" "Nope, we don't have no weapons." "I'm going to search you." "Get in there. Search it." "Where you going?" "I'm going to Hopedale and if I find my weapons I'll have them." I left all my guns in the house. "Well, you got to give them to us." "You don't need them." You ain't getting them. I know what they'll do. They'll confiscate them and give them away or whatever. So, he let us go and I told him, I says, "You didn't see anything."

Later, Richie added:

There's no way in hell you're going to find out how we're coming back out.

We knew the water a lot better than he did and we went around to Hopedale and my house was standing. The outer side of the house was in good shape. Two steel doors were twisted in figure eight. There was nothing inside my house. Nothing! The office was gone. The slates in the kitchen and dining room all were gone. All the sheetrock in the house was gone. The sheets were wrapped around a two by four and you couldn't get them off. . . . They [the insurance company] said the water did this. You couldn't make the water do that. You can't make water go in circles.

We talked in greater depth about his property and the hurricane damage. Here is what else Richie said concerning the impact of his losses due to the storm:

It hurt me deeply. It hurt me very, very deeply. All of my tools. . . . I had welding machines, and glasses and hand saws, air compressors. . . . All that's gone. I had boxes of welding rod that I had put in the attic. When I'd be getting ready to retire, I knew I'd need them, because they expensive. We lost all that. We lost everything. I tried to salvage some of the tools. No good. No good at all. . . . The insurance company will not pay for stuff like that. . . . They won't pay you. Lord,

I lost a lifetime collection of tools. All my albums that had been around the world with . . . Germany, Japan, Newfoundland, Korea . . . brought things back from Korea. We lost all that . . . I lost everything pertaining to the military that I had and I have a deep, deep love for the military. I respect it. I give praise to the boys that go.

At this point in our conversation, his daughter Sherri asked him if he cried over these losses, and he said no, that he did not cry. He explained that he did not think crying would make any difference. His wife added, "His focus is on what has got to be done more than what has . . . what's lost." For clarification, I asked Richie if his focus was more on actions than feelings. Sherri nodded in agreement, adding, "Oh, yes. Daddy always was like that. Daddy's tough. He don't show it too much, you know, we know he's got [a heart]. . . . We know he's tenderhearted, very tough in mind though. . . . Always was. But, you know, as far as like the storm's concerned, I mean I don't know if he actually went to bed and cried." Richie flatly responded, "No."

I didn't want to interrupt the family dialogue, but I silently concurred with Sherri's speculation. I personally could not imagine enduring such tremendous lifetime losses without leaving a trail of tears. As he continued, Richie illustrated his point that tears are ineffective for solving problems by drawing on an experience from his past. In his own words:

But you got to start thinking about what you have to do to rectify the situation as much as you can. Crying don't help. . . . It does not help, Sherri, it does not help. . . . The fact is, it makes it worse. It stops your mind from thinking. You lose your sense of direction and pay more attention to your crying. . . . I know it does. I tried that when I was a kid and that's all it ever did. It did nothing. My Daddy divorced when I was a young kid and I love my Dad. Crying didn't help. Did not help. I found him forty years later. . . . I found him just in time to bury him. He was in an old folk's place. I was glad I got to see him. I'm thankful I got to see him. . . . I knocked on his door, and I had the police and everybody looking for him. . . . And I knocked on his door and he opened it and I said, "Mr. Byrd?" And he said, "I am." "Do you have any idea who I am?" "You're one of them God damn men that's been bothering me all the time, huh?" I said, "No, sir." "Well, who in the hell are you?" I said, "I'm your son, Richard Byrd." [And the father said,] "Oh my God, I've been looking for you all my life."

As the story unfolded, Richie Byrd, now in his late seventies, referenced his early childhood. He was told that he had been adopted. He was given his stepfather's last name, not learning his true birth name until he enlisted in the service, which required a birth certificate. On the day he enlisted, he changed his name back to Byrd, his true birth name, and it has been that way ever since. Putting together the missing pieces of his family puzzle seemed so fundamental, clearly a meaningful event with developmental implications for his identity as an emerging adult enlisting in the service. Coming forward in time, one can also sense how his early life experiences also contributed to his present-day position on the futility of tears in a post-disaster situation.

In summary, the lingering presence of grief associated with prior negative life events is a reality which calls for sensitivity, consideration, and respect (see Chapter 6). The memory of losses from the past may creep into the present, often when least expected. Some individuals may already know this about past losses based on lived experience, while others have yet to learn this life lesson. The late Elisabeth Kübler-Ross, who is known widely for her contributions on death and dying, as well as on the processes of grief and grieving, understood this life lesson from a medical point of view. Her five stages of grief, referenced in Chapter 7, may be quite familiar to families of cancer patients or to medical personnel who work in hospice settings. To the point, Dr. Kübler-Ross would not be at all surprised by the observation that grief from long ago resurfaces from time to time. In her own words:

> The reality is that you will grieve forever. You will not "get over" the loss of a loved one; you will learn to live with it. You will heal and you will rebuild yourself around the loss you have suffered. You will be whole again but you will never be the same. Nor should you be the same nor would you want to.[21]

Acknowledging the loss and impact of disaster-related losses on everyday life is a step in the direction of grief resolution. To my way of thinking, adopting a lifespan perspective on current life circumstances might be helpful, too. By taking a long view, the potential influence of prior sorrow on one's current life can be accounted for. Ideally, grief over significant losses will play out over time with trusted family members and friends who provide support for this process. Practically, the resolution of grief over significant losses in the past may not unfold so neatly or predictably. Under such circumstances, the possibility of lingering and perhaps crippling grief from prior negative life events could be addressed safely in a therapeutic context. In short, counseling resources and therapeutic intervention from trained professionals within their area of specialization should not be overlooked as people move forward into a new normal after disaster.

RECOGNIZE OBSTACLES TO HEALING

Life is never the same after a disaster or other tragedy. Throughout this chapter and elsewhere,[22] Katrina survivors have made the point that their lives will not return to a pre-Katrina "normal." The issue, then, is not whether the world will ever return to "normal" or even come close to what it was before disaster. In fact, there may be little agreement among survivors concerning what life really was like before disaster. People are unique. Most will remember the world that existed prior to disaster from their own frame of reference.

One's position or "take" on a given situation may also evolve over time as new information becomes available. Moreover, the veracity of peo- ples' personal reflections—and doubts about how good the "good old days" really were—are not at issue either. Personal recollections are *not* infallible: simply put, our memories of past events are subject to biases, distortions, and reconstructions over time.[23] We also lose ground with memory as we age.[24] To the point, the issue to be resolved can be reduced to a simple question: Does our take on a situation—the private musings and the stories we tell ourselves and others—help us overcome an ordeal? Or do these thoughts and stories create obstacles to healing, pushing the peace of a contented heart just beyond our reach?

Psychologists, social workers, and other health and wellness professionals use the term "rumination" in reference to negative thought processes that hinder recovery and may threaten emotional health. In short, *negative musings* over past events delay grief resolution and are likely to negate the healing process after a tragedy has taken place. By negative musings, I refer to personal sentiments or declarations that may dominate survivors' thoughts. Such musings can be heard in conversation, or they may re- main unvoiced, a private thought not shared with others. Regardless, such musings or repetitive thoughts can and often do hold people in a place of sorrow—sometimes indefinitely. Learning to recognize negative thoughts as a cerebral bad habit is important after disaster. Greater insight, where negative musings can be seen as an obstacle to healing, is an important first step in the direction of recovery. Recognizing the potential for per- sonal growth and experiencing joy in everyday life despite changing life circumstances are also critical for the success of long-term recovery after disaster or other tragedy.

In overview, four potential obstacles to healing after exposure to a natural disaster are presented next: (1) "This is not fair. Why me?" (2) "I wish things were like they used to be," (3) "I should be over this by now," and (4) "I can't let it go." Here, I suggest that these obstacles may block the normal processes of grief over significant loss. As agents of inaction, these obstacles are dangerous in that they can bring paralysis to survivors, slowing or completely stalling post-disaster recovery. Consequently, readers may find that these four obstacles provide a context within which the principles of healing presented in Chapters 5–7 can be applied.

"This Is Not Fair. Why Me?"

There are times when the circumstances of life have changed abruptly, deviated from the expected course, and adjustments become necessary. An overwhelming sense of "unfairness" may follow. The insistent feeling of "Not fair!" is an understandable, if not typical response to disaster or other tragedy. "Not fair" makes sense. Sometimes "not fair" is wholly accurate, too. "Not fair" may fit the circumstances when negative life events are unquestionably outside of one's personal control. In other words, there is nothing that could have been said or nothing that could have been done differently to avoid or reverse a life-changing event. Evidence in line with this obstacle may be heard in the rhetorical questions people ask themselves after an unforeseen and calamitous event: "This (circumstance) is not fair—what did I ever do to deserve this?"

It is curious to note that at the heart of this obstacle is a four-letter F word: *fair*. Perhaps people can relate to this sentiment of a situation being patently "unfair." In truth, most people could admit to having felt this way at least once or twice over the course of a lifetime. When survivors have no say or choice about negative life events that have happened, the cry of "unfair" may be factually accurate and justified from a legalistic point of view. Problems arise when people become stuck in this mindset, though. That is, a rigid adherence to a violated sense of fairness associated with events from the past can quickly become a dead end. For some people, it is easy to become trapped in dead-end thinking, and it is often quite hard to extricate oneself from the perils of self-absorption or self-righteousness.

The second part of this obstacle—"Why me?"—makes a certain amount of sense, too, if one begins his or her day assuming that the world is a fair place. From an academic point of view, this notion is known as the "just world hypothesis."[25] People who begin with the assumption that life is inherently fair may believe that good people are rewarded for their positive actions, prosocial deeds, or inherent goodness, while bad people are punished for their misdeeds, evil actions, or crimes. The problem with this way of thinking is that everyday life seldom unfolds this neatly. As Rabbi Harold Kushner has pointed out in his best-selling book, *When Bad Things*

Happen to Good People, life is unfair sometimes, and seeking the answer to why tragic events happen may not be helpful. In his own words,

> Is there an answer to the question of why bad things happen to good people? That depends on what we mean by "answer." If we mean "Is there an explanation which will make sense of it all?"—Why is there cancer in the world? Why did my father get cancer? Why did the plane crash? Why did my child die?—then there is probably no satisfying answer. We can offer learned explanations, but in the end, when we have covered all the squares on the game board and are feeling very proud of our cleverness, the pain and the anguish and the sense of unfairness will still be there.
>
> But the word, "answer" can mean "response" as well as "explanation" and in that sense, there may well be a satisfying answer to the tragedies in our lives. . . . In the final analysis, the question of why bad things happen to good people translates itself into some very different questions, no longer asking why something happened, but asking how we will respond, what we intend to do now that it has happened.[26]

Most would agree that hurricanes, floods, tornadoes, and other disasters that bring catastrophic destruction, destroying homes and disrupting lives are "not fair." The "why me?" part of this obstacle may indeed reflect a youthful or naïve assumption about the world as a fair place, as previously discussed. The "why" did this happen or "why me" musings may also bring another assumption to the surface: that is, the notion that everything happens for a reason. If that reason could be known, then the post-disaster outcomes that people have to live through perhaps could be easier to live with and eventually accept.

From a scientific point of view, a climatologist or other professional with expertise in severe weather events can likely provide a very unequivocal reason or explanation for why hurricanes happen, as Katrina did over the US Gulf of Mexico in August of 2005. Through modeling, experts can also predict the likely path of a storm and provide fair warning of the impending doom and what damage might be expected when winds of up to 150 miles per hour make landfall. Based on a scientific approach, the "whys" of hurricanes can be understood simply: the reason why has to do with water temperature and the forces of nature.

In contrast to an objective, scientific argument, some people may attribute hurricanes or other destructive events of nature to individuals or certain groups of people. That is, it may be tempting for some to interpret disaster as a cosmic punishment for wrong-doing or bad behavior. Yet, to my knowledge, there is no scientific basis, real or imagined, for associating the occasion of a disaster with an individual's behavior, personality, or social status. Taking it personally or making it personal for others does not help and may make post-disaster recovery even worse than it already is. Surely disaster survivors didn't bring an event of nature on themselves. Simply put, taking disaster losses personally would not appear to be accurate scientifically speaking, or helpful either, practically speaking.

At some point, people may realize and come to accept that life is not always fair nor circumstances just. Nevertheless, the notion of "fairness" remains relevant and merits further consideration in my view. Why? Simply because negative musings (rumination) fueled by a misguided adherence to the notion of fairness can block or completely derail the healing process after disaster.

To counter negative thinking where a tendency to take disasters personally prevails (i.e., "Why me?"), it may be helpful to look at catastrophic events of nature on a grander scale, even a worldwide stage. By definition, disasters are global events that happen with an increasing frequency that may be related to global climate change (see Chapter 1). Given the number and sheer magnitude of these events, there is a certain statistical probability that a person may not live the rest of his or her natural life without exposure to a natural disaster. In short, the experience of a disaster is becoming an increasingly likely occurrence across the globe today.

* * *

Thinking about the concept of fairness brings up a closely related question: Who is at fault for the unfortunate life circumstances that happen from time to time? A variation on the obstacle, "This is not fair, why me?" comes into view. Such a variation might be grounded in blame: "This is not my fault. This is your fault." A knee-jerk reaction to sudden setbacks or painful detours in life is to point the accusatory finger: someone else is surely to blame for great misfortune.

In the wake of Katrina, playing this "blame game" was all too common an occurrence. The nail upon which Katrina-related suffering was hung varied considerably at that time. Blame for this collective misery has been assigned to a variety of sources from local and state politicians, to national elected officials, to the US Army Corps of Engineers, and the federal government.

Playing the blame game may offer temporary reprieve or perhaps the illusion of closure on life-changing events that bring the perpetual torment of regret. Finitude or the presumed end of suffering for one who is playing the blame game might sound like this: "It is your fault that this happened!" or, "This is your fault! This wouldn't have happened if you had only . . ." (fill in the blank). Such statements, whether voiced openly or left unsaid on a slow burn, reflect pain. Assigning blame to others is understandable after a calamity. Statements of blame may be factually accurate in some cases, too. However, I suggest that spiteful accusations, where others are blamed for misfortune—whether culpability is real or imagined—are counterproductive. Simply put, playing the blame game imposes barriers that hinder grief resolution. As long as we are blaming others and harboring hostility (or hatred), we are delaying acceptance. Blaming others can also blind individuals to potential silver linings that may be associated with traumatic events, as discussed earlier in Chapter 7. Sadly, reluctance to accept life-changing circumstances postpones grief resolution, which is a necessary step in post-disaster recovery. At the risk of gross oversimplification, one may come to realize that healthy coping (which leads to positive outcomes) focuses on what people can do well in the present and future and not on what others have done poorly in the past.

To summarize, crying "unfair" and clinging to a feeling of being wronged, playing the blame game, and holding on to anger (or hatred) related to loss are dangerous distractions that interfere with the healing process. Distractions can be insidious, too, especially when an injustice has taken place and there is no logic or sensible explanation for terrible suffering imposed by the actions of another person(s) or faceless entity. When people are ready to release these distractions, let go of simmering anger, and move beyond the blame game, they may begin to sense greater meaning in suffering, which may facilitate acceptance and eventual recovery. Herein lies the rub: acceptance of a tragedy may set survivors on a higher spiritual plane. Paradoxically, acceptance may bring survivors closer to healing, becoming whole again, and being freed of relentless sorrow or perpetual regret that weakens the spirit. In the words of Viktor Frankl, the Viennese psychiatrist who suffered in four Nazi death camps during World War II,

> The way in which a man accepts his fate and all of the suffering it entails, the way in which he takes up his cross, gives him ample opportunity—even under the most difficult circumstances—to add a deeper meaning to his life.[27]

"I Wish Things Were Like They Used To Be"

At first glance, this second obstacle could be interpreted as an indicator of resistance to change among survivors. It is also possible that this obstacle may reflect an intolerance of uncertainty, a personality trait or general response tendency that can lead to difficulties with managing changes in the environment. This particular individual difference characteristic, where people may struggle with uncertainty, can complicate adjustment to new life circumstances. Taking a scientific approach, one may recognize that there are many possible reasons why survivors may feel this way after disaster. For instance, *wishing things were like they used to be* may have less to do with personality characteristics or individual differences (i.e., resistance to change, intolerance of uncertainty) and more to do with maturity. That is, the wisdom that comes in later life with age and experience for some people—maturity—may bring about the realization that certain seasons of life really were quite nice. Sometimes people do not understand what they had or appreciate what life was like until it is gone. In the words of Kim Nunez, a coastal resident who lost her home in Katrina, "Make sure you cherish what you have because you never, ever know when it can all disappear."

Regardless of the reason(s) why survivors may wish things were like they used to be, a feeling of longing for the "old normal" is understandable after disaster or other tragic event. When challenged by the sudden and comprehensive lifestyle changes that natural disasters set into motion, seeking the comfort of the familiar makes sense and may be the "go to" coping strategy of choice. Yet reliance on this strategy (and only this strategy) to manage a constellation of new post-disaster stressors can be frustrating and counterproductive. To illustrate, consider John Tesvich who lived within a few miles of where Katrina made landfall in south Louisiana. He and his family returned to recover their property and rebuild their home. In time, utility services were restored to the area. All he wanted was to have his original telephone number back. Under the circumstances, seeking the comfort of the familiar—having one's old phone number back and in working order—is understandable. It was a simple request which, in retrospect, seems perfectly reasonable.

Despite the simplicity of John's request, the telephone company denied it. As he was told, new grids mean new service. The old service was destroyed and no longer existed, so new numbers were issued, and there were no exceptions. A statement of fact, perhaps, but also a blistering reminder of the magnitude of how much was lost in Katrina—everything was gone, even the old telephone number.

From an objective standpoint, implementing new telephone service in the years after a disaster would be logistically challenging, so simplifying this process by issuing new telephone numbers is also understandable. Nevertheless, being on the receiving end of a dismissive statement from a stranger employed by the telephone company brings the persistence of pain into full focus. The appeal for the old telephone number that was denounced so swiftly was one more painful reminder of storm-related losses unexpectedly thrust into awareness. Surely the telephone company's operator meant no harm, yet the fact remains that an old phone number may have held personal meaning as well as a tie to a former existence now erased by the storm and horrendous flooding that followed.

In brief, despite one's best effort at rebuilding and renovation after disaster, it may not be possible to recreate the physical and social worlds exactly as they used to be prior to disaster. Stated differently, trying to re-create the "old normal" that existed before disaster in the "new normal" of present-day circumstances can be seen as a variation on the "square pegs don't fit into round holes" idiom.

Yet people can and do move forward into a new normal after disaster. To illustrate a sense of comfort in the familiar (sort of) yet now quite different home and community environments, consider this quote from Ralph Grayson, a twenty-one-year-old man. He was a high school student at the time of the 2005 hurricanes. His recollection of life after Katrina follows:

> Normal living. . . . I could tell you probably when it came back the most, but I'm not sure that I can really say that we ever got back to full, normal living because so much of what we had known before the storm had changed. We were able to get back into our old house, you know, two years after the storm had hit. It was, but even then it was renovated, so it was new. And, I was able to go back to the same school that I had gone to before the storm, but the people who were there were different. You know, some people had left. Some new people had come in. So it was always this process of getting refamiliarized with everything, because nothing was normal. So I mean, I guess the, the most normal was when we were finally able to get back into our house and go back to my old school. But even then I, I think there was never a point when things were fully normal because things had changed too much for that.

In earlier chapters, I pointed out that suffering may seem endless for natural disaster survivors owing to the collapse of physical and social worlds. Consequently, there may be no sense of familiarity or normalcy to be found in one's hometown after disaster. Yet there is ample evidence in the disaster science literature to support the contention that post-disaster resilience is real and that most people will "bounce back."[28] There is genuine healing to experience and a new normal to embrace, with comfort to be found in a transformed social and physical environment in the years after disaster.

In summary, wishing things were like they used to be is an understandable reaction to catastrophic loss. From an academic perspective, however, *wishful thinking* is considered a maladaptive coping strategy.[29] Reliance on wishful thinking as a primary method of coping—or just getting stuck in this mindset—is an obstacle to healing that may have untoward emotional consequences for survivors. To the point, this strategy seldom brings about the desired outcome and may also delay grief resolution. Wishful thinking makes it harder to accept current changes and adjust to the present circumstances which comprise "the new normal" after disaster.

"I Should Be Over This by Now"

Ironically, a third obstacle that hinders the healing process after disaster is holding onto a self-imposed timetable, with deadlines for the various steps to occur during the recovery process. While it may be tempting to lay out a timetable for recovery from a natural disaster, such an exercise may not be helpful. Why? Simply because the recovery process nearly always takes longer than most people expect or could imagine it would.

With respect to physical recovery, individual and community-wide construction projects run into roadblocks and setbacks that take time to resolve, pushing back stages so that entire projects often take longer than the general public realizes or expects. Disaster recovery may also exceed external expectations imposed by the Federal Emergency Management Agency (FEMA) or other nameless, faceless governmental entities involved in the disaster recovery process. In truth, no one may have a real answer to the question of how long will it take to recover from a natural disaster in the physical sense.

What may take even longer to recover than the community infrastructure and physical landscape of neighborhoods and homes pertains to that which is not so readily visible or easily measured. *Emotional recovery*, defined as the feeling of rightness with the world or belongingness within the community where one now resides, may take longer to achieve than disaster recovery in a physical sense. False expectations for the duration of post-disaster adversity are likely to prolong the pain for individuals, families, and community leaders, increasing rather than reducing everyone's frustrations.

* * *

On the other hand, thinking about timetables for recovery could be productive, even valuable for some individuals. I'll never forget the crisp and unequivocal words of Kim Nunez, the coastal resident who told me, "I'll give myself five years, and then we close the book on Katrina." For disaster survivors, contemplating timetables for recovery may prompt discussion with family and friends. Open communication may bring differing expectations into focus and increase the awareness of needs and issues related to the pace of the recovery process.

As discussed in Chapter 6, *respect* for the process of recovery after disaster warrants further discussion in the context of self-imposed expectations such as "I should be over this by now." I say this because the realization that recovery is a process that calls for respect may help survivors manage the emotions that arise after disaster, such as frustration, disappointment, regret, and sorrow. Whether this realization happens suddenly or moves into one's awareness gradually, *respect for the process of disaster recovery* may act as a measuring stick by which survivors can calibrate (or recalibrate) their expectations to more closely align with the realities of current circumstances and one's post-disaster life. Most would agree that recovery of any sort is a dynamic process, with ups and downs along with good days and bad days. Despite the comprehensive devastation, disaster recovery can be conceptualized as a process that has a beginning (usually defined by the date of the disaster), a middle part, and, eventually, an end. Adapting to new life circumstances after having lost everything in a catastrophic disaster is a lengthy process. Gauging post-disaster expectations accordingly is an important consideration that can bolster psychological health.

Those who have lived through hurricanes or a tragic event of any sort may have greater insight into the process of disaster recovery and the difficulties of adjustment than do people without such prior life experiences. In fact, it was Selma Campbell, a ninety-year old coastal resident, who told me that she worried for her son who was still displaced and living inland at that time because he "doesn't know about losing a home." She did, though. Katrina was her third home to be destroyed by a hurricane. Through a lifetime of personal experience, she knew about destructive hurricanes and starting over. The process of working through the loss, overcoming obstacles and setbacks, rebuilding, restoring, and resuming her life was new to her son but certainly not unfamiliar territory for her. In short, this nonagenarian understood a simple truth: life goes on after disaster. From the unnamed storm of 1947, to Hurricane Betsy in 1965, then to Katrina in 2005, she had nearly a century of severe weather experiences to draw on for comparison. Interestingly, Selma also remarked that she was grateful for the governmental assistance she had received after Katrina. Never before had anyone given her a trailer to live in while she, an octogenarian at the time, and her multigenerational family rebuilt their coastal parish home. Gratitude, despite one's circumstances, seemed to work for her (see Chapter 6).

"I Can't Let It Go"

I'll never forget the day Zoe Crawford looked me square in the eye during a research interview in November of 2010. She said, without hesitation, "I want the world to know how much I have suffered." An uncomfortable, penetrating silence followed as I tried to absorb what Zoe had said. I could only imagine how painful and difficult the Katrina tragedy must have been for her. I didn't ask what happened to her or her family. I didn't ask why she felt that way. To probe further just seemed disrespectful to me in that moment in time.

Looking back, maybe I should have asked why she wanted the world to know how much she had suffered. Did I miss an opportunity to learn about a different dimension of post-disaster grief that I had not yet considered? Probably; yet upholding ethical standards in research should always trump scientific curiosity. Exercising *disaster respect*, as discussed in Chapter 6, should also be kept in mind while talking with survivors who have endured catastrophic events. I made a mental note to remember that some Katrina survivors may want others to acknowledge or at least know about their experiences, however painful.

In retrospect, there may have been many reasons why Zoe Crawford wanted the world to know what she had endured and how much she had suffered. Perhaps she needed recognition or validation: "Yes, catastrophic losses are profoundly painful. Yes, you have been very brave in the face of great tragedy." Or maybe it was not validation that Zoe wanted, but sympathy. Perhaps all that moment called for was a kind and reassuring pat on the arm, a comforting, gratuitous gesture coupled with soft words of encouragement, sounding perhaps grandmotherly: "There, there, dear, you've been through a hard time, but things will get better."

Last, maybe the real reason why Zoe wanted "the world to know how much she suffered" was not for validation, support, or sympathy, but instead, it was her way of calling for *disaster respect* (see Chapter 6). Maybe her words, "I want the world to know how much I have suffered" can be translated to sound something like this: "I want the world to respect this catastrophic experience I have had."

For survivors, sensing others' respect for their personal experiences and struggles, especially those who were not directly impacted by the Katrina disaster, can be gratifying. Respect from others can be helpful also, providing a fresh perspective that may facilitate recovery. For instance, *respect* for the disaster experience may prompt survivors to look at their current circumstances differently. By evaluating post-disaster life from a different angle or in a different light, one's personal narrative or "stories" may evolve over time. In contrast, disrespect, in whatever form it takes, can prolong a painful experience, as discussed in Chapter 6. I could speculate endlessly, yet a simple truth remains: unwillingness or an inability to release negative life events is counterproductive, if not debilitating. Holding on to painful experiences can be hurtful and harmful. So can allowing a single, bad experience to define us as individuals.

In short, it may take much longer than expected for some survivors to reach closure after a disaster or other calamitous event. Variations in timetables for healing as well as different routes to recovery are all too common after a tragedy, sometimes causing friction among family and friends. If not friction, these differences certainly provide grist for frustration and harsh judgment among people who presumably care about each other. Resilience, pertaining to a natural tendency to bounce back from adversity, varies among individuals. After a tragedy, some people seem to recover relatively quickly, regaining their footing and moving forward in a new normal. In contrast to people who bounce back with seeming ease, others may take a more circuitous route, possibly cycling through red-flag coping strategies that are destructive, unhealthy, and do not promote long-term recovery. Simply put, healing is not linear, at least not for most people.

Recognizing individual differences among survivors and respecting variations in their timetables for healing is imperative. The topic of respect as a principle of healing was addressed in Chapter 6, where I made the point that the relationship between disaster exposure and long-term recovery is multifaceted and dynamic. How this relationship plays out over time may depend on a combination of temperamental tendencies and individual difference characteristics, such as the age of the individual and where he or she may have been in life when the tragic event took place (e.g., a child, a young adult just starting out, a middle-aged adult contemplating retirement, or a senior facing later life issues, such as health, finances, independence, and so forth).

Authentic healing that promotes well-being, a feeling of wholeness, and rightness with the world is an individual journey that will unfold incrementally: a series of small steps that people must take on their own. These steps may be both frightening and painful, although, in time, survivors may find themselves in a better place. Sometimes, there may be a developmental transition in self-awareness as an individual sheds the label of "victim" and adopts the more efficacious self-view of "survivor." The transformation, from victim to survivor, among other adjustments that may take place after disaster or other tragedy, will be addressed more fully in the final chapter.

SUMMARY

Throughout this chapter, I have made the point that the experience of a natural disaster is a lot like *death*. With death, there is irreversible loss. With disaster, there are irreversible losses, too. Taking the long view, coping and adjustment to life after disaster resembles the grief resolution process that takes place after the death of a loved one. There is at least one key difference, though. With disaster, survivors' physical and social worlds collapsed—homes and neighborhoods are gone, friends and family are scattered, and there is no larger community with familiar sights to see, places to go, and things to do. Thus, not one but many attachments have been strained or severed on multiple levels—to special people and places, as well as to personal possessions and other things individuals may hold dear.

Severed attachments associated with severe weather effects may play a role in promoting and perpetuating grief after disaster. From an adult developmental point of view, severed attachments to special people and places that were destroyed by disaster can thwart the healing process, delaying grief resolution and slowing the discovery of finding a "new normal" after disaster. Temporal aspects of recovery warrant special consideration in a disaster context, too. For disaster survivors, the sense of loss may be overwhelming, defying imagination. How long will it last? It's hard to say. For some people, the duration of suffering may be measured in weeks. For others, it may be months or even years, depending on the person and his or her life circumstances.

Academically speaking and perhaps contrary to personal beliefs which are deeply rooted in faith (see Chapter 5), it is conceivable that the sense of loss after disaster will be infinite. For some individuals, the feeling of loss may have a well-defined beginning but no real ending. Under these circumstances, a survivor will get on with life, moving forward and learning how to live with the loss—or not. To illustrate learning how to live with loss, I borrow once again from American history. Many will remember Rose Fitzgerald Kennedy as the matriarch of a political family and mother of nine children, including John F. Kennedy, the Thirty-fifty President of the United States. When I think of Rose Kennedy, I remember that she lived to be 104 years old, a remarkable accomplishment. Centenarians are fascinating in their own right, having lived well beyond statistical projections for life expectancy.[30] Centenarians may also bring to the table a worldly wisdom that comes with age and experience. As an example, Rose Kennedy's quote comes to mind: "It has been said, 'time heals all wounds.' I do not agree. The wounds remain. In time, the mind, protecting its sanity, covers them with some scar tissue and the pain lessens. But it is never gone."[31]

Disaster experiences are likely to stay with survivors. Stepping back to see a "bigger picture," the duration of post-disaster grief (i.e., how long it lasts) is likely to differ widely depending on the individual and his or her life circumstances at the time of the event. Survivors may remember difficult times when daily life felt so slow, where the passage of time seemed more like an hour-to-hour existence. Or maybe there were times when the pace of life slowed down to moment by moment, dragging to a near standstill at times. Most will never forget their losses or what they went through on the long road to recovery. Yet survivors may also nod in agreement with the sentiment that life goes on after disaster, as will be discussed more fully in the next chapter.

NOTES

1. Keri L. Kytola, Katie E. Cherry, Loren D. Marks, and Trevan G. Hatch, "When Neighborhoods Are Destroyed by Disaster: Relocate or Return and Rebuild?," in *Traumatic Stress and Long-Term Recovery: Coping with Disasters and Other Negative Life Events,* ed. Katie E. Cherry (New York: Springer International Publishing Switzerland, 2015), 211–229.
2. Katie E. Cherry, Loren D. Marks, Rachel Adamek, and Bethany A. Lyon, "Younger and Older Coastal Fishers Face Catastrophic Loss After Hurricane Katrina," in *Traumatic Stress and Long-Term Recovery: Coping with Disasters and Other Negative Life Events,* ed. Katie E. Cherry (New York: Springer International Publishing Switzerland, 2015), 327–348
3. Kytola, "When Neighborhoods Are Destroyed by Disaster," 219–227.
4. Yuval Neria, Sandro Galea, and Fran H. Norris, eds., *Mental Health and Disasters* (New York: Cambridge University Press, 2009).
5. M. Katherine Shear, Katie A. McLaughlin, Angela Ghesquiere, Michael J. Gruber, Nancy A. Sampson, and Ronald C. Kessler, "Complicated Grief Associated with Hurricane Katrina," *Depression and Anxiety* 28 (2011): 648–657.
6. M. Katherine Shear, "Complicated Grief," *New England Journal of Medicine* 372, no. 2 (2015): 406.
7. M. Katherine Shear and Susan Delaney, "On Bereavement and Grief: A Therapeutic Approach to Healing," in *Traumatic Stress and Long-Term Recovery: Coping with Disasters and Other Negative Life Events,* ed. Katie E. Cherry (New York: Springer International Publishing Switzerland, 2015), 403–418.
8. Katie E. Cherry, Laura Sampson, Sandro Galea, Loren D. Marks, Pamela F. Nezat, Kayla H. Baudoin, and Bethany A. Lyon, "Optimism and Hope After Multiple

Disasters: Relationships to Health-Related Quality of Life. *Journal of Loss and Trauma* 22, no. 1 (2017): 61–76.

9. Trevan G. Hatch, Katie E. Cherry, Keri L. Kytola, Yaxin Lu, and Loren D. Marks, "Loss, Chaos, Survival, and Despair: The Storm After the Storms," in *Traumatic Stress and Long-Term Recovery: Coping with Disasters and Other Negative Life Events*, ed. Katie E. Cherry (New York: Springer International Publishing Switzerland, 2015), 231–245.

10. Kytola, "When Neighborhoods Are Destroyed by Disaster."

11. Hatch, "Loss, Chaos, Survival, and Despair."

12. Robert A. Neimeyer, Laurie A. Burke, Michael M. Mackay, and Jessica G. van Dyke Stringer, "Grief Therapy and the Reconstruction of Meaning: From Principles to Practice," *Journal of Contemporary Psychotherapy* 40 (2010), 73–83.

13. John Bowlby, *Attachment and Loss, Vol. 1. Attachment* (New York: Basic Books, 1969).

14. George A. Bonnano, *The Other Side of Sadness: What the New Science of Bereavement Tells Us About Life After Loss* (New York: Basic Books, 2009).

15. Elisabeth Kübler-Ross and David Kessler, *On Grief and Grieving* (New York: Scribner, 2005).

16. Clive Staples Lewis, *A Grief Observed* (New York: HarperCollins, 1961).

17. Shear and Delaney, "On Bereavement and Grief," 406.

18. Krzysztof Kaniasty and Fran H. Norris, "Distinctions That Matter: Received Social Support, Perceived Social Support, and Social Embeddedness After Disasters," in *Mental Health and Disasters,* eds. Yuval Neria, Sandro Galea, and Fran H. Norris (New York: Cambridge University Press, 2009), 175–200.

19. Katie E. Cherry, Laura Sampson, Pamela F. Nezat, Ashley Cacamo, Loren D. Marks, and Sandro Galea, "Long-Term Psychological Outcomes in Older Adults After Disaster: Relationships to Religiosity and Social Support," *Aging & Mental Health* 19, no. 5 (2015): 430–444.

20. Lincoln to Fanny McCullough, Washington, December 23, 1862, in *Abraham Lincoln: His Speeches and Writings,* ed. Roy P. Basler (New York: Universal Library Grosset & Dunlap, 1962), 688–689.

21. Kübler-Ross and Kessler, *On Grief and Grieving*, 230.

22. Kytola, "When Neighborhoods Are Destroyed by Disaster," 216–219.

23. Daniel L. Schacter, *The Seven Sins of Memory: How the Mind Forgets and Remembers* (New York: Houghton Mifflin Company, 2001).

24. Katie E. Cherry and Anderson D. Smith, "Normal Memory Aging," in *Handbook of Clinical Geropsychology*, eds. Michel Hersen and Vincent B. Van Hasselt (New York: Plenum Press, 1998): 87–110.

25. Jennifer L. Silva, Loren D. Marks, and Katie E. Cherry, "The Psychology Behind Helping and Prosocial Behaviors: An Examination from Intention to Action," in *Lifespan Perspectives on Natural Disasters: Coping with Katrina, Rita and Other Storms,* ed. Katie E. Cherry (New York: Springer Science + Business Media, 2009), 219–240.

26. Harold S. Kushner, *When Bad Things Happen to Good People* (New York: Anchor Books, 1981), 161.

27. Viktor E. Frankl, *Man's Search for Meaning* (Boston: Beacon Press, 2006), 67.

28. George A. Bonnano, "Loss, Trauma, and Human Resilience: Have We Underestimated the Human Capacity to Thrive After Extremely Aversive Events?" *American Psychologist* 59 (2004): 20–28.

29. Susan Folkman and Judith Tedlie Moscowitz, "Coping: Pitfalls and Promise," *Annual Review of Psychology* 55 (2004): 745–774.
30. Leonard W. Poon and Jiska Cohen-Mansfield, *Understanding Well-Being in the Oldest-Old* (New York: Cambridge University Press, 2011).
31. Jean Kennedy Smith, *The Nine of Us: Growing up Kennedy* (New York: HarperCollins, 2016), 237.

CHAPTER 9

∿

Life Goes On

New Routines, Looking Back, and Looking Ahead

Good things do come out of tragedy, and there's always a light at the end of the tunnel. Always.

—Kim Nunez

"Life goes on" is a phrase that most people have probably heard before. Or maybe we have spoken these words when trying to console a sorrowful person in the depths of despair. With sad endings, like divorce or death of a loved one, words of encouragement often sound something like this: "Chin up, dear. Life goes on." In fact, one can imagine that well-meaning people say these words after disruptive and painful events almost as automatically as they may say "Gesundheit!" or "God bless you!" after someone sneezes.

Experience may teach survivors that life does go on after disaster, providing confirmation that lends validity to this common sense notion. While most would agree, fewer people stop to ponder the question that disaster survivors may have asked for many years. That is, if "life goes on," then just how does one get on with it when the "life" we have known many years, if not a whole lifetime, doesn't exist anymore? In the midst of heartache and grief associated with tragic events, it may not be possible to resume daily life, at least not at first. And when daily life does resume, it may be quite different from before. People refer to this life as "the new normal," as discussed in Chapter 8.

Despite losing the "old normal," survivors will develop a new script for daily living. Maybe their new script will provide a sense of direction, or perhaps it will bring feelings of wholeness and rightness with the world. As an example, consider the following quote from Shelly Postman, a coastal resident. Her remarks reflect new routines for coastal living, acceptance, and a positive outlook.

> As far as our normal living, that new normal for us, I think came for me mentally, emotionally when we got back here [St. Bernard]. It didn't feel right any place else that we were and when we came back here, it finally . . . it did. And we quickly established routines, things that we still follow now, that now we call it, everyone does, your "new normal." . . . It's not the old normal, but it is the new normal, and that's what we follow now. It's as normal as it's going to be, and I think we've reached a level of acceptance.

For current and former coastal residents alike, the emergence of a "new normal" included negative experiences and unpleasant social encounters. Many participants spoke of their displacement and how difficult it was to be a stranger in a new town (see Chapter 4). Unfortunately, dark times and negative social interactions are a part of the Katrina story that should not be overlooked or downplayed. The following quote is illustrative. Ashley Bowen, a former coastal resident, relocated permanently to Baton Rouge, Louisiana, in the fall of 2005. Her remarks reflect a pervasive feeling that other people don't understand the Katrina experience: they just don't get it. One can also sense frustration and pain. In Ashley's own words:

> Since coming to Baton Rouge, I cannot begin to tell you how many times I have been referred to as "a Katrina person." I am so much more than that. I am a person who loves her family dearly and that we are struggling to put our lives back together again, one day at a time. A lot of my neighbors are victims of Katrina. Someone once referred to my neighborhood as "Katrina Village." I wish the community would be more enlightened to the struggles of displaced victims and how they really feel, and the struggles and obstacles that they have had to overcome.

Ashley Bowen brings up a good point. To my way of thinking, Ashley's words cast a spotlight on the destructive power of negativity while underscoring the very real need for compassion, understanding, and respect for the disaster experience. For everyone, those who returned and those who relocated permanently, disaster respect is a critical piece of the recovery puzzle (see Chapter 6). An important challenge for university researchers who study the human impact of disasters is to understand the dynamic role that disaster respect may play in the recovery process.

Whether directly or indirectly affected by severe weather events, respect for the disaster experience can be gratifying for some people and possibly a life line for others. Consequently, we would do well to remember the principle of respect when talking with survivors socially or in a professional capacity (i.e., first responders, service providers, governmental officials, educators, lawyers). As discussed in Chapter 6, respect may go hand in hand with gratitude. Both principles support healing in a post-disaster environment. Coming full circle, Ashley Bowen, who resented the label of "Katrina person," closed with the following sentiment about what matters in life and her appreciation for her family:

> And that's one thing that I am thankful, that I can wake up every day and I get to talk to my son and my husband and play with Pearl [the dog; see Chapter 7] and can call [my son], and say, "You got a break in between classes? You want to meet for lunch?" And so those are important things . . . And living in a big fancy house, that's not important to me. Your family's more important. . . . And if you have your family, you have everything.

*   *   *

Whether relocating permanently to a different city or returning to reclaim flooded property and rebuild homes, neighborhoods, and communities, most disaster survivors will develop a sense of order, purpose, and wholeness to life as they inch forward in the recovery process.[1] It doesn't happen overnight, though. Seasoned storm survivors will tell you that post-disaster recovery is a lengthy process. Like Selma Campbell, the ninety-year-old who worried for her son who lost his own home for the first time in 2005, recovery takes time. Just how long this process may take is difficult, if not impossible to answer definitively.

In October of 2010, I was talking with coastal resident Tim Hartigan about the volunteer groups who were still helping with community-wide restoration projects. I remembered seeing teenagers in matching chartreuse shirts planting trees in St. Bernard. They had traveled from Wisconsin in the summer of 2010 to advance the recovery effort in St. Bernard Parish. Many people who I have talked to were profoundly grateful for the volunteers who came to provide disaster relief at first and community restoration later on, as discussed in Chapter 6. Tim also pointed out that the recovery effort takes much longer than the world may realize. In his own words:

. . . a lot of people don't realize that this thing [Katrina recovery] is not over. Someone early, very early, on said, "It'll take about ten years." They were in some major disaster I forgot what it was but he said, "Yes, it takes about ten years to start seeing the light."

At that time, the ten-year estimate seemed about right to me. Looking around the towns and neighborhoods of St. Bernard Parish, I could see for myself that a good deal of progress had been made in the five years since Katrina—schools and churches were open, stores and businesses were restored—even a hair salon and coffee shop were in full swing and open for business. In July of 2010, the local movie theater had just reopened. Civic and community leaders participated in a ground-breaking ceremony on the site where construction for a new hospital would soon commence. The list of improvements around the coastal community of St. Bernard goes on today, which can be interpreted as evidence of *community resilience*, underscoring a simple truth that life goes on after a disaster.

Despite the progress, blighted property and abandoned buildings remained while I was there, too, a haunting reminder of the community-wide destruction that happened in August of 2005. My favorite fast food restaurant, a busy hub and last stop for coffee or to refresh when traveling "down the road" to southeastern St. Bernard, was located next to an expansive, empty parking lot. While waiting in the car line for drive-through service, I frequently gazed off to the right at that empty parking lot, cordoned off and completely encircled by a six-foot chain link fence. A few hundred feet back or so stood a cavernous, cement structure without a storefront or signage of any sort. A public place of commerce where people used to come and go, perhaps a shopping center or maybe a department store, although I never was quite sure just what the concrete shell of a building had been before Katrina. I studied the tufts of green and brown grass reaching skyward through large cracks in the empty cement parking lot. These tall weeds added some texture and color to the forbidding and unkempt appearance of the fenced off, now blighted property, I thought. This ruined site, among many others, will one day be cleared, remnants of vacant buildings will be razed and their expansive parking lots removed in large, broken cement pieces, lifted by backhoe and carted off by industrial dump trucks. Sadly, abandoned buildings and other lifeless structures with boarded or broken windows will remain in flooded communities for some time, a somber reminder of a former community and lifestyle now gone forever owing to the forces of severe weather.

Regardless of the pace of disaster recovery, a simple truth remains: life goes on. Earlier I brought up a question: How do survivors get on with life when homes and communities are gone, families are scattered, and lifestyles are uprooted? Is this a rhetorical question? No, not really. When lives have been disrupted by disaster or torn apart by tragedy, the recovery of familiar routines, together with the establishment of new ones, may provide direction and a glimpse of hope that things will get better. To my way of thinking, new routines and traditions offer a formula for daily living that helps when moving forward in a post-disaster reality, as discussed next.

ROUTINES AND TRADITIONS: FOUNDATIONAL FOR LIFE AFTER DISASTER

Routines may be thought of along a continuum, ranging from the simple mundane tasks of daily living (i.e., household chores, like cooking and cleaning) to the pursuit of happiness through hobbies or leisure activities. By routines, I'm referring to activities that are carried out in the context of everyday living in an ordered, repetitive manner. Traditions, by comparison, may be more encompassing, extending beyond individuals within their nuclear families and including sociocultural events or religious practices. Daily routines and time-honored traditions help order our lives, providing stability and predictability.

When routines and traditions are severely disrupted, as is the case with disaster, daily life becomes uncertain and chaotic.[2] Consequently, the recovery of routines and traditions may be of greater importance to disaster survivors' sense of rightness with the world than most people realize. In time, routines that incorporate special people—family, old friends and maybe new ones, too—can be reclaimed after disaster. When old routines are recovered and new routines implemented, a sense of comfort and rightness of the world may follow. As an example, I am reminded of Kim Nunez, who, like many others, had lost her home and all of her material possessions in Katrina, including her guitar and other musical instruments. For Kim, playing the guitar was not only a solitary leisure activity but also a source of entertainment and enjoyment for her extended family. Playing music and singing together with her sisters and their children had been a regular event at family gatherings before the 2005 storm. The first Christmas after Katrina, her nieces and nephews pooled their money and everyone chipped in to purchase a new guitar for Kim. She spoke of the delight she saw in the faces of the children and their excitement over watching their aunt playing guitar again. Strumming familiar chords with her family singing along brought the joy of music back into the house. When the "guitar came online," as Kim put it, a sense of normalcy followed. Whether on an individual or family level, recovery of routines and traditions is associated with disaster resilience, promoting psychological health after tragedy strikes.

More on Routines and Traditions: The Special Case of Holidays

Routines and traditions are fundamental to family life as well as to the life of a community. So are holidays. From a strictly academic point of view (and regardless of the geographic area in which one may reside), holidays provide an ordered way to conceptualize the passage of time.

From January to December, holidays happen. Throughout the calendar year, some holidays are well known and observed widely (e.g., the Fourth of July/Independence Day), while other holidays may be less familiar, perhaps obscure, or of local significance only (e.g., the Fourteenth of April/ National Crawfish Day). Thinking about holidays across a calendar year, there are several diverse and culturally rich examples during the months of November and December. Depending on location, ethnic background, and denominational preferences, seasonal holidays that are celebrated in November include Veterans Day and Thanksgiving. December holidays include Christmas, Hanukkah, and Kwanzaa, among others.

Holiday traditions invite sociological contemplation, representing an interesting blend of society's sacred and secular tendencies. Advent wreaths, nativity scenes, and the festival of lights, among other sacred traditions, are perfectly interleaved with the commercial world of shopping malls, holiday sales, and Santa Claus's magical sleigh filled to capacity with beautifully wrapped gifts with brightly colored bows for children all over the world. At one level of analysis, routines and traditions propel the holidays, as do other events that are celebrated annually, such as birthdays and anniversaries. At a deeper level of analysis, however, routines and traditions may provide more than just a script for celebration. Routines and traditions lend order and predictability to day-to-day living throughout the calendar year. For some people, having a firm and clear sense of order in their lives is familiar and comforting. For others, order in everyday living is a necessity—something they just cannot do without—perhaps fostering an illusion of personal control over day-to-day circumstances.

Looking back to November of 2005, only a few months had passed since Hurricane Katrina devastated the US Gulf Coast region. Across the nation, people were gearing up for the holidays. For many people, holiday plans and preparations begin with Thanksgiving, an annual event celebrated among family and friends with a traditional dinner including turkey, cranberries, sweet potatoes, and pumpkin pie. Images of Santa Claus and his reindeer, among other festive decorations, appear in public places. Brightly colored lights are seen at night, wrapped around trees and hung from rooftops. Neighborhoods and businesses are adorned with signs of the yuletide season. Sounds of Christmas music can be heard everywhere, played in department stores, in the shopping malls and on the radio. Holiday greeting cards are mailed to friends and family, bringing updates of activities and newsworthy accomplishments throughout the year. Parties, dinners, and other events of the season fill personal and professional calendars.

By December, holiday traditions are in full swing. After long weeks of rehearsal, children's programs are held at schools. Choirs sing cantatas, liturgical dancers perform, and segments of Handel's *Messiah* can be heard in churches or other places of worship. In theaters and sometimes on television, ballerinas dance the *Nutcracker* with orchestral accompaniment, among other visual and performing artists' contributions to the season. On the last day of December, people stay up late to watch the ball drop at midnight in Times Square, where thousands of New Year's Eve revelers cluster in a chilly New York City to welcome January 1—the start of a new calendar year which begins with great celebration, promise, and hope.

For many people, the months of November and December are filled with anticipation, excitement, and yuletide cheer. Holiday festivities unfold according to well-established routines and traditions—from baking cookies, to decorating homes both inside and outside, hanging ornaments on a Christmas tree, donating to charities, sending gift cards and baked goods to special people, and exchanging presents with loved ones.

Holiday routines and traditions were severely disrupted for coastal residents and their families who were directly affected by the 2005 Atlantic Hurricanes Katrina and Rita. Most had evacuated to different cities and states, holing up in other people's homes, hotels, church gymnasiums, community centers, or trailers provided by the Federal Emergency Management Agency (FEMA). Neighbors, friends, and extended family were gone. Homes, schools, and places of worship were profoundly damaged or destroyed completely. For these individuals, there would be no going up to the attic to retrieve holiday decorations. For some, there was no attic left or a place to call home at all. One participant who had stayed for the storm, choosing to shelter in place rather than evacuate for Katrina, spoke of watching an artificial Christmas tree blow out of his neighbor's attic among other storm debris hurdled skyward by 120 mile per hour winds on August 29, 2005.

ILLUSTRATION: THANKSGIVING AT SEA AND CHRISTMAS CAROLING ANYWAY

Despite the upheaval and losses, some people whose lives were forever changed by Katrina found a way to preserve holiday routines in 2005. Perhaps the familiar holiday traditions offered some reprieve from the cascade of ongoing disaster stressors. To speculate, holiday routines may have provided a foothold for moving ahead in dark and uncertain times. The following examples are illustrative.

Croatian families have fished oysters in the bayous and natural waterways of south Louisiana for generations, as discussed in Chapter 2. In the fall of 2005, there were no habitable dwellings in lower Plaquemines Parish. With significant damage to her home in Buras, Louisiana, where Hurricane Katrina made landfall, Jane Tesvich, a Croatian mother, thought to herself, "What would I normally be doing at this time of year? I would be having Thanksgiving dinner with my family." Despite the devastation and war zone-like conditions in her community, that is exactly what they did—gathered the family and enjoyed a traditional Thanksgiving dinner with twenty-seven in attendance. A very different celebration that year owing to the great distances that displaced family members traveled to reunite and the location of their meal, which was served on the *Sea Pearl*, a sixty-five-foot oyster boat, instead of their home.

Other coastal residents had returned to their storm-ravaged communities, living in FEMA trailers parked on their property or clustered in common areas on public ground. For essential personnel and first responders in St. Bernard Parish, a centralized FEMA trailer camp was established. Several participants lived among coworkers and colleagues during those first months after the storm. On a dark December evening, Hazel Alfonso described an incredulous sound: she heard voices singing merrily outside of her FEMA trailer! To her amazement, there on her doorstep stood Dr. Bryan Bertucci, a medical professional who had worked tirelessly through Katrina under desperate circumstances at the local hospital. Dr. Bertucci was singing Christmas carols with his family, their faces illuminated by the bright strings of festive lights which hung from her FEMA trailer. For Dr. Bertucci, the yuletide tradition of Christmas caroling—bringing the joy of the season to neighbors' doorsteps with music—was not at all stymied by Katrina's devastation. Through this simple holiday tradition, these carolers brought the peace of the season and a glimmer of hope to their neighbors, which Hazel remembered so vividly six years after the desolation and despair that defined the Katrina experience for so many people in 2005. For individuals and families, hope for better times ahead can help carry us through, offering the possibility of a meaningful future despite calamity.

Looking Back: Storm Mementos and Commemorative Activities

Many participants had storm mementos in their home: recovered glass marbles kept in a jar on the counter; a round porcelain vase with bright yellow sunflowers painted on its side, tucked safely in a corner shelf by a kitchen window; and a fiberglass statue of a little black dog—a dachshund complete with a collar. The dog statue had been lodged in a tree but now stands near the front door like a sentry. A shard of thick, blue stained glass salvaged from the rubble of St. Mark, a bulldozed Catholic Church, was given to a retired teacher who had taught school there many years ago. Among my favorites is a shadow box with storm mementos placed inside, thoughtfully arranged with artistry and grace. Outlined with delicate lace and matching white rope was a color photograph of this family's home as it looked before Hurricane Katrina pulverized it on August 29, 2005. Beside the photograph was the original house key on a ring, a child's silver toothbrush, and a poem, which brought warmth and meaning to the montage. Written by Rosiland White, this beautiful poem is reprinted with permission in Chapter 5.

Storm mementos varied in size, too. From small objects that can be held in the hand to pieces of original timber from the Los Isleños museum incorporated into the newly rebuilt and revitalized structure in southeastern St. Bernard. The largest storm memento that I saw is the *Ellie Margaret*, a fifty-foot wooden shrimping boat. This boat, a double rigger with large, horizontal nets protruding from both sides, had sunk in Katrina. The *Ellie Margaret* was later pulled to the surface, restored, and returned to its dock on the bayou. Today, this once sunken shrimping boat can now be seen in action on the water in St. Bernard Parish,[3] recapturing a multigenerational legacy of commercial fishing in the natural waterways of south Louisiana (see Chapter 2).

Storm mementos can be meaningful for survivors. Whether small in size or quite large, these treasured objects may call to mind a former life that was taken away by an environmental event that happened on August 29, 2005. There are annual ceremonies to commemorate the particular day when the world changed for this coastal community.

A Day of Reflection Breakfast was implemented at Chalmette High School, the shelter of last resort in August of 2005 (see Chapter 3). In 2010, former First Lady Laura Bush and then US Senator Mary Landrieu were honored guests at the Day of Reflection, commemorating the fifth anniversary of Hurricane Katrina. A tasteful and somber video presentation displayed images of the 2005 storm's devastation. The room was filled with current and former residents, high school students and teachers, merchants, politicians, and the news crews from local television stations, among other media representatives. Mrs. Bush gave a warm and compassionate keynote address, noting the progress and how far the parish had come since the storm, when she and her husband, then US President George W. Bush had visited briefly during Katrina's immediate aftermath five years before.

The mood in the room varied on that Day of Reflection, as did the look on peoples' faces—somber and pained for some—cheerful and upbeat for others. Some approached this event with funereal reverence. For others, it was more like a happy reunion, a refreshing opportunity to visit with neighbors and friends, especially those who had relocated elsewhere but returned for this event. I thought about those who were not in attendance, too. Perhaps some of them pass the day without notice. Others do not need or want a reminder of August 29: they remember that day all too well. How could they possibly forget the day their lives changed so abruptly? Or maybe some people just need a break. Ceremonies and commemorative activities may be simply too much Katrina rehashing for their taste. As I have been told, some residents leave town for a few days in the last week of August, finding the storm anniversary—the day their life changed forever—simply too overwhelming or painful to tolerate standing in place.

Surely, commemorative events, activities, and days set aside for remembrance have their rightful place in the healing process. If anything, they can serve as a benchmark for measuring progress, showing survivors how far they have come and how different the world is today than it was before. The presence of honored guests and visitors at such events also sends a strong message that people still care about the survivors and what happened to them, as well as those who perished, regardless of how long ago the life-changing event occurred. In short, community-wide events can provide a rich and meaningful venue for social support, an important variable that predicts well-being in the years after a disaster.[4]

A note of caution is in order, however. Just as survivors have experienced a tragic event and felt its impact in a manner possibly different from coworkers, family, and friends, so will they mark the anniversary of this event in their own way, in a manner that is consistent with their frame of reference, belief system, and broader ideas about the nature of the world in which they live. In a nutshell, commemorative events, as a community-wide forum for looking back, may be helpful for some but not for others. Note, too, that there may be a thin line separating reminiscence from rumination, a potentially unhealthy behavior which negates the healing process, as discussed in Chapter 8. In keeping with the "one size doesn't fit all principle" of healing after a disaster (see Preface and Chapter 4), it is prudent to recognize that not everyone finds such commemorative activities helpful, worthwhile, or enjoyable.

Coming forward in time, a change in format was implemented for the Day of Reflection Breakfast in observance of the tenth Katrina anniversary. As I was told, a traditional, New Orleans jazz funeral theme in 2015 marked the end of an era centered exclusively on Katrina reflections. Today, the annual Day of Reflection Breakfast is still held on August 29 at Chalmette High School, but now with a different theme selected at the end of the preceding school year. The 2018 theme was "St. Bernard Strong" reflecting a new era of community resilience and growth.

Stepping away from storm mementos and commemorative ceremonies, a broader question emerges: How does one respectfully mark the past and all that was lost while staying in touch with the present and keeping an eye to the future? Most would agree that respect for what was is a necessity. However, respect for what is to come, a new future unfolding differently than expected, may be equally important to long-term recovery. One can visualize a metaphorical scale with two sides in balance. On one side are past events which may weigh heavily in the minds and hearts of survivors. Yet on the other side of the scale is the present, coupled with a future that has yet to happen. For individuals and families (event planners, too), the challenge becomes one of balance—how to respect the past while honoring the present. The following illustration speaks to this challenge.

Illustration: Remembering the Past and Honoring the Present

It was a Saturday afternoon in June of 2010. Mass would start at 4:00 P.M., so I knew I needed to be mindful of the hour while conducting Patsy Shapiro's interview so she wouldn't be late for church. We were sitting at a table in the dining area of her home. I glanced around the room. Behind where I was sitting—just over my right shoulder—stood a magnificent grandfather clock. It was exquisite. I studied its features. An old and stately piece, I wondered if it was a treasured family heirloom. The hands of the clock were perfectly positioned as its pendulum swung in slow and steady arcs, yet the time indicated did not quite match that on my wristwatch. Patsy noticed me studying her clock. She quickly explained that it ran slowly, always a bit behind the correct time. I told her I could sympathize, quipping that I was often a bit behind schedule, too, running late myself on most days.

Patsy went on to explain that the clock had been a gift to her from her brother and had stood through Katrina's onslaught. Fascinated and wondering how this stately clock could have possibly survived the brutal forces of wind and water, she pointed to a faint line on its side. On closer examination, I could see for myself the horizontal water line that stretched across its wooden exterior, marking for all time precisely how deep the water had been inside her home in August of 2005. Her grandfather clock was a treasured gift certainly, but also a noteworthy storm memento—a reminder of what had happened in 2005. On further reflection, it occurred to me that Patsy's special clock is unique for another reason. This grandfather clock lends a physical image to a more fundamental and powerful message that time does not stop—it slows maybe, but it moves perpetually on in spite of tragedy. We finished the interview well in advance of 4:00 P.M. Mass—another reminder that Saturday routines fall back into place as life goes on after the monstrous storm of 2005.

LOOKING AHEAD: CURRENT AND FUTURE CHALLENGES

In the fall of 2010, a public forum was held at the Sigur Civic Center in Chalmette, Louisiana. During the opening remarks, the speaker, then St. Bernard Parish President, Craig Taffaro said "five major events in five years." As I listened, I paused to mentally count the five major events: Hurricanes Katrina and Rita were number 1 and 2 in August and September of 2005, respectively. Hurricanes Gustav and Ike followed in 2008, as number 3 and 4. Gustav and Ike struck portions of south Louisiana and Texas, bringing additional losses for those still struggling with post-Katrina damage. In conversation with Doogie Robin, I learned that Gustav reflooded lower St. Bernard, bringing an estimated eight feet of water to Delacroix Island, Yscloskey, Hopedale, and Shell Beach. Doogie lost his FEMA trailer in Gustav's floodwaters in 2008. His only complaint to me was that FEMA would not tell him where they had taken his ruined trailer, nor would a replacement trailer be issued. Another gentleman spoke of Gustav reflooding southeastern St. Bernard. Katrina had taken his home on Delacroix Island. His new home, a double-wide trailer, was raised on stilts eighteen feet above ground. This home was high in the air and safely above the floodwaters below, although Gustav had also brought an unwanted guest to his front door. There, on the landing to his porch, sat an alligator lounging the sun.

Event number 5 was the Deepwater Horizon oil spill in the Gulf of Mexico, which happened off of Louisiana's coast on April 20, 2010.

Tragically, eleven men died in the fire that erupted on the platform when the rig exploded. As I was told, it wasn't an oil spill, it was an oil geyser, sending 4.9 million barrels of oil into the Gulf over a three-month period.

A devastating technological disaster, the oil spill has dealt a crippling blow to the commercial fishing industry in St. Bernard and Plaquemines Parishes, among many other coastal communities in south Louisiana and the other four Gulf states directly affected. Scores of marine biologists and other scientists are studying the impact of this event on the sealife, marshes, and ecosystems of the Gulf. Social scientists are studying the human side of this tragedy in an effort to understand the toll this event is taking on the people for whom water is a way of life.[5,6] At the time of this writing, the long-term impact of the oil spill remains unclear. What is clear is that this terrible event has introduced yet another layer of significant adversity to those who have already suffered so greatly in the wake of four major weather events within a five-year period.

And yet life goes on. The hurricane season of 2012 brought Isaac, a tropical storm upgraded to a Category 1 hurricane at landfall on August 29, 2012, a chilling reminder of the storm that pummeled the Gulf Coast on the seventh Katrina anniversary. For residents inside of the newly reconstructed levee protection system, Isaac was not so bad. The damages were minimal. For those in Braithwaite and other areas in St Bernard and Plaquemines Parishes outside of the levee protection system, Isaac's effects were far more devastating, with some homes taking on twelve feet of water. Displaced again, residents from those outlying areas affected by Hurricane Isaac faced an uncertain future as the decision to return and rebuild or re-locate elsewhere loomed menacingly overhead. An outpouring of goodwill from those who were not severely impacted by Isaac was also evident, with donation centers filled with supplies, goods, and clothes to help those who were suddenly homeless—again.

CONCLUDING THOUGHTS

For people who have not experienced disaster, as well as for those who have, Kim Nunez's words of wisdom are worth keeping in mind. When I asked her what she wanted others to know about her experiences with Katrina, here is what Kim told me (emphasis added):

> And, I know this is probably just so broad, but as far as what you want people to know, I would just say in general, not something that was just because of Katrina or just because of a hurricane, I think this can be if you live in Tornado

Alley or, whatever you do [or where ever you live], *make sure you cherish what you have because you never, ever know when it can all disappear.*

There is ample scientific evidence that catastrophic events of nature occur with increasing frequency today. Other types of negative life events that can pull the rug out from under our lives happen, too. Negative life events can be devastating, leaving individuals feeling lost, alone, and separate or quite different from others. Whether at the time or in the years after a negative life event, there is value in realizing that other people have been exposed to disasters and lived through them—and some people have lived through more than one.

I recall a conversation I had with Catherine Serpas as she reflected on her home and property after Katrina's floodwaters had receded. She looked at her yard and asked her husband, "How are we going to clean this up?" He said, quite simply, "We have to pick up one stick at a time," as discussed in Chapter 4. This brave couple and their "one stick at a time" approach to post-Katrina recovery calls to mind a Chinese proverb: "A journey of a thousand miles begins with a single step."[7] I should admit that I know very little about Eastern philosophy (and nothing more than a survey course I had in college many years ago). Nonetheless, I believe that the origin of this proverb can be traced to Lao Tzu, a Chinese philosopher who was born in 604 BC and is considered by many to be the author of *Tao Teh Ching.*[8] Whether picking up one stick at a time or taking one step in the direction of a thousand-mile journey, seasoned disaster survivors will tell you not to give up and that things do get better.

As a university researcher studying severe weather impacts over time, listening to coastal residents who lost homes in 2005 has provided a wealth of information and new insights concerning long-term recovery after a natural disaster. Throughout this volume, I have given voice to an assumption that suffering is finite, having a beginning, a middle, and an ending. A closely related assumption is that there is a way through it, a pathway to the other side of dark and painful events. In truth, there is likely more than one pathway. The challenge, then, is to find one's own way, which is easy to say and hard to do. To further complicate matters, people will have different ideas and opinions concerning the best way to get to the other side of suffering.

Authentic healing is an individual journey that unfolds incrementally, a series of steps that people take on their own. These steps may be frightening and painful, although in time, people may discover that they are in a better place. For some individuals, there may be a developmental transition in self-awareness as one sheds the label of victim and adopts the more efficacious self-view of a survivor. This transformation, from victim to survivor, is one among many adjustments that may take place after a natural disaster or other heart-rending tragedy.

Healing Principles: A Recap

Based on more than a decade of research on health and well-being after a natural disaster (see Appendix A), I believe that there are at least six variables that matter in a post-disaster context. To my way of thinking, these variables can be thought of as evidence-based principles that support the healing process after disaster. Presented in pairs across Chapters 5–7, they are: faith and humor, respect and gratitude, acceptance and silver linings. These principles of healing support daily living, helping survivors find their way to the other side of suffering, a thousand-mile journey taken one step at a time.

In thinking through the best words I can to choose to close this volume, I am reminded of the late Reverend Richard C. Halverson, a Presbyterian minister and Chaplain of the US Senate (1916–1995). Here is what Rev. Halverson had to say about the practice of sharing ideas with other people:

> You can offer your ideas to others as bullets or as seeds. You can shoot them, or sow them; hit people in the head with them, or plant them in their hearts. Ideas used as bullets will kill inspiration and neutralize motivation. Used as seeds, they take root, grow, and become reality in the life in which they are planted. The only risk in the seed approach: Once it grows and becomes part of those in whom it's planted, you probably will get no credit for originating the idea. But if you're willing to do without the credit . . . you'll reap a rich harvest.[9]

In this spirit, I offer the six healing principles in Chapters 5–7 as seeds and not bullets. In closing, I shall offer one a last seed, a final idea for consideration.

In truth, there are many seeds that could be proffered here, tantalizing tidbits or officious directives for those who suffer today—in other words, the "disaster soundbite" equivalent of written text. In contrast, I prefer to close with a simple thought—a seventh seed to sow for future reference. The takeaway message that I have in mind is this: *disasters happen, but there is hope.* Based on the voices of Katrina survivors, I know there is authentic reason for hope.

The 2012 hurricane season also brought Superstorm Sandy crashing into New England, causing unimaginable destruction across multiple states in the northeast. Making landfall on October 29, 2012, Sandy has been described as New Jersey's Katrina. It may be tempting to compare and contrast the two catastrophic storms—for instance, Katrina's sweltering heat and death toll that exceeded 1,800 versus Sandy's chilling temperatures with 285 deaths directly attributed. Nonetheless, such academic exercises may not be particularly useful, especially for those directly affected by these events.

For the survivors of catastrophic disaster, comparisons are likely to have emotional consequences. That is, comparing prior storms may set in motion a cascade of feelings that may be counterproductive, prolonging the pain, driving despair, and delaying recovery. In the wake of Superstorm Sandy, Lorena Hadley, a seasoned coastal resident in St. Bernard, shared this observation (emphasis added):

> [S]eeing what the people are going through up north. And I just wish I had the finances and the ability to go there. Even if it would just be to give out water or food or hug them and tell them it's going to be okay. You're going to make it. Don't give up. *There is hope.* And with God, nothing is impossible.
>
> And it breaks my heart that I'm unable to contribute to that because so many people contributed to us when we were in that state that I would love to be able to give back just a portion of what I received from complete strangers. People we never knew greeted us, took care of us, you know? The Red Cross, the Salvation Army. Donating money is one thing, but being there to hug somebody . . . Jesus always touched people . . . He physically touched them. He didn't talk to them before . . . He always physically touched them. And He's comforting them and knowing that somebody else has been where you are gives you hope, I believe.

I close with Lorena's last words concerning the 2012 Superstorm Sandy. She told us:

> And seeing them going through their houses trying to find things, what's left. . . . It seems hopeless . . . it seems like it will never happen . . . your life will never, ever be the same again. And it won't be . . . in some ways it stays changed forever because you don't experience something traumatic like that and you can't come out the same person. You're either going to come out bitter and angry or you're going to come out with more compassion and more feeling and more love [sniffles with emotion]. And I choose the latter. . . . It does get better. Patience and baby steps, it does get better.

NOTES

1. Keri L. Kytola, Katie E. Cherry, Loren D. Marks, and Trevan G. Hatch, "When Neighborhoods Are Destroyed by Disaster: Relocate or Return and Rebuild?," in *Traumatic Stress and Long-Term Recovery: Coping with Disasters and Other Negative Life Events*, ed. Katie E. Cherry (New York: Springer International Publishing Switzerland, 2015), 211–229.
2. Trevan G. Hatch, Katie E. Cherry, Keri L. Kytola, Yaxin Lu, and Loren D. Marks, "Loss, Chaos, Survival, and Despair: The Storm after the Storms," in *Traumatic Stress and Long-Term Recovery: Coping with Disasters and Other Negative Life Events*, ed. Katie E. Cherry (New York: Springer International Publishing Switzerland, 2015), 231–245.
3. "The Everyday Effect," accessed August 16, 2018, https://www.youtube.com/watch?v=xtAaW5z-lHQ
4. Katie E. Cherry, Laura Sampson, Pamela F. Nezat, Ashley Cacamo, Loren D. Marks, and Sandro Galea, "Long-Term Psychological Outcomes in Older Adults After Disaster: Relationships to Religiosity and Social Support," *Aging & Mental Health* 19, no. 5 (2015), 430–444.
5. Katie E. Cherry, Laura Sampson, Pamela F. Nezat, Sandro Galea, Loren D. Marks, and Bethany A. Lyon, "Prior Hurricane and Other Lifetime Trauma Predict Coping Style in Older Commercial Fishers After the BP Deepwater Horizon Oil Spill," *Journal of Applied Biobehavioral Research* (June 22:2, 2017), 1–18, https://doi.org/10.1111/jabr.12076
6. Bethany A. Lyon, Pamela F. Nezat, Katie E. Cherry, and Loren D. Marks, "When Multiple Disasters Strike: Louisiana Fishers in the Aftermath of Hurricanes and the British Petroleum Deepwater Horizon Oil Spill," in *Traumatic Stress and Long-Term Recovery: Coping with Disasters and Other Negative Life Events*, ed. Katie E. Cherry (New York: Springer International Publishing Switzerland, 2015), 57–70.
7. Andrei G. Zavaliy, "Dao De Jing: ca. 300-200 BCE," in *Milestone Documents of World Religions: Exploring Traditions of Faith Through Primary Sources, Vol. 1*, ed. David M. Fahey (Ipswich, MA: Salem Press, 2010), 240–262.
8. Witter Bynner, trans., *The Way of Life According to Lao Tzu* (New York: Putnam, 1944), 11–27.
9. Alice Gray, *Stories for the Heart: The Original Collection* (New York: Multnoma Books, 1996), 122.

ACKNOWLEDGMENTS

First and foremost, the present volume reflects many lives—beginning with the people who lost their homes, neighborhoods, and way of life in the wake of two terrible hurricanes, Katrina and Rita. The swath of Katrina's destruction and massive flooding following the levee breaches in 2005 will linger in the hearts and minds of US Gulf Coast residents for many years, if not in perpetuity. Back then and now, too, my core idea has been that disaster survivors have something of great value: an insiders' perspective on the disaster experience. They have important things to say to those who will listen. In a nutshell, they can teach the world about recovery: how one can get on with life and gain (or regain) a sense of purpose and direction when all that he or she has acquired in life has been taken away by the forces of nature and severe weather events.

In a spirit of humility and profound gratitude, I thank the scores of people who agreed to participate in a research project designed to reveal post-Katrina risk and resilience characteristics. I am indebted to many current and former coastal residents of south Louisiana who have taken the time and put in the effort to fill out surveys and answer questions, opening their hearts and lives to scientific inquiry. It is hard to convey in words the depth of respect and admiration that I have for those who have shared their personal experiences. I am deeply grateful for the generosity of spirit and time they have spent on my behalf to further the research process. It is my high hope that survivors of current and future disasters, severe weather events, and tragedies of any sort will find comfort in the stories of hope and healing contained within this volume.

I also wish to express my heartfelt thanks for the kindness many research participants have extended to me and the student research assistants involved with this project. Acknowledging human frailties, especially limitations of memory, I readily admit that I may have forgotten a few names here—please forgive me if that name is yours. Setting frailties aside, let me first recognize Sr. Mary Keefe and the late Fr. John Arnone, whose warm welcome at Our Lady of Lourdes Catholic Church in Violet, Louisiana, and the quaint St. Bernard Catholic Church down the road set in motion the next two and a half years of field work. I thank Mary Ann Bazile, Peggy Schifano, Kim Nunez, Catherine Serpas, Dave and Vicki Brubaker, Lori Hix, Lou and Lorena Hadley, Duke and Lucy Collins, Gayle Buckley, Roy and Pam Mathews, Rose Lent, Barbara Manuel, Janet Tamor, and Mary Beth Tamor. In addition, I am deeply grateful for many friendships that have formed over the past decade in connection with this project. I am truly grateful for the remarkable generosity and friendship offered by Ashley, Mike, and Brandon Bowen; Violet Ragusa; Sandra Lopez; Judy and Vivian Chiappetta; Claire Landry; Jeannette Abadie; and many more.

The 2010 Deepwater Horizon Oil Spill in the Gulf of Mexico, eighty-five miles off the coast of south Louisiana, introduced a technological disaster to the US Gulf states of Florida, Alabama, Louisiana, and Texas just five years after Katrina. At that time, we reached out to commercial fishers and their families, adding a new dimension to the research project to account for the impact of the oil spill on post-Katrina recovery. I express my sincere thanks to the fishing families in southeastern St. Bernard who taught me about water as a way of life: George Barisich and his wife, Debbie; F. J. Campo and his family (Mabel, Robert, Michael, Blake); Charlie Robin III and his family (Celie, Ricky, Sue, Charlie IV); and the late Edward ("Doogie") Robin, a true legend in the minds and hearts of many. I am also deeply grateful to Theresa Denley and family (her parents, Ramona and Jerry Alfonso; her husband, Jammie; and their daughters, Lauren and Emma). I also thank Rosiland and Robert White, and Pam Mones and her family (the late Anna Melerine and Barry Melerine).

Plaquemines Parish lies on the other side of the Mississippi River, across from St. Bernard as the crow flies. I am grateful to the Croatian fishing families of Plaquemines Parish who introduced me to their culture and furthered my understanding of oysters and the harvesting process. As John and Jane Tesvich patiently explained, the world of oysters likens to farming. Think agriculture: oyster beds, like large tracts of farmland, require certain environmental conditions for the proper growth of the delicate baby oysters ("spat"). It takes years to build (and rebuild) oyster beds after natural and technological disasters. I thank the Croatian fishers and their families who have contributed to the research: John and Jane Tesvich, Domenica and Luke Cibilich, Eva Vujnovich and her family (Peter, Mary Jane, Ashley, Rita and Jonathan Frelich, and Nada and Raymond Vath).

The Louisiana Healthy Aging Study (LHAS), an interdisciplinary research project, offered a unique opportunity for me to investigate Katrina's impact on older adults (including nonagenarians) beginning in October of

2005. I thank LHAS Program Project Director S. Michal Jazwinski for his guidance as I embarked on my first hurricane assessment, which brought a deeper appreciation of the human impacts of the Katrina disaster. I am also grateful to my colleagues, Sandro Galea and Laura Sampson, whose statistical expertise and years of thoughtful consultation and guidance enabled me to fully develop the quantitative results that have emerged from this project. A special note of thanks is also due to Loren D. Marks, a qualitative researcher and wonderful colleague who introduced me to the art of qualitative analysis of narrative text. A sampling of the quantitative and qualitative journal articles and book chapters that have emerged from this project appears in Appendix A.

Many helping hands have contributed to the execution of the research on which this book is based. More than two dozen student research assistants have been involved in different aspects of the project over the past decade, from assembling paper-and-pencil response forms to conducting research interviews, to data entry and compiling results. I thank Kelli Broome, Erin Jackson Walker, Pamela M. Forest, Ashley Cacamo Brien, and Susan Brigman for their many and varied contributions to this project. I also thank Kayla Holland Baudoin, Sarah Finney, Trevor Johnson, Savannah Ballard, Emily Allen, Bethany Pinkston, Kyle Ryker, Dina Anbinder, Rachel Adamek, S. Devon Walsh, Kristina Fitzgerald, Claire Bernacchio, Keri Kytola, Trevan Hatch, and many others for the time they spent transcribing interviews and carrying out qualitative analyses of the written narratives.

As the chapters of this book began to take shape, I benefitted greatly from the helpful feedback and critical comments that many friends and colleagues have offered to me. I recognize and greatly appreciate the time and effort involved in critically reading early chapter drafts. This book is a better piece thanks to the discerning eyes of Sr. Mary Keefe, Pamela M. Forest, Kim Nunez, Lori Hix, Loren D. Marks, Claire Landry, Joyce Komraus, Ruth Rogas, Katelyn McKneely, and my dear friend Peggy Buquoi who proofread each and every page in this book. I also want to thank Dana Bliss, senior editor at Oxford University Press, for patiently answering many questions and illuminating the steps I needed to take to bring this book from a sketchy idea to fruition. I remain deeply grateful for his expertise and guidance and for this opportunity to publish with Oxford University Press.

Last, I thank my family for their encouragement and support of my academic endeavors: my mother, Elaine Cherry, and brother, John Cherry. I could not be the person I am today or do the things I do without the love and support of my dear husband, James Harvey and our son, John Arthur ("Jack") Harvey. Looking back, I will always be indebted to my father, the late John C. Cherry, Jr., for instilling a love of science and introducing me to the scientific method as a way of looking at the world when I was a child in elementary school. My grandfather, the late Francis S. ("Pat") Strawser instilled in me a lifelong admiration and respect for older people, as well as a certain fascination with severe weather events. My grandmother, Selma F. Strawser, who, by example and occasionally direct instruction, taught me to never give up, no matter what.

APPENDIX A

Annotated Bibliography

OVERVIEW

This volume is based on knowledge gained within the context of a research program which began in the first weeks after Hurricane Katrina devastated the US Gulf Coast in 2005. As noted in the Preface, we tested an indirectly affected sample of adults living in Baton Rouge, Louisiana, during Katrina's immediate aftermath. These participants were enrolled in the Louisiana Healthy Aging Study (LHAS), an interinstitutional and multidisciplinary study of the determinants of longevity and healthy aging. We were in the third year of a multiyear program project grant funded by the National Institute on Aging in 2005 when Katrina struck, so there was some urgency at the time to determine how the storm had impacted LHAS nonagenarians and their younger counterparts. With pre-disaster data for these participants, who ranged in age from forty-five to older than ninety years, we were also in a unique position to generate new knowledge about disaster impacts on multiple cognitive and psychosocial health indicators in midlife and later life.[1,2]

This early work during Katrina's immediate aftermath is noteworthy for at least two reasons. First, the prospective design (with pre-hurricane data) is unusual in disaster research. As is typical with most disaster assessments, researchers rush to gather data in the immediate aftermath, yet nothing is known about the participants before the disaster struck. Consequently, it is not possible to unequivocally attribute outcomes to the disaster as these differences may have existed before the event. With a prospective design, salient information about participants is known beforehand, which permits clearer and more meaningful inferences about post-disaster outcomes. Second, the LHAS hurricane assessment provided a foundation for the 2010–2012 post-Katrina resilience study. The major findings from this study on post-disaster health and well-being among current and former coastal parish (county) residents are summarized next. Interested readers are directed elsewhere for further information on the LHAS Katrina disaster assessment.[3,4,5,6,7,8]

Readers should also know that the 2005–2006 LHAS hurricane assessment and the 2010–2012 post-Katrina resilience study both employed mixed-method designs in which participants were given survey measures (i.e., "quantitative") and open-ended questions to answer aloud (i.e., "qualitative"). In mixed-method designs, the survey measures are paper-and-pencil questionnaires with clear-cut response options that usually involve checking off boxes or filling in bubbles on prepared forms. The use of survey measures to quantify participants' responses is advantageous, given the ease of administration and scoring. Data analysis is relatively straight forward, too: participants' responses are entered into a statistical software package where widely practiced conventions for the analyses of quantitative data are carried out. To be precise, analyses of variance (ANOVAs), multiple linear regressions, and logistic regressions provide new evidence to inform scholarly hypotheses about post-disaster psychological outcomes. Furthermore, surveys and questionnaires usually contain scales with well-established psychometric qualities that ensure the reliability of measurement and speak to the validity of outcomes. As discussed later, select articles from the 2010–2012 post-Katrina resilience research are presented to illustrate this quantitative approach to knowledge generation.

Mixed-method designs also include open-ended questions that afford greater flexibility and richer depth of responses on topics that may be sensitive. With an open-ended format, participants have the freedom to elaborate their spoken responses in as little or as much detail as desired. Oral responses to open-ended questions are digitally recorded and transcribed verbatim, thus creating written protocols that can be content analyzed for meaning and recurrent themes using qualitative methods of analysis.

Participants in the LHAS hurricane assessment and the post-Katrina resilience study responded to a set of open-ended questions that were formulated to yield new evidence about coping resources and resilience after a natural disaster. Participants' narrative responses to these questions were digitally recorded, transcribed, and audited for accuracy, a process which took more than two years to complete. Across many semesters, these transcripts were content analyzed in weekly meetings by teams of Louisiana State University (LSU) undergraduate and graduate students.

Emergent themes with supportive quotes were identified using established procedures for qualitative analyses. As is often the case with statistical analyses of quantitative data, there is more than one way to carry out qualitative analyses to capture emergent themes from narrative data, too. For both the 2005–2006 and 2010–2012 projects, narrative data were content analyzed based on the tenets of grounded theory using open and axial coding, as documented in greater detail elsewhere.[9]

This annotated bibliography provides a glimpse into select journal articles (all peer reviewed) and book chapters where quantitative and qualitative analyses of primary data from the 2010–2012 post-Katrina resilience study are reported. In the next section, four journal articles utilizing quantitative data analytic methods are presented first. These articles, in order, showcase the slate of post-disaster outcomes assessed in this study. We included measures of (1) mental health (symptoms of depression, posttraumatic stress, anxiety), (2) resilience (pertaining to one's ability to "bounce back" after adversity), (3) health-related quality of life (including physical and mental health composite scores), and (4) an index of coping (commercial fishers only, to assess ongoing styles of coping with the 2010 Deepwater Horizon Oil Spill). Next, six book chapters and two peer-reviewed journal articles where qualitative analyses were carried out are presented. In all cases, the emergent themes arose from team-based coding and were published with excerpts of the original, primary data. For brevity, only the emergent themes are presented here. Interested readers are referred to the original sources for verbatim quotes and narrative text that support these themes.

To summarize, this set of twelve published articles and book chapters covers a wealth of empirical data that can be interpreted as support for the healing principles described in Chapters 5–7. For expository convenience, a structured abstract format with three rubrics is provided for each journal article and book chapter (i.e., background and purpose, method, results and implications). By adopting this convention, readers can compare study outcomes across the quantitative and qualitative data in the 2010–2012 post-Katrina resilience study.

Quantitative Research Illustration

(1) Katie E. Cherry, Laura Sampson, Pamela F. Nezat, Ashley Cacamo, Loren D. Marks, and Sandro Galea, "Long-Term Psychological Outcomes in Older Adults After Disaster: Relationships to Religiosity and Social Support," *Aging & Mental Health* 19, no. 5 (2015): 430–444.

Background and Purpose. This article is the lead paper for the 2010–2012 post-Katrina resilience research. Participants were former coastal residents of St. Bernard and Plaquemines Parishes (counties) in south Louisiana who permanently relocated inland after the 2005 storms and current coastal residents who returned and rebuilt homes in storm-devastated communities. A group of thirty persons living outside of the severely devastated areas was included as a control group for comparison purposes. Other methodological features (principle dependent measures) and first findings are briefly described here.

Our primary purpose was to examine religiosity and perceived social support as predictors of mental health among current and former coastal residents with catastrophic losses after the 2005 Hurricanes Katrina and Rita. Religiosity is a multidimensional variable including personal and social factors that may be associated with resilience and vulnerability after a disaster. In the earlier LHAS hurricane assessment, religious beliefs and practices and religious coping were both negatively correlated with health-related quality of life (i.e., the SF-36 physical health composite and physical function subscale scores[10]) at Wave 1 (<5 months after the 2005 storms) and Wave 2 (6–14 months post-event). These early findings imply greater reliance on religiosity as a coping mechanism among less physically capable individuals, although this was an indirectly affected sample. In the severely devastated coastal communities, many churches and formal places of worship were destroyed and never rebuilt after the 2005 hurricanes. Consequently, we hypothesized that personal factors (religious beliefs and practices) may be more important to psychological outcomes (depression, anxiety, posttraumatic stress symptoms) than attendance at a formal place of worship or involvement with others in a faith community in the years after the 2005 hurricanes.

A second purpose was to assess the impact of the 2010 Deepwater Horizon Oil Spill on Katrina recovery. A devastating technological disaster, an estimated 4.9 million barrels of oil were released into the Gulf of Mexico off the coast of south Louisiana over a three-month period, threatening the seafood industry and culture of Louisiana's coastal parishes. Data collection was in progress when the oil spill began, so we added a comparison group of commercial fishers. They were also lifelong coastal residents with catastrophic losses in 2005 (e.g., homes, boats, docks, equipment). We hypothesized that commercial fishers with additional economic stressors related to the 2010 oil spill disaster would show greater symptom prevalence than current and former coastal residents without strong economic ties to the spill.

Method. In all, 219 individuals participated in this study. They completed measures of storm exposure and stressors, religiosity, perceived social support, and multiple mental health indicators (i.e., symptoms of depression, anxiety, posttraumatic stress). The twelve-item religiosity questionnaire (RQ) was developed in March of 2006 for the LHAS hurricane assessment and administered here to measure faith community involvement, nonorganizational religiosity, and religious beliefs and coping.[11]

Results and Implications. Low income and being a commercial fisher were significant predictors of depression symptoms in bivariate and multivariate regression models. Importantly, nonorganizational religiosity was a significant predictor of symptoms of posttraumatic stress disorder (PTSD) in bivariate and multivariate logistic regressions. Follow-up analyses revealed that more frequent participation in nonorganizational religious behaviors was associated with a heightened risk of PTSD. Perceived social support had a protective effect for all mental health outcomes, which also held for symptoms of depression and generalized anxiety disorder in multivariate regression models. These data show that people with natural and technological disaster exposure are at risk for adverse psychological outcomes in the years after these events. Individuals with low income, low social support, and high levels of nonorganizational religiosity are also at greater risk.

(2) Katie E. Cherry, Laura Sampson, Sandro Galea, Loren D. Marks, Pamela F. Nezat, Kayla H. Baudoin, and Bethany A. Lyon, "Optimism and Hope After Multiple Disasters: Relationships to Health-Related Quality of Life," *Journal of Loss and Trauma* 22, no. 1 (2017): 61–76.

Background and Purpose. Natural and technological disasters are devastating events with long-term consequences that are poorly understood. This study utilized the 2010–2012 post-Katrina resilience study dataset to examine personal factors hypothesized to be important to health-related quality of life in the years after multiple disaster exposures.

Our primary purpose was to examine the role that dispositional optimism may play in health-related quality of life after multiple back-to-back disasters. Optimism has been defined as one's expectation for positive outcomes despite obstacles. We hypothesized that optimism would be associated with post-disaster health based on prior work showing that optimism was related to posttraumatic growth, flexible and adaptive coping, and perceived ability to manage potentially traumatic events.[12]

A second purpose was to examine associations among state hope and health-related quality of life after multiple disaster exposures. We relied on Snyder et al.'s conceptualization of hope as comprised of agency (i.e., one's capacity to initiate and carry out personal goals) and pathways (i.e., one's ability to construct routes to obtain goals).[13] Prior research with Hurricane Katrina survivors has shown that state hope was negatively associated with posttraumatic stress symptoms.[14] We hypothesized that optimism and hope, although different constructs, are both important to physical and mental health outcomes in the years after multiple disasters.

Method. In all, 219 individuals participated in this study. The control group of thirty (indirectly affected persons) did not differ from the sixty-two former coastal residents who relocated permanently to the Baton Rouge, Louisiana, area on nearly all measures, so we combined these groups for the analyses reported here. All had completed measures of optimism, hope, and the Medical Outcomes Study Short Form-36 Health Survey, which provides summary scores for mental and physical health based on eight health indicators.[15]

Results and Implications. We statistically controlled for the known influences of age, gender, education, income, and prior lifetime trauma in the logistic regression analyses to permit more precise inferences on optimism and hope as predictors of health-related quality of life. These results indicated that optimism and hope were independently and positively associated with better mental health (i.e., the SF-36 MCS composite scores). To be precise, the odds ratio (OD) for optimism was 1.21 with a 95% confidence interval (CI: 1.10, 1.32). The odds ratio for hope was 1.11 with a 95% confidence interval (CI: 1.05, 1.17). Neither optimism nor hope was significantly associated with physical health when considered alone. However, optimism interacted with the prior lifetime trauma variable, where optimism only significantly predicted physical health for those with higher previous trauma scores. We interpreted this finding to suggest that prior trauma or potentially traumatic events (PTEs) may strengthen optimistic expectancies for recovery and positive appraisals of physical health.

These findings provide new evidence of optimism and hope as protective factors for mental health after multiple disasters. The present results imply that optimism may only matter for reported physical health among disaster survivors with prior trauma, while both optimism and hope matter for mental health.

(3) Katie E. Cherry, Laura Sampson, Sandro Galea, Loren D. Marks, Katie E. Stanko, Pamela F. Nezat, and Kayla H. Baudoin, "Spiritual Support and Humor Are Associated with Resilience After Multiple Disasters," *Journal of Nursing Scholarship* (2018): 1–22.

Background and Purpose. Natural and technological disasters are stressful events for individuals and communities. *Resilience*, defined as the ability to "bounce back" or respond positively to adversity, implies successful adaptation when challenged by stressful life events.[16] The primary purpose in this study was to examine spiritual support as a protective factor for post-disaster resilience. Ai and her colleagues[17] defined spiritual support as "a form of perceived support that derives from a deep connection with a higher power or a spiritual relationship in a faith, which encompasses intimacy, emotional, cognitive, and resource aspects of this relation." We hypothesized that spiritual support in the years after Katrina and the Deepwater Horizon Oil Spill would act as a coping resource to promote post-disaster resilience.

A second purpose was to examine humor as a variable that may be important for post-disaster resilience. Humor is a complex social behavior that can serve many different purposes. In this study, humor was conceptualized as a secular coping resource. We hypothesized that humor would be associated with resilience after multiple disasters.

Method. In all, 219 participants from original dataset comprised three groups (noncoastal residents, current coastal residents, and current coastal fishers). Psychosocial predictors of central interest were spiritual support and humor. Both were hypothesized to be associated with resilience. Covariates included group, gender, education, income, social engagement, charitable work done for others, and prior lifetime trauma.

Results and Implications. Logistic regression analyses confirmed that spiritual support (OR = 1.11, $p \leq 0.01$) and use of coping through humor (OR = 1.17, $p \leq 0.01$) were independently and positively associated with resilience. This finding supports the hypotheses that both spiritual and secular coping resources would be associated with post-disaster resilience. We also found that disruption in charitable work done for others in a typical year before the hurricanes (OR = 0.49, $p \leq 0.05$) and income of less than \$2,000 per month were negatively associated with resilience (OR = 0.47, $p \leq 0.05$).

Experiencing one or more disasters can create chronic psychosocial stress, with long-term threats to health and well-being. Recognizing which coping resources bolster resilience rather than harm it is important for improving quality of life in disaster victims. These data show that spirituality, humor, disruptions in charitable work, and low income were all independently associated with resilience in the years after consecutive disasters.

(4) Katie E. Cherry, Laura Sampson, Pamela F. Nezat, Sandro Galea, Loren D. Marks, and Bethany A. Lyon, "Prior Hurricane and Other Lifetime Trauma Predict Coping Style in Older Commercial Fishers After the BP Deepwater Horizon Oil Spill," *Journal of Applied Biobehavioral Research* (June 22:2, 2017): 1–18.

Background and Purpose. Fishing communities along the US Gulf Coast have had devastating losses in connection with the 2005 Hurricanes Katrina and Rita and the 2010 Deepwater Horizon Oil Spill. Natural and technological disaster exposures and subsequent losses are known to be associated with psychological distress. This distress may be lessened through adaptive coping behaviors, although little is known about how prior lifetime trauma may affect coping responses.

In this study, we examined the impact of multiple disasters on mental health outcomes in commercial fishers who lost homes and property in the 2005 Hurricanes Katrina and Rita and whose lives were now interrupted by the 2010 oil spill. The primary purpose was to determine whether storm-related stressors from the 2005 hurricanes and other lifetime traumatic events were associated with coping responses and whether coping styles in turn were associated with psychological outcomes. We hypothesized that avoidant emotional coping would be more strongly associated with symptoms of depression and posttraumatic stress than would problem-focused and active emotional coping styles.

Method. Participants were sixty-four south Louisiana commercial fishers and their family members from the 2010–2012 dataset (age range of 21–90 years). All completed the Brief COPE[18] to assess strategies for coping with oil spill stress twelve to twenty-six months after the spill. Additional measures were storm-related stressors associated with the 2005 hurricanes, other lifetime traumatic events, and mental health.

Results and Implications: Regression analyses indicated that Katrina-related stressors and lifetime traumatic events predicted different styles of coping. However, only avoidant coping was associated with increased risk of depression and posttraumatic stress. These data confirm that multiple disaster exposures are devastating for coastal residents, particularly those in the commercial fishing industry with recent trauma related to the 2010 BP oil spill.

Qualitative Research Illustration

(1) Keri L. Kytola, Katie E. Cherry, Loren D. Marks, and Trevan G. Hatch, "When Neighborhoods Are Destroyed by Disaster: Relocate or Return and Rebuild?," in *Traumatic Stress and Long-Term Recovery: Coping with Disasters and Other Negative Life Events*, ed. Katie E. Cherry (New York: Springer International Publishing Switzerland, 2015), 211–229.

Background and Purpose. After Katrina, some coastal residents relocated permanently inland. Others returned to rebuild their homes in directly affected communities. An ecological systems approach, among other contextual theories, provides a useful guide for thinking about survivors nested within the broader social contexts of family, community, and cultural traditions and heritage. In this chapter, Bronfenbrenner's ecological systems theory[19] was used as a conceptual framework to examine the long-term consequences of catastrophic destruction across multiple ecologies. Our primary purpose was to provide insight into post-disaster resilience by comparing and contrasting narrative data from former (relocated permanently) and current coastal residents who had returned to rebuild homes after Katrina. A second purpose was to document the methodology (i.e., interview procedures, team-based coding, qualitative analyses) noted briefly here and reported in greater detail elsewhere.[20]

Method. In all, this sample consisted of 125 participants who ranged in age from eighteen to eighty-nine years. All had experienced catastrophic damage and displacement from their coastal parish (county) homes after Katrina. They were tested individually in their homes or in a community location across two (or more) sessions. In the first session, informed consent was obtained and the quantitative measures (paper-and-pencil surveys) were administered. All were given seven open-ended questions on a prepared page to consider and discuss in the next research session.

During the second session, the same questions were presented individually on prepared cards. Participants' oral responses were digitally recorded and transcribed verbatim. Transcriptions were audited for accuracy. Print copies were produced for team-based coding by LSU student research assistants. Here and in the chapter that follows, we focus on participants' responses to these four questions:

"People who lived through Hurricanes Katrina and Rita experienced a variety of challenges, obstacles, and setbacks. Please tell us how you coped with the challenges you faced after the storms."
"What kinds of things did you do to establish a new daily routine?"
"When did 'normal living' come back for you?"
"What would you like others to know about your experiences with Hurricanes Katrina and Rita?"

Results and Implications. Qualitative analyses yielded five themes pertaining to the challenges faced after Hurricanes Katrina and Rita in 2005; two are presented here and three appear in the next chapter.

Theme 1, *There's no going back: the "old normal" is gone forever*, captured the life-changing effects of Hurricanes Katrina and Rita expressed by many participants in the study. Both those who relocated permanently and those who returned to rebuild mourned the passing of the *old normal*. Theme 2, *"You don't understand unless you were there"* conveyed a sense of great loss, which was often accompanied by the feeling that *no one understands*. Whether one's challenge was to find a new town in which to live or to rebuild a hurricane-damaged hometown, the importance of having a sense of belonging in a community and a perceived social support network was often mentioned by this sample of Katrina survivors.

The two themes presented in this chapter have theoretical and practical implications. Theoretically, these results are consistent with an ecological systems perspective, highlighting the need for further research on the impacts of disruption across multiple nested ecologies. Practically, feelings of loss and frustration persist over time for disaster survivors. These findings underscore the need for support services in disaster-affected areas and in the receiving communities that have become a new home for former coastal residents.

(2) Trevan G. Hatch, Katie E. Cherry, Keri L. Kytola, Yaxin Lu, and Loren D. Marks, "Loss, Chaos, Survival, and Despair: The Storm After the Storms," in *Traumatic Stress and Long-Term Recovery: Coping with Disasters and Other Negative Life Events*, ed. Katie E. Cherry (New York: Springer International Publishing Switzerland, 2015), 231–245.

Background and Purpose. The US Gulf Coast experienced catastrophic damage when Hurricanes Katrina and Rita struck in August and September of 2005, respectively. Our primary purpose in this chapter was to report the remaining three themes mentioned in Kytola et al. (2015). These themes covered the challenges participants faced after having lost property, homes, and communities in the 2005 hurricanes.

Method. These primary data were obtained from the same 125 directly affected coastal residents in a mixed-method study on post-disaster Katrina resilience in 2010–2012.

Results and Implications. Narrative responses to the same four questions noted in the preceding chapter yielded three emergent themes which reflect participants' anguish, fatigue, and discouragement after Katrina. The themes include (1) *"I don't want to lose another friend": a loss of more than material possessions*; (2) *"No coping, just surviving": chaos and the* *crushing burden of survival*; and (3) *"[Katrina] made me a weaker person:"* anguish and despair after the storms.

At least five years after Katrina and Rita, participants spoke of many losses, spanning from material possessions to their "entire community" (i.e., houses, jobs, neighbors, businesses, schools, churches, government buildings, and even the hospital). Many seemed overwhelmed with the task of trying to adjust to their new circumstances. They stressed that the infrastructure of the parish and the way of life they had known for forty years or more was destroyed. Sorrow associated with loss of neighbors and community seemed to linger much more than sorrow from the loss of houses, furniture, and automobiles.

The participants' voices provide authentic images of post-disaster losses, coupled with the lingering and pervasive sense of sorrow. Prolonged grief associated with post-disaster losses highlights a critical need for disaster mental health services and interventions to lessen post-disaster distress (see Chapter 8, this volume, for discussion).

(3) Loren D. Marks, Yaxin Lu, Katie E. Cherry, and Trevan G. Hatch, "Faith and Coping: Spiritual Beliefs and Religious Practices After Hurricanes Katrina and Rita," in *Traumatic Stress and Long-Term Recovery: Coping with Disasters and Other Negative Life Events,* ed. Katie E. Cherry (New York: Springer International Publishing Switzerland, 2015), 369–387.

Background and Purpose. In the lead (quantitative) article summarized here, Cherry and her colleagues reported that religiosity and perceived social support were associated with post-disaster psychological outcomes at least five years after Katrina. In this chapter and the next, we used a qualitative approach to address the questions of *why* and *how* religiosity mattered to some disaster survivors. Two open-ended questions were developed based on an earlier theoretical formulation[21] where "religion" was conceptualized along three separate dimensions: (a) *spiritual beliefs* (personal, internal beliefs, framings, meanings, and perspectives), (b) *religious practices* (outward, observable expressions of faith such as prayer, scripture study, rituals, traditions, or less overtly sacred practice or abstinence that is religiously grounded), and (c) *faith communities* (support, involvement, and relationships grounded in one's congregation or religious group).

In this chapter, our purpose was to shed new light on the first two dimensions, spiritual beliefs and religious practices, as coping resources in the wake of the Katrina tragedy. Team-based coding of narrative text from Katrina survivors allowed deeper insights about *what* sacred beliefs and practices were helpful and also *why* they mattered as Katrina survivors faced multiple stressors in the immediate aftermath and in the years following the 2005 storms. The role that faith communities played in the Katrina disaster is covered in the companion chapter presented next.

Method. In all, 125 persons (all directly affected) from the original sample responded to an open-ended question concerning whether religious beliefs and practices helped them cope with the challenges they faced after the storms. The question, verbatim, was as follows:

> In times of trouble, people often turn to their religion and spiritual beliefs to help them cope with life stresses. Have your religious beliefs and practices helped you cope with Hurricanes Katrina and Rita? If so, in what way?

Results and Implications. Qualitative analyses of participants' narrative responses yielded five emergent themes, three of these related to spiritual beliefs and two related to religious practices. These first three themes reflected sacred beliefs that reportedly helped many participants cope with the short- and long-term effects of the hurricanes. These themes were *"I couldn't have done it without my God's help": God as a personal and relational being"* (Theme 1); *"God is in control": conceptualizations and characteristics of God* (Theme 2); *"The Katrina experience renewed your faith": spiritually framing the storm* (Theme 3). The last two themes reflected religious *practices* and their connection with hurricanes, stress reactions, and coping responses. These themes were: *"Praying helped me cope": prayer in the immediate Katrina/Rita aftermath* (Theme 4) and *"I prayed a lot for guidance": God as a guide in post-storm decision making* (Theme 5). Taken together, these five themes yield new insights on spiritual beliefs and religious practices (especially prayer) in coping with the immediate and long-term aftermath of two catastrophic hurricanes.

(4) Loren D. Marks, Trevan G. Hatch, Yaxin Lu, and Katie E. Cherry, "Families and Faith-based Communities After a Disaster: Successes and Failures in the Wakes of Hurricanes Katrina and Rita," in *Traumatic Stress and Long-Term Recovery: Coping with Disasters and Other Negative Life Events,* ed. Katie E. Cherry (New York: Springer International Publishing Switzerland, 2015), 247–270.

Background and Purpose. The role of churches and faith-based communities in disaster relief is widely recognized and well-known in the

Katrina era.[22] The primary purpose of this chapter was to explore whether faith communities were perceived as helpful by directly affected survivors coping with the aftermath of these hurricanes or whether these organizations contributed to their frustrations and misery. A second purpose was to address the deeper issues of *why* and *how* faith communities helped (or harmed) coastal residents of south Louisiana whose lives were forever changed by the 2005 storms.

Method. Participants were the same 125 current and former residents of two coastal parishes (counties) in south Louisiana. Here we focus on their responses to an open-ended question designed to tap the role of faith-based communities in helping them cope with the personal challenges they faced after the storms. The question, verbatim, was as follows:

> In times of trouble, people may turn to a faith community to help them cope with life stresses. Has a church or faith community helped you cope with Hurricanes Katrina and Rita? If so, in what way?

Results and Implications. Four themes emerged in connection with a church or faith-based community after Katrina. The first theme, *"The hunger for faith community,"* reflected a pressing need for faith community that some participants reported after the storms. The second theme, *"My church family kept me going,"* captured how and why the faith community was an important coping resource that served as a meaningful source of support. The third theme, *"I felt like my church abandoned me,"* stood in stark contrast to the preceding two themes. Some participants were deeply disappointed with their faith community's response (or lack of response) after Katrina and conveyed a *negative* attitude toward their faith community. The fourth theme, *"Helping others: am I my brother's keeper?"* reflected the impact of receiving assistance from a faith community to which the beneficiaries had no prior ties. Participants described faith communities that offered much to help disaster survivors in need without regard for denomination or belief. This theme was consistent with the well-documented outpouring of goods and services in the Katrina relief efforts orchestrated by most of the major denominations at local and national levels.

These four themes have implications for disaster preparedness and the coordination of relief efforts after a catastrophic disaster. In particular, these themes imply that faith-based institutions may occupy both a helpful and harmful place in the psychological experience of trauma-exposed hurricane survivors. Briefly, this dualistic (helpful/harmful) nature could be viewed as a threat to people's core beliefs and assumptions about their own faith traditions in times of great need. Alternatively, the complex nature of faith-based community presence (or absence) presents a unique opportunity for multidisciplinary collaborations to be formed among religious leaders, disaster relief personnel, and mental health professionals to help individuals and families cope with catastrophic losses that accompany severe weather events.

(5) Katie E. Stanko, Laura Sampson, Katie E. Cherry, Sandro Galea, and Loren D. Marks, "When Reliance on Religion Falters: Religious Coping and Posttraumatic Stress Symptoms in Older Adults After Multiple Disasters," *Journal of Religion, Spirituality, and Aging* 30 (2018): 292–313.

Background and Purpose. Ample evidence indicates that religiosity is associated with better physical and mental health outcomes. Cherry and colleagues (2015) had expected to replicate this well documented outcome in the 2010–2012 post-Katrina resilience study, where several dimensions of religiosity were assessed quantitatively (i.e., faith community involvement, nonorganizational religiosity, religious beliefs and practices, religious coping). Contrary to expectation, they found that nonorganizational religiosity was significantly associated with an *increased* prevalence of posttraumatic stress (PTS) symptoms. Follow-up analyses that compared the upper third of the sample ("high scorers") to the lowest third ("low scorers") on the nonorganizational religiosity scale revealed that high scorers were more than *nine times* as likely to report PTS symptoms compared to their low-scoring counterparts. Cherry et al. (2015) interpreted this finding to indicate that persons who suffer most severely from PTSD may seek solitary forms of religious coping to strengthen their sense of well-being. They may also turn to nonorganizational religiosity in response to emotional distress when former places of worship were destroyed by Katrina.

The purpose of this study was to discover possible reasons for the nine-fold increase in PTS symptoms for those with high nonorganizational religiosity scores using a qualitative approach. Here we compared the extreme low and high scorers' narrative responses to two open-ended questions on (1) the involvement of faith communities and (2) religious beliefs and practices as coping resources after disaster.

Method. The original sample had 219 individuals. We removed the 30 non-coastal controls, then divided that sample (189) into thirds (tertiles) based on their nonorganizational religiosity scores: 66 had low scores (scores of 3–7), 70 had medium scores (8–10), and 53 reported high scores (scores of 11–15). Only the low (*n* = 66) and the high (*n*=53) scorers were compared here, so the final sample size was 119.

Results and Implications. Qualitative analyses were carried out on narrative responses to the two open-ended questions using the same method as described in Kytola et al. (2015). The four recurring, core themes were (1) *Use of prayer and belief in God as coping*, (2) *The importance of going to church*, (3) *Reliance on a faith community*, and (4) *Disappointment with the Catholic Church*. Note that this fourth theme likely reflected both frustration and disappointment that this predominantly Catholic sample experienced in the wake of Katrina, as noted earlier in Marks, Hatch, Lu, and Cherry's (2015) chapter.

Some common themes emerged for the high and low scorers, and key differences were apparent as well. To be precise, the low scorers more often described secular coping strategies and were less reliant on a church community after Katrina. Of special interest were the group differences in religious coping. Greater positive religious coping was evident for the low scorers than the high scorers. In contrast, high scorers referenced a greater need for God and faith, highly valued their church as a coping resource, and described passive religious coping strategies. These data indicate that disruptions in familiar religious routines after a disaster may be negatively impactful for some persons more than others. With respect to practical implications of these data, assessing a disaster survivor's religious needs, beliefs, and coping strategies may be critical for the design of interventions to lessen post-disaster suffering.

(6) Katie E. Cherry, Loren D. Marks, Rachel Adamek, and Bethany A. Lyon, "Younger and Older Coastal Fishers Face Catastrophic Loss After Hurricane Katrina," in *Traumatic Stress and Long-Term Recovery: Coping with Disasters and Other Negative Life Events*, ed. Katie E. Cherry (New York: Springer International Publishing Switzerland, 2015), 327–348.

Background and Purpose. Louisiana's commercial fishers and their family members have endured five major hurricanes in seven years; Katrina and Rita in 2005, Gustav and Ike in 2008, and Isaac in 2012. The environmental realities of coastal erosion and the progressive loss of barrier islands and marshland which have historically buffered the impact of deadly hurricanes are worrisome for commercial fishers who depend on natural resources to make a living.

Our primary purpose in this chapter was to examine Katrina's impact on younger (<55 years of age) and older (55+ years) commercial fishers and their family members. Conceivably, cultural heritage and tradition may hold greater meaning for older fishers than for their younger counterparts.

Furthermore, older fishers who have lived in hurricane-prone coastal regions for over a half-century have likely developed hurricane preparedness techniques and methods of coping that may promote individual and family resilience. Thus, a second purpose was to provide new insights concerning age differences in coping responses in the years after natural disaster exposures.

Method. The sample was comprised of 64 commercial fishers and their family members from the 2010–2012 post-Katrina resilience study. Four couples responded jointly to the open-ended questions and one participant declined for a total of 59 responses. To examine age-related differences in responses, the sample was split at the median age. Younger adults ranged in age from 21 to 54 years (M = 43.2, SD = 10.9 years). Older adults were 55–90 years of age (M = 66.5, SD = 10.5 years). Here we focused on fishers' answers to three open-ended questions, the same two questions concerning spiritual beliefs and religious practices listed in the Marks et al. (2015) chapters presented earlier, and one question concerning "silver linings," which was designed to shed new light on benefit finding as a coping strategy in the years after Katrina. The "silver lining" question, verbatim, is as follows:

> They say every cloud has a silver lining and even the most awful events can have positive outcomes. Do you think there are any positive outcomes that can come from Hurricanes Katrina and Rita? If so, what are they?

Results and Implications. Qualitative analyses of younger and older fishers' narratives yielded three core themes: (1) *Materialism and true colors revealed: despicable deeds and acts of grace after the storm*; (2) *Helping efforts across denominations: God was using his people to help his [other] people*; and (3) *Historical ties that bind: old roots and new connections.* Themes 1 and 2 captured similar responses across the two age groups. Younger and older fishers alike reported material losses and shifts in outlook and priorities after the storms, along with an outpouring of support from volunteers associated with faith-based disaster relief efforts. They described the organized disaster relief efforts carried out by faith-based communities. Many spoke of receiving assistance without regard to traditional denominational boundaries (e.g., Baptists, Amish, and many others). They also referenced humanitarian gestures and good will extended by strangers, some of whom have emerged as emotionally meaningful new friends.

Theme 3 captured pronounced age differences between the two groups. For younger fishers, salient trends were new friendships with displacement hosts and social opportunities in noncoastal communities to which they had evacuated. In contrast, the older fishers more often spoke of environmental concerns, bringing awareness to the problem of coastal erosion and the pervasive loss of land witnessed by generations of fishing families over the past century.

Ties to family and their coastal homeland were well represented in both age groups' narratives, providing a generationally rich perspective on natural disaster. Culture and tradition would appear to affect both younger and older fishers' coping responses and adjustment in the years after a devastating natural disaster.

(7) Trevan G. Hatch, Katie E. Cherry, Yaxin Lu, and Loren D. Marks, "Seeing Silver Linings After Catastrophic Loss: Personal Growth, Positive Adaption, and Relationships That Matter," in *Traumatic Stress and Long-Term Recovery: Coping with Disasters and Other Negative Life Events,* ed. Katie E. Cherry (New York: Springer International Publishing Switzerland, 2015), 389–402.

Background and Purpose. Benefit finding is a coping strategy that some disaster survivors use to manage stressors associated with catastrophic losses (see Chapter 7, this volume). The purpose of this chapter was to provide new evidence concerning perceived silver linings (defined as benefits and blessings) in connection with the 2005 Hurricanes Katrina and Rita.

Method. Participants were the same 125 former and current coastal residents described in Kytola et al.'s (2015) chapter. Our focus here centers on participants' responses to the same silver lining question just reported in the summary of Cherry et al.'s (2015) chapter: *They say every cloud has a silver lining and even the most awful events can have positive outcomes. Do you think there are any positive outcomes that can come from Hurricanes Katrina and Rita? If so, what are they?* Participants' responses to this question were digitally recorded, transcribed verbatim, and subjected to qualitative analyses using the same open and axial coding procedures described earlier in Kytola et al. (2015).

Results and Implications. Despite having experienced catastrophic losses, participants mentioned positive outcomes in connection with the Katrina disaster. Qualitative analyses yielded three emergent themes. The first theme, *"Personal growth and change in perspective,"* reflected participants' new attitude on life. They were reportedly grateful for life and family and had developed a new perspective on materialism (see Chapter 6, this volume, on gratitude as a principle of healing). In particular, participants spoke of shifting away from investing time and energy into acquiring and maintaining "things." Instead, some talked about placing a new emphasis on developing and enjoying more meaningful (and less tangible) aspects of life, which included spirituality, improved relationships, peace of mind, and a clear conscience.

The second theme, "*Appreciation for a new positive social environment*," captured participants' appreciation for their new environment, whether they returned to rebuild their coastal neighborhood or relocated permanently. Some were reportedly glad to resettle in new and different communities with greater opportunities for entertainment and educational advancement. Others expressed gratitude that they could return to rebuild the old neighborhood.

The third theme, "*Relationships with friends and family are what matter most*," was arguably the most salient silver lining observed here. Many described a heightened awareness of the importance of social relationships in the immediate aftermath of the storm. They spoke about forming lasting new friendships (e.g., new neighbors and volunteers) and realizing that family relationships were important to them. Although the disaster scattered their friends and neighbors widely, the displacement experience also brought new people into their social networks, many of whom have become close friends. Natural disasters may unify families and communities, a unique silver lining and a potentially important direction for future research.

(8) Katie E. Stanko, Katie E. Cherry, Kyle S. Ryker, Farra Mughal, Loren D. Marks, Jennifer Silva Brown, Patricia F. Gendusa, Marisa C. Sullivan, John Bruner, David A. Welsh, L. Joseph Su, and S. Michal Jazwinski, "Looking for the Silver Lining: Benefit Finding After Hurricanes Katrina and Rita in Middle-Aged, Older, and Oldest-Old Adults," *Current Psychology* 34 (2015): 564–575.

Background and Purpose. Looking for potentially positive outcomes is one way that people cope with stressful events. In this article, two studies are reported where we examined perceived "silver linings" associated with the 2005 Hurricanes Katrina and Rita among indirectly affected adults living in Baton Rouge, Louisiana. Study 1 was conducted within the first two years after these hurricanes made landfall. The primary purpose was to determine whether perceived silver linings varied by age group. A longitudinal design was used with two points of measurement to determine whether participants' perceived silver linings would change over time. Study 2 was a conceptual replication with a new sample of adults living in Baton Rouge at the time of Katrina. These adults served as the indirectly affected control group for comparison purposes in the 2010–2012 post-Katrina resilience study.

Method. In Study 1, middle-aged (ages 47–64 years), older (ages 65–89 years), and oldest-old (ages 90–95 years) adults in the LHAS responded to an open-ended question on perceived silver linings in a longitudinal assessment carried out during the immediate impact (1–4 months after landfall) and post-disaster recovery phase (6–14 months post-storm). In Study 2, a new sample of indirectly affected adults (ages 31–82 years) was recruited at least five years after the storms. Narrative data were analyzed using the same qualitative methods described in Kytola et al. (2015).

Results and Implications. In Study 1, team-based coding of participants' responses yielded three reliable and replicable themes across assessments: (1) *A learning experience and better preparedness for future disasters*, (2) *Having improved cities* (Baton Rouge and New Orleans), and (3) *An increase in "Good Samaritan" acts*, such as strangers helping one another. Responses were similar across age groups, although older adults were the least likely to report positive outcomes. In Study 2, a learning experience and preparedness core theme replicated Study 1's findings. Additionally, a new core theme emerged in Study 2, which was improved social cohesion among family and friends.

Taken together, these studies provide new evidence of perceived "silver linings" after the Katrina disaster. The inclusion of a longitudinal assessment (Study 1) and conceptual replication (Study 2) were strengths of this study. These data indicate that identifying lessons learned and potentially positive outcomes may foster post-disaster resilience for indirectly affected adults in the years after disaster.

NOTES

1. Katie E. Cherry, Sandro Galea, L. Joseph Su, David A. Welsh, S. Michal Jazwinski, Jennifer L. Silva, and Marla J. Erwin, "Cognitive and Psychosocial Consequences of Hurricanes Katrina and Rita on Middle Aged, Older, and Oldest-Old Adults in the Louisiana Healthy Aging Study (LHAS)," *Journal of Applied Social Psychology* 40 (2010): 2463–487.
2. Katie E. Cherry, Jennifer Silva Brown, Loren D. Marks, Sandro Galea, Julia Volaufova, Christina Lefante, L. Joseph Su, David A. Welsh, and S. Michal Jazwinski, "Longitudinal Assessment of Cognitive and Psychosocial Functioning After Hurricanes Katrina and Rita: Exploring Disaster Impact on Middle-Aged, Older, and Oldest-Old Adults," *Journal of Applied Biobehavioral Research* 16 (2011): 187–211.
3. Katie E. Cherry, Sandro Galea, and Jennifer L. Silva, "Successful Aging in Very Old Adults: Resiliency in the Face of Natural Disaster," in *Handbook of Clinical*

Psychology: Vol. 1, eds. Michel Hersen and Alan M. Gross (New York: John Wiley & Sons, Inc., 2008), 810–833.

4. Katie E. Cherry, Jennifer L. Silva, and Sandro Galea, "Natural Disasters and the Oldest-Old: A Psychological Perspective on Coping and Health in Late Life," in *Lifespan Perspectives on Natural Disasters: Coping with Katrina, Rita and Other Storms*, ed. Katie E. Cherry (New York: Springer Science+Business Media, 2009), 171–193.

5. Loren D. Marks, Katie E. Cherry, Jennifer L. Silva, "Faith, Crisis, Coping and Meaning Making After Katrina: A Qualitative, Cross-Cohort Examination," in *Lifespan Perspectives on Natural Disasters: Coping with Katrina, Rita and Other Storms*, ed. Katie E. Cherry (New York: Springer Science+Business Media, 2009), 195–215.

6. Jennifer L. Silva, Loren D. Marks, and Katie E. Cherry, "The Psychology Behind Helping and Prosocial Behaviors: An Examination from Intention to Action," in *Lifespan Perspectives on Natural Disasters: Coping with Katrina, Rita and Other Storms*, ed. Katie E. Cherry (New York: Springer Science+Business Media, 2009), 219–240.

7. Christina Tausch, Loren D. Marks, Jennifer Silva Brown, Katie E. Cherry, Tracey Frias, Zia MacWilliams, Miranda Melancon, and Diane D. Sasser, "Religion and Coping with Trauma: Qualitative Examples from Hurricanes Katrina and Rita," *Journal of Religion, Spirituality and Aging* 23 (2011): 236–253.

8. Jennifer Silva Brown, Katie E. Cherry, Loren D. Marks, Erin M. Jackson, Julia Volaufova, Christina Lefante, and S. Michal Jazwinski, "After Hurricanes Katrina and Rita: Gender Differences in Health and Religiosity in Middle-Aged and Older Adults," *Health Care for Women International* 31 (2010): 997–1012.

9. Loren D. Marks, "A Pragmatic, Step-by-Step Guide for Qualitative Methods: Capturing the Disaster and Long-Term Recovery Stories of Katrina and Rita," *Current Psychology* 34 (2015): 494–505.

10. John E. Ware and Cathy Donald Sherbourne, "The MOS 36 Item Short-Form Health Survey (SF-36): I. Conceptual Framework and Item Selection," *Medical Care* 30 (1992): 473–483.

11. Cherry, "Longitudinal Assessment of Cognitive and Psychosocial Functioning After Hurricanes Katrina and Rita," 191.

12. Gabriele Prati and Luca Pietrantoni, "Optimism, Social Support, and Coping Strategies as Factors Contributing to Posttraumatic Growth: A Meta-Analysis," *Journal of Loss and Trauma* 14, no. 5 (2009): 364–388.

13. C. R. Snyder, Susie C. Sympson, Florence C. Ybasco, Tyrone F. Borders, Michael A. Babyak, and Raymond L. Higgins, "Development and Validation of the State Hope Scale," *Journal of Personality and Social Psychology* 70 (1996): 321–335.

14. Kerrie Glass, Kate Flory, Benjamin L. Hankin, Bret Kloos, and Gustavo Turecki, "Are Coping Strategies, Social Support, and Hope Associated with Psychological Distress Among Hurricane Katrina Survivors?" *Journal of Social and Clinical Psychology* 28 (2009): 779–795.

15. Ware, "The MOS 36 Item Short-Form Health Survey (SF-36)," 473–483.

16. Katie E. Cherry and Sandro Galea, "Resilience After Trauma," in *Resiliency: Enhancing Coping with Crisis and Terrorism*, NATO Science for Peace and Security Series—E Human and Societal Dynamics, eds. Dean Ajdukovic, Shaul Kimhi, and Mooli Lahad (Amsterdam: IOS Press, 2015), 35–40.

17. Amy L. Ai, Terrence N. Tice, Christopher Peterson, and Bu Huang, "Prayers, Spiritual Support, and Positive Attitudes in Coping with the September 11 National Crisis," *Journal of Personality* 73 (2005): 767.

18. Charles S. Carver and Michael F. Scheier, "Situational Coping and Coping Dispositions in a Stressful Transaction," *Journal of Personality and Social Psychology* 66 (1994): 184–195.

19. Uri Bronfenbrenner, *The Ecology of Human Development* (Cambridge, MA: Harvard University Press, 1979).

20. Katie E. Cherry, ed., *Lifespan Perspectives on Natural Disasters: Coping with Katrina, Rita and Other Storms* (New York: Springer, 2009).

21. Loren D. Marks, "Religion and Bio-Psycho-Social Health: A Review and Conceptual Model," *Journal of Religion and Health* 44 (2005): 173–186.

22. Katie E. Cherry, Priscilla D. Allen, and Sandro Galea, "Older Adults and Natural Disasters: Lessons Learned from Hurricanes Katrina and Rita," in *Crisis and Disaster Counseling: Lessons Learned from Hurricane Katrina and Other Disasters,* ed. Priscilla Dass-Brailsford (Thousand Oaks, CA: Sage, 2010), 115–130.

APPENDIX B

In Everlasting Memory
of Katrina Victims

ST. BERNARD, LOUISIANA: AUGUST 29, 2005

Bertha Acosta

Hollis Alford

Angela Alviar

Eveleyn Ancar

Douglas Arceneaux

Betty Arceneaux

Joseph Banks

Lillian Banta

Walter Barcellona

John Bekkner

Carmen Bennett

Lucille Besnard

Sarah Bosarge

Eugenie Boyle

Eunice Breaux

Jospeh Brossette

Thomas Burke

Evelyn Burns

Benny Butler, Jr.

Leroy Butler

Robert J. Caire

Frank Chambers

Charles Chauppetta

Harold Cordes

Walter Cosse

Adele Cousins

Ned Couvillion

Frances Cox

Irene Daigle

Mary Darsam

Rosemary Davis

Robert Delafosse

Zerelda Delatte

Alan Delaune

Jane Denley

Agnes Depascual

Rita Drury

Guiomar Duarte

Edward "Pete" Dugas

Harrison A. Duhon

Loveless Dupuy

Patsy Eaton

Mary Ellis

Russell Embry

Joan Emerson

Helen Fahrenholtz

Ervin Farzande

John Farzande

Maxine Frischhertz

Joyce Fonseca

Brenda Fontaintte

Charles Gagliano

Shirley Gagliano

Arthur Galatas

Tufanio Gallodoro

Mario Gardener

Catherene Godwin

Thelma Godwin

Mary Gourges

Rita Green

William Gregg

George Grunik

Ura Gurtner

Shirley Hartdegen

Wilbur A. Hebert, Jr.

Rosemary Herndon

Dorothy Hingle

George Huard

Alice Hutzler

Myrtle Jackson

Virginia James

Georgia Jenkins

Joseph Jenkins

Josephine Johnson

Mabel Johnson

Vicki Jordan

Mertha Kaminsky

Iris Knight

Mildred Kramer

Edith Krennerich

Harold Kurz

Laura Lae

Helen Larre

Mary Labat

Gladys LeBlanc

Mary Lind

Dominique Liuzza

Oralie Lobre

Todd J. Lopez

Shirley Lott

Harry Louros

Peggy Mahaney

Joseph Major

William Manson

Shirley Mares

August Martinolich

Joyce McGuire

Lucille Melerine

Shirley Meyer

Earl Meyer

Helen Meyer

Arthur Miller

Helen Montalbano

Lauretta Morales

Curtis Morrow

Stephen Mosgrove

Matthew Muhoberac, Jr.

Joel C. Mumphrey

Frances Navis

Denise Newman

William Noote

Janet Parker

Carol Parr

Norman Parr

Gregory Patrolia

Richard Patrolia

Helen Perret

Rosemary Pino

Emile Poissenot

Glenn Rambo

Gladys Randall

Janet Rashkin

Richard Reysack

Rufus Rivers

Rebecca Roark

Lynda Robin

Bernice Robino

Eva Rodrique

Elizabeth Ross

John Russell

Georgia Ryan

Van Ryan

Darlene Saia

Antonia Sanfilippo

Rosemary Savoie

Anna Schielder

Cynthia Schiro

Dolores Schiro

Jake Schiro, Jr.

Henry Seifker

David Selbe

Mary Simpson

Louise Sires

Matthew Smallwood

Freddie Smith

Carole Spano

Robert Spinks

Henry Stafford, Sr.

Marion Stearnes

John Sullivan

Alvin Swan

Dorothy Taguino

Charlie Taylor

Michael Thomason

Donna Thomopolous

George Torrence

Mary Ann Trentecosta

Anna Marie Uroquhart

Almeda Verret

Inex Vidrios

Mary Wagner

Thelma Wall

Lawrence Williams

Gloria Young

BIBLIOGRAPHY

Ai, Amy L., Terrence N. Tice, Christopher Peterson, and Bu Huang. "Prayers, Spiritual Support, and Positive Attitudes in Coping with the September 11 National Crisis." *Journal of Personality* 73 (2005): 767.

American Veterinary Medical Association. "PETS Act (FAQ)." *AVMA*, last modified 2018. Accessed August 3, 2018. https://www.avma.org/KB/Resources/Reference/disaster/Pages/PETS-Act-FAQ.aspx?PF=1

Baard, Henricus P. *Frans Hals*. Translated by George Stuyck. London: Thames and Hudson Ltd., 1981.

Bacher, Renee, Teresa Devlin, Kristine Calongne, Joshua Duplechain, and Stephanie Pertuit. *LSU in the Eye of the Storm*. Baton Rouge: LSU Press, 2005.

Baltes, Paul B., and Margret M. Baltes. *Successful Aging: Perspectives from the Behavioral Sciences*. New York: Cambridge University Press, 1990.

Beevers, John. *The Autobiography of St. Thérèse of Lisieux: The Story of a Soul*. New York: Doubleday, 1957.

Bonanno, George A. "Loss, Trauma, and Human Resilience: Have We Underestimated the Human Capacity to Thrive After Extremely Aversive Events?" *American Psychologist* 59 (2004): 20–28.

Bonanno, George A. *The Other Side of Sadness: What the New Science of Bereavement Tells Us About Life After Loss*. New York: Basic Books, 2009.

Bonanno, George A., Chris R. Brewin, Krzysztof Kaniasty, and Annette M. La Greca. "Weighing the Costs of Disaster: Consequences, Risks, and Resilience in Individuals, Families, and Communities." *Psychological Science in the Public Interest* 11 (2010): 1–49.

Bonanno, George A., and Sumati Gupta. "Resilience After Disaster." In *Mental Health and Disasters*, edited by Yuval Neria, Sandro Galea, and Fran H. Norris, 145–160. New York: Cambridge University Press, 2009.

Bonhoeffer, Dietrich. *I Want to Live These Days with You: A Year of Daily Devotions*. Louisville: Westminster John Knox Press, 2007.

Bowlby, John. *Attachment and Loss, Vol. 1. Attachment*. New York: Basic Books, 1969.

Bremner, J. Douglas. "Effects of Traumatic Stress on Brain Structure and Function: Relevance to Early Responses to Trauma." *Journal of Trauma Dissociation* 6 (2005): 51–68.

Brinkley, Douglas. *The Great Deluge: Hurricane Katrina, New Orleans, and the Mississippi Gulf Coast*. New York: Harper Collins Publishers, 2005.

Bremner, J. Douglas and Lai Reed. *You Can't Just Snap Out of It*. Laughing Cow Books, 2014.

Bronfenbrenner, Uri. *The Ecology of Human Development*. Cambridge, MA: Harvard University Press, 1979.

Brulliard, Karin. "How the Chaos of Hurricane Katrina Helped Save Pets from Flooding in Texas." *Washington Post*, August 31, 2017. https://www.washingtonpost.com/news/animalia/wp/2017/08/31/how-the-chaos-of-hurricane-katrina-helped-save-pets-from-flooding-in-texas/?noredirect=on&utm_term=.81c39ec73337

Brumley, Cade. *Leadership Standards in Action: The School Principal as a Servant-Leader*. New York: Rowman & Littlefield Publishers, 2012.

Brunsma, David L., David Overfelt, and J. Steven Picou. *The Sociology of Katrina: Perspectives on a Modern Catastrophe* (2nd ed.). Lanham: Rowman & Littlefield Publishers, 2010.

Bush, Laura. *Spoken from the Heart*. New York: Scribner, 2010.

Buuck, Michelle Mahl. *Firestorm: Hurricane Katrina and the St. Bernard Fire Department*. Xlibris Corporation, 2007.

Bynner, Witter, trans. *The Way of Life According to Lao Tzu*. New York: Putnam Publishing Group, 1944.

Carr, Kelly, and Patricia L. Weir. "A Qualitative Description of Successful Aging Through Different Decades of Older Adulthood." *Aging & Mental Health* 21, no. 12 (2017): 1317–1325.

Carver, Charles S., and Michael F. Scheier. "Situational Coping and Coping Dispositions in a Stressful Transaction." *Journal of Personality and Social Psychology* 66 (1994): 184–195.

Cherry, Katie E., ed. *Lifespan Perspectives on Natural Disasters: Coping with Katrina, Rita and Other Storms*. New York: Springer Science + Business Media, 2009.

Cherry, Katie E., ed. *Traumatic Stress and Long-Term Recovery: Coping with Disasters and Other Negative Life Events*. New York: Springer International Publishing Switzerland, 2015.

Cherry, Katie E., Priscilla D. Allen, and Sandro Galea. "Older Adults and Natural Disasters: Lessons Learned from Hurricanes Katrina and Rita." In *Crisis and Disaster Counseling: Lessons Learned from Hurricane Katrina and Other Disasters*, edited by Priscilla Dass-Brailsford, 115–130. Thousand Oaks, CA: Sage, 2010.

Cherry, Katie E., and Sandro Galea. "Resilience After Trauma." In *Resiliency: Enhancing Coping with Crisis and Terrorism*, NATO Science for Peace and Security Series— E Human and Societal Dynamics, edited by Dean Ajdukovic, Shaul Kimhi, and Mooli Lahad, 35–40. Netherlands: IOS Press, 2015.

Cherry, Katie E., Sandro Galea, and Jennifer L. Silva. "Successful Aging in Very Old Adults: Resiliency in the Face of Natural Disaster." In *Handbook of Clinical Psychology: Volume 1*, edited by Michel Hersen and Alan M. Gross, 810–833. New Jersey: John Wiley & Sons, 2008.

Cherry, Katie E., Jennifer L. Silva, and Sandro Galea. "Natural Disasters and the Oldest-Old: A Psychological Perspective on Coping and Health in Late Life. In *Lifespan Perspectives on Natural Disasters: Coping with Katrina, Rita and other Storms*, edited by Katie E. Cherry, 171–193. New York: Springer Science+Business Media, 2009.

Cherry, Katie E., Sandro Galea, L. Joseph Su, David A. Welsh, S. Michal Jazwinski, Jennifer L. Silva, and Marla J. Erwin. "Cognitive and Psychosocial Consequences of Hurricanes Katrina and Rita on Middle Aged, Older, and Oldest-Old Adults in the Louisiana Healthy Aging Study (LHAS)." *Journal of Applied Social Psychology* 40 (2010): 2463–2487.

Cherry, Katie E., Bethany A. Lyon, Emily O. Boudreaux, Alyse B. Blanchard, Jason L. Hicks, Emily M. Elliott, Leann Myers, Sangkyu Kim, and S. Michal Jazwinski. "Memory Self-Efficacy and Beliefs About Memory and Aging in Very Old Adults in the Louisiana Healthy Aging Study (LHAS)." *Experimental Aging Research* 45, no. 1 (2019): 28–40.

Cherry, Katie E., Loren D. Marks, Rachel Adamek, and Bethany A. Lyon. "Younger and Older Coastal Fishers Face Catastrophic Loss After Hurricane Katrina." In *Traumatic Stress and Long-Term Recovery: Coping with Disasters and Other Negative Life Events*, edited by Katie E. Cherry, 327–348. New York: Springer International Publishing Switzerland, 2015.

Cherry, Katie E., Loren D. Marks, Tim Benedetto, Marissa Sullivan, and Alyse Barker. "Perceptions of Longevity and Successful Aging in Very Old Adults." *Journal of Religion, Spirituality and Aging* 25 (2013): 288–310. https://doi.org/10.1080/15528030.2013.765368

Cherry, Katie E., Laura Sampson, Sandro Galea, Loren D. Marks, Pamela F. Nezat, Kayla H. Baudoin, and Bethany A. Lyon. "Optimism and Hope After Multiple Disasters: Relationships to Health-Related Quality of Life." *Journal of Loss and Trauma* 22, no. 1 (2017): 61–76.

Cherry, Katie E., Laura Sampson, Sandro Galea, Loren D. Marks, Katie E. Stanko, Pamela F. Nezat, and Kayla H. Baudoin. "Spiritual Support and Humor are Associated with Resilience After Multiple Disasters." *Journal of Nursing Scholarship* (2018): 1–22.

Cherry, Katie E., Laura Sampson, Pamela F. Nezat, Ashley Cacamo, Loren D. Marks, and Sandro Galea. "Long-Term Psychological Outcomes in Older Adults After Disaster: Relationships to Religiosity and Social Support." *Aging & Mental Health* 19, no. 5 (2015): 430–444.

Cherry, Katie E., Laura Sampson, Pamela F. Nezat, Sandro Galea, Loren D. Marks, and Bethany A. Lyon. "Prior Hurricane and Other Lifetime Trauma Predict Coping Style in Older Commercial Fishers After the BP Deepwater Horizon Oil Spill." *Journal of Applied Biobehavioral Research* 2 (2017, June 22): 1–18. https://doi.org/10.1111/jabr.12076

Cherry, Katie E., Jennifer L. Silva Brown, Loren D. Marks, Sandro Galea, Julia Volaufova, Christina Lefante, L. Joseph Su, David A. Welsh, and S. Michal Jazwinski. "Longitudinal Assessment of Cognitive and Psychosocial Functioning After Hurricanes Katrina and Rita: Exploring Disaster Impact on Middle-Aged, Older, and Oldest-Old Adults." *Journal of Applied Biobehavioral Research* 16 (2011): 187–211.

Cherry, Katie E., and Anderson D. Smith. "Normal Memory Aging." In *Handbook of Clinical Geropsychology*, edited by Michel Hersen and Vincent B. Van Hasselt, 87–110. New York: Plenum Press, 1998.

Cooper, Christopher, and Robert Block. *Disaster Hurricane Katrina and the Failure of Homeland Security*. New York: Times Books, Henry Holt and Company, 2006.

Cosco, Theodore D., A. Matthew Prina, Jamie Perales, Blossom C. M. Stephan, and Carol Brayne. "Operational Definitions of Successful Aging: A Systematic Review." *International Psychogeriatrics* 26, no. 3 (2014): 373–381.

Crich Baptist Church, Derbyshire, UK (website). "It Is Well with My Soul: The Hymn and the Story." Accessed June 20, 2019. https://www.crichbaptist.org/articles/christian-poetry-hymns/it-is-well-with-my-soul/

Duay, Deborah L., and Valerie C. Bryan. "Senior Adults' Perceptions of Successful Aging." *Educational Gerontology* 32 (2006): 423–445.

Emmons, Robert A. *Thanks! How Practicing Gratitude Can Make You Happier.* New York: Houghton-Mifflin, 2007.

Emmons, Robert A., and Michael E. McCullough. *The Psychology of Gratitude.* New York: Oxford University Press, 2004.

Finney, Jr., Peter. "Prince of Peace Deacon Tells Harrowing Tale of Survival." *Clarion Herald Archive* (August 26, 2006).

Floris, Odelia. *Inspiration and Wisdom from the Pen of Ralph Waldo Emmerson.* CreateSpace Independent Publishing Platform, June, 2015.

Folkman, Susan, and Richard S. Lazarus. "If It Changes It Must Be a Process: Study of Emotion and Coping During Three Stages of a College Examination." *Journal of Personality and Social Psychology* 48 (1985): 150–170.

Folkman, Susan, and Judith Tedlie Moscowitz. "Coping: Pitfalls and Promise." *Annual Review of Psychology* 55 (2004): 745–774.

Frankl, Viktor E. *Man's Search for Meaning.* Boston: Beacon Press, 2006.

Gerhart, James I., Daphna Canetti, and Stevan E. Hobfoll. "Traumatic Stress in Overview: Definition, Context, Scope, and Long-Term Outcomes." In *Traumatic Stress and Long-Term Recovery: Coping with Disasters and Other Negative Life Events*, edited by Katie E. Cherry, 3–24. New York: Springer International Publishing Switzerland, 2015.

Ghost Rider Pictures. *Forgotten on the Bayou.* Last modified 2008, http://www.ghostriderpictures.com/RockeyTrailer.html

Glass, Kerrie, Kate Flory, Benjamin L. Hankin, Bret Kloos, and Gustavo Turecki. "Are Coping Strategies, Social Support, and Hope Associated with Psychological Distress Among Hurricane Katrina Survivors?" *Journal of Social and Clinical Psychology* 28 (2009): 779–795.

Gray, Alice, *Stories for the Heart: The Original Collection.* New York: Multnoma Books, 1996.

Grimm, David. "How Pets of Hurricane Harvey Are Benefitting from the Lessons of Katrina." *Huffington Post*, September 5, 2017. http://actionnews.ca/newstempch.php?article=/entry/how-pets-of-hurricane-harvey-are-benefiting-from-the-lessons-of-katrina_us_59af1f02e4b0b5e53101cf02

Hancock, Mark. "Many in Louisiana, Texas Lament Rita 'Amnesia.'" *USA Today,* January 25, 2006. https://usatoday30.usatoday.com/news/nation/2006-01-25-rita_x.htm

Harper, Anna R., and Kenneth I. Pargament. "Trauma, Religion, and Spirituality: Pathways to Healing." In *Traumatic Stress and Long-Term Recovery: Coping with Disasters and Other Negative Life Events*, edited Katie E. Cherry, 349–367. New York: Springer International Publishing Switzerland, 2015.

Hatch, Trevan G., Katie E. Cherry, Keri L. Kytola, Yaxin Lu, and Loren D. Marks. "Loss, Chaos, Survival, and Despair: The Storm After the Storms." In *Traumatic Stress and Long-Term Recovery: Coping with Disasters and Other Negative Life Events*, edited by Katie E. Cherry, 231–245. New York: Springer International Publishing Switzerland, 2015.

Hatch, Trevan G., Katie E. Cherry, Yaxin Lu, and Loren D. Mark. "Seeing Silver Linings After Catastrophic Loss: Personal Growth, Positive Adaption, and Relationships That Matter." In *Traumatic Stress and Long-Term Recovery: Coping with Disasters and Other Negative Life Events*, edited by Katie E. Cherry, 389–402. New York: Springer International Publishing Switzerland, 2015.

Heckhausen, Jutta, and Richard Schultz. "A Life-Span Theory of Control." *Psychological Review* 102, no. 2 (1995): 284–304.

Henderson, Tammy L., Karen A. Roberto, and Yoshinori Kamo. "Older Adults' Responses to Hurricane Katrina: Daily Hassles and Coping Strategies." *Journal of Applied Gerontology* 29 (2010): 48–69, doi: 10.1177/0733464809334287.

Henry, Jacques. "Return or Relocate? An Inductive Analysis of Decision-Making in a Disaster." *Disaster* 37, no. 2 (2013): 294–316.

Horne, Jed. *Breach of Faith: Hurricane Katrina and the Near Death of a Great American City.* New York: Random House, 2006.

Horst, Jerald, and Glenda Horst. *The Louisiana Seafood Bible: Oysters.* Gretna: Pelican Publishing Company, 2011.

Johnson, Jennifer, and Sandro Galea. "Disasters and Population Health." In *Lifespan Perspectives on Natural Disasters: Coping with Katrina, Rita and Other Storms,* edited by Katie E. Cherry, 281–326. New York: Springer Science+Business Media, 2009.

Jopp, Daniella S., Dagmara Wozniak, Amanda K. Damarin, Melissa De Feo, Seojung Jung, and Sheena Jeswani. "How Could Lay Perspectives on Successful Aging Complement Scientific Theory? Findings from a US and a German Life-Span Sample." *The Gerontologist* 55 (2015): 91–106.

Kamo, Yoshinori, Tammy L. Henderson, and Karen A. Roberto. "Displaced Older Adults' Reactions to and Coping with the Aftermath of Hurricane Katrina." *Journal of Family Issues* 30 (2011): 1346–1370.

Kaniasty, Krzysztof, and Fran H. Norris. "Distinctions That Matter: Received Social Support, Perceived Social Support, and Social Embeddedness After Disasters." In *Mental Health and Disasters,* edited by Yuval Neria, Sandro Galea, and Fran H. Norris, 175–200. New York: Cambridge University Press, 2009.

Kern, Emily. "Manganos Not Guilty." *Baton Rouge The Advocate,* September 8, 2007.

Kilmer, Ryan P., Virginia Gil-Rivas, Richard G. Tedeschi, and Lawrence G. Calhoun, eds. *Helping Families and Communities Recover from Disaster: Lessons Learned from Hurricane Katrina and Its Aftermath.* Washington, DC: American Psychological Association, 2010.

Koenig, Harold G., Dana King, and Verna B. Carson, eds. *Handbook of Religion and Health* (2nd ed.). New York: Oxford, 2012.

Kübler-Ross, Elisabeth. *On Death and Dying.* New York: Scribner, 1969.

Kübler-Ross, Elisabeth, and David Kessler. *On Grief and Grieving.* New York: Scribner, 2005.

Kushner, Harold S. *When Bad Things Happen to Good People.* New York: Anchor Books, 1981.

Kytola, Keri L., Katie E. Cherry, Loren D. Marks, and Trevan G. Hatch. "When Neighborhoods Are Destroyed by Disaster: Relocate or Return and Rebuild?" In *Traumatic Stress and Long-Term Recovery: Coping with Disasters and Other Negative Life Events,* edited by Katie E. Cherry, 211–229. New York: Springer International Publishing Switzerland, 2015.

Lewis, Clive Staples. *A Grief Observed.* New York: HarperCollins, 1961.

Lincoln, Abraham. "Lincoln to Fanny McCullough." Washington, December 23, 1862. In *Abraham Lincoln: His Speeches and Writings,* edited by Roy P. Basler. New York: Universal Library Grosset & Dunlap, 1962.

Littleton, Heather, Samantha Horsley, Siji John, and David V. Nelson. "Trauma Coping Strategies and Psychological Distress: A Meta-Analysis." *Journal of Traumatic Stress* 20, no. 6 (2007): 977–988.

Lyon, Bethany A., Pamela F. Nezat, Katie E. Cherry, and Loren D. Marks. "When Multiple Disasters Strike: Louisiana Fishers in the Aftermath of Hurricanes and the British Petroleum Deepwater Horizon Oil Spill." In *Traumatic Stress and Long-Term Recovery: Coping with Disasters and Other Negative Life Events*, edited by Katie E. Cherry, 57–70. New York: Springer International Publishing Switzerland, 2015.

Maeda, Masaharu, and Misari Oe. "The Great East Japan Earthquake: Tsunami and Nuclear Disaster." In *Traumatic Stress and Long-Term Recovery: Coping with Disasters and Other Negative Life Events*, edited by Katie E. Cherry, 71–90. New York: Springer International Publishing Switzerland, 2015.

Marks, Loren D. "A Pragmatic, Step-by-Step Guide for Qualitative Methods: Capturing the Disaster and Long-Term Recovery Stories of Katrina and Rita." *Current Psychology* 34, no. 3 (2015): 494–505. https://doi.org/10.1007/s12144-015-9342-x

Marks, Loren D. "Sacred Practices in Highly Religious Families: Christian, Jewish, Mormon, and Muslim Perspective." *Family Process* 43 (2004): 217–231.

Marks, Loren D. "Religion and Bio-Psycho-Social Health: A Review and Conceptual Model. *Journal of Religion and Health* 44 (2005): 173-86.

Marks, Loren D., Katie E. Cherry, Jennifer L. Silva. "Faith, Crisis, Coping and Meaning Making after Katrina: A Qualitative, Cross-Cohort Examination." In *Lifespan Perspectives on Natural Disasters: Coping with Katrina, Rita and Other Storms*, edited by Katie E. Cherry, 195–215. New York: Springer Science+Business Media, 2009.

Marks, Loren D., Trevan G. Hatch, Yaxin Lu, and Katie E. Cherry. "Families and Faith-Based Communities After a Disaster: Successes and Failures in the Wakes of Hurricanes Katrina and Rita." In *Traumatic Stress and Long-Term Recovery: Coping with Disasters and Other Negative Life Events*, edited by Katie E. Cherry, 247–270. New York: Springer International Publishing Switzerland, 2015.

Marks, Loren D., Yaxin Lu, Katie E. Cherry, and Trevan G. Hatch. "Faith and Coping: Spiritual Beliefs and Religious Practices After Hurricanes Katrina and Rita." In *Traumatic Stress and Long-Term Recovery: Coping with Disasters and Other Negative Life Events*, edited by Katie E. Cherry, 369–387. New York: Springer International Publishing Switzerland, 2015.

Martin, G. "The Meaning and Origin of the Expression: Every Cloud Has a Silver Lining." *The Phrase Finder*. Accessed January 2, 2014. http://www.phrases.org.uk/meanings/every-cloud-has-a-silver-lining.html

Martin, Rod A. *The Psychology of Humor: An Integrative Approach*. Burlington: Elsevier Academic Press, 2007.

Masten, Ann S. *Ordinary Magic: Resilience in Development*. New York: Guilford Press, 2014.

Masten, Ann S., and Angela J. Narayan. "Child Development in the Context of Disaster, War, and Terrorism: Pathways of Risk and Resilience." *Annual Review of Psychology* 63 (2012): 227–257.

Moye, Dorothy. "The X-Codes: A Post-Katrina Postscript." *Southern Spaces* (August 26, 2009). http://www.southernspaces.org/2009/x-codes-post-katrina-postscriptcontent_top

Neimeyer, Robert A., Laurie A. Burke, Michael M. Mackay, and Jessica G. van Dyke Stringer. "Grief Therapy and the Reconstruction of Meaning: From Principles to Practice." *Journal of Contemporary Psychotherapy* 40 (2010): 73–83.

Neria, Yuval, Sandro Galea, and Fran H. Norris, eds. *Mental Health and Disasters*. New York: Cambridge University Press, 2009.

Oriol, William E. *Psychosocial Issues for Older Adults in Disasters*. Washington, DC: US Department of Health and Human Services, Substance Abuse and Mental Health Services Administration, Center for Mental Health Services, 1999.

Osbeck, Kenneth W. *Amazing Grace: 366 Inspiring Hymn Stories for Daily Devotions* (2nd ed.). Grand Rapids: Kregel Publications, 2002.

P&G (Proctor and Gamble). "The Charmin Effect." Filmed April 2016. YouTube video, 3:00. Posted April 2016. https://www.youtube.com/watch?v=xtAaW5z-lHQ

Pargament, Kenneth I. *The Psychology of Religion and Coping: Theory, Research, and Practice*. New York: Guilford Press, 1997.

Penley, Julie A., Joe Tomaka, and John S. Wiebe. "The Association of Coping to Physical and Psychological Health Outcomes. A Meta-Analytic Review." *Journal of Behavioral Medicine* 25 (2002): 551–603.

Perez, Samantha. *The Isleños of Louisiana: On the Water's Edge*. Charleston: The History Press, 2011.

Poon, Leonard W., and Jiska Cohen-Mansfield. *Understanding Well-Being in the Oldest-Old*. New York: Cambridge University Press, 2011.

Prati, Gabriele, and Luca Pietrantoni. "Optimism, Social Support, and Coping Strategies as Factors Contributing to Posttraumatic Growth: A Meta-Analysis." *Journal of Loss and Trauma* 14, no. 5 (2009): 364–388.

Pruchno, Rachel, and Deborah Carr. "Successful Aging 2.0: Resilience and Beyond." *The Journals of Gerontology: Series B* 72, no. 2 (2017): 201–203. https://doi.org/10.1093/geronb/gbw214

Ranzijn, Rob, and Mary A. Luszcz. "Acceptance: A Key to Well-Being in Older Adults?" *Australian Psychologist* 34 (1999): 94–98.

Robin, Cecile Jones. *Remedies and Lost Secrets of St. Bernard's Isleños*. St. Bernard Village: Los Isleños Heritage and Cultural Society, 2000.

Rogers, Fred. *The World According to Mister Rogers: Important Things to Remember*. New York: Hatchette Books, 2003.

Rose, Chris. *1 Dead in Attic*. New York: Simon & Schuster, 2005.

Roth, Susan, and Lawrence J. Cohen. "Approach, Avoidance, and Coping with Stress." *American Psychologist* 41 (1986): 813–819.

Ryff, Carol D. "In the Eye of the Beholder: Views of Psychological Well-Being Among Middle-Aged and Older Adults." *Psychology and Aging* 4, no. 2 (June 1989): 195–210.

Ryff, Carol, Elliott Friedman, Thomas Fuller-Rowell, Gayle Love, Yuri Miyamoto, Jennifer Morozink, Barry Radler, and Vera Tsenkova. "Varieties of Resilience in MIDUS." *Social and Personality Compass* 6/11 (2012): 792–806.

Sacks, O., *Gratitude*. New York: Alfred A. Knopf, 2015.

Sankey, Ira David. *My Life and the Story of the Gospel Hymns and of Sacred Songs and Solos*. London: Forgotten Books, 2012, originally published 1907.

Schacter, Daniel L. *The Seven Sins of Memory: How the Mind Forgets and Remembers*. New York: Houghton Mifflin Company, 2001.

Schaefer, Mikel. *Lost in Katrina*. Gretna: Pelican Publishing Company, 2007.

Schnider, Kimberly R., Jon D. Elhai, and Matt J. Gray. "Coping Style Use Predicts Posttraumatic Stress and Complicated Grief Symptom Severity among College Students Reporting a Traumatic Loss." *Journal of Counseling Psychology* 54, no. 3 (2007): 344–350.

Schnurr, Paula P., and Bonnie L. Green. *Trauma and Health: Physical Health Consequences of Exposure to Extreme Stress*. Washington, DC: American Psychological Association, 2004.

Schroeder, Alison. "St. Bernard Parish Hospital Is a Final Piece of Katrina Recovery." *Times-Picayune*, June 24, 2012. http://www.nola.com/health/index.ssf/2012/06/st_bernard_parish_hospital_a_f.html

Shear, M. Katherine. "Complicated Grief." *New England Journal of Medicine* 372, no. 2 (2015): 406.

Shear, M. Katherine, and Susan Delaney. "On Bereavement and Grief: A Therapeutic Approach to Healing." In *Traumatic Stress and Long-Term Recovery: Coping with Disasters and Other Negative Life Events,* edited by Katie E. Cherry, 403–418. New York: Springer International Publishing Switzerland, 2015.

Shear, M. Katherine, Katie A. McLaughlin, Angela Ghesquiere, Michael J. Gruber, Nancy A. Sampson, and Ronald C. Kessler. "Complicated Grief Associated with Hurricane Katrina." *Depression and Anxiety* 28 (2011): 648–657.

Silva Brown, Jennifer, Katie E. Cherry, Loren D. Marks, Erin M. Jackson, Julia Volaufova, Christina Lefante, and S. Michal Jazwinski. "After Hurricanes Katrina and Rita: Gender Differences in Health and Religiosity in Middle-Aged and Older Adults." *Health Care for Women International* 31 (2010): 997–1012.

Silva, Jennifer L., Loren D. Marks, and Katie E. Cherry. "The Psychology Behind Helping and Prosocial Behaviors: An Examination from Intention to Action." In *Lifespan Perspectives on Natural Disasters: Coping with Katrina, Rita and Other Storms.* Edited by Katie E. Cherry, 219–240. New York: Springer Science+Business Media, 2009.

Smith, Jean Kennedy. *The Nine of Us: Growing up Kennedy.* New York: HarperCollins, 2016.

Snyder, Charles R., and Kimberley M. Pulvers. "Dr. Seuss, the Coping Machine, and 'Oh, the Places You'll Go.'" In *Coping with Stress: Effective People and Processes,* edited by C. R. Snyder, 3–29. New York: Oxford University Press, 2001.

Snyder, Charles R., Susie C. Sympson, Florence C. Ybasco, Tyrone F. Borders, Michael A. Babyak, and Raymond L. Higgins. "Development and Validation of the State Hope Scale." *Journal of Personality and Social Psychology* 70 (1996): 321–335.

Sparks, Susan. *Laugh Your Way to Grace: Reclaiming the Spiritual Power of Humor.* Woodstock: Skylight Paths, 2010.

Spera, Keith. "Katrina's Lives Lost: The Life Stories Behind the Storm Victims." *New Orleans Times-Picayune*, October 20, 2005.

Stanko, Katie E., Katie E. Cherry, Kyle S. Ryker, Farra Mughal, Loren D. Marks, Jennifer Silva Brown, Patricia F. Gendusa, Marisa C. Sullivan, John Bruner, David A. Welsh, L. Joseph Su, and S. Michal Jazwinski. "Looking for the Silver Lining: Benefit Finding After Hurricanes Katrina and Rita in Middle-Aged, Older, and Oldest-Old Adults." *Current Psychology* 34 (2015): 564–575.

Stanko, Katie E., Laura Sampson, Katie E. Cherry, Sandro Galea, and Loren D. Marks. "When Reliance on Religion Falters: Religious Coping and Post-Traumatic Stress Symptoms in Older Adults after Multiple Disasters." *Journal of Religion, Spirituality, and Aging* 30 (2018): 292–313.

Tausch, Christina, Loren D. Marks, Jennifer Silva Brown, Katie E. Cherry, Tracey Frias, Zia MacWilliams, Miranda Melancon, and Diane D. Sasser. "Religion and Coping with Trauma: Qualitative Examples from Hurricanes Katrina and Rita." *Journal of Religion, Spirituality and Aging* 23 (2011): 236–253.

Tennen, Howard, and Glenn Affleck. "Finding Benefits in Adversity." In *Coping: The Psychology of What Works,* edited Charles. R. Snyder, 279–304. New York: Oxford University Press, 1999.

US Census Bureau. *QuickFacts St. Bernard Parish, Louisiana* (2017a), retrieved on August 8, 2018. https://www.census.gov/quickfacts/fact/map/stbernardparishlouisiana,US/PST045217

US Census Bureau. *QuickFacts Plaquemines Parish, Louisiana* (2017b), retrieved August 8, 2018. https://www.census.gov/quickfacts/fact/map/plaqueminesparishlouisiana,stbernardparishlouisiana,USviewtop

Viada, Sally E. Interview by Katie E. Cherry, June 20 and July 5, 2018.

Vujnovich, Milos M. *Yugoslavs in Louisiana.* Gretna: Pelican Publishing Company, 1974.

Ware, Carolyn E. "Croatians in Southeast Louisiana: An Overview." *Louisiana Folklore Miscellany* 11 (1996): 67–85.

Ware, Carolyn E. "Louisiana's Croatian American Society: A Case Study in Adaptation and Resilience." *Louisiana Folklore Miscellany* 23 (2013): 97–128.

Ware, Carolyn E. "Neda Jurisich, Eva Vujnovich, and Mary Jane Munsterman Tesvich: Three Generations of Croatian-American Women in Louisiana." In *Louisiana Women: Their Lives and Times, Vol. 2,* edited by Shannon Frystak and Mary Farmer-Kaiser, 149–172. Athens: University of Georgia Press, 2016.

Ware, John E., and Cathy Donald Sherbourne. "The MOS 36 Item Short-Form Health Survey (SF-36): I. Conceptual Framework and Item Selection." *Medical Care* 30 (1992): 473–483.

Webster's New Compact Office Dictionary. Cleveland: Wiley Publishing, Inc., 2003.

Weems, Carl F., and Stacy Overstreet. "An Ecological-Needs-Based Perspective of Adolescent and Youth Emotional Development in the Context of Disaster: Lessons from Katrina." In *Lifespan Perspectives on Natural Disasters: Coping with Katrina, Rita and Other Storms,* edited by Katie E. Cherry, 27–44. New York: Springer Science+Business Media, 2009.

Wells, Ken. *The Good Pirates of the Forgotten Bayous.* New Haven: Yale University Press, 2008.

Wilcox, Ella Wheeler. *Poems of Passion.* Chicago: Albert, Whitman & Co., 1883.

Wilson-Genderson, Maureen, Rachel Pruchno, and Allison R. Heid. "Modeling Successful Aging Over Time in the Context of a Disaster." *The Journals of Gerontology: Series B* 72, no. 2 (2017): 328–339.

Winchester, Simon. *A Crack in the Edge of the World: Earthquake of 1906.* New York: Harper Collins, 2005.

Wright, Margaret O'Dougherty, Ann S. Masten, and Angela J. Narayan. "Resilience Processes in Development: Four Waves of Research on Positive Adaptation in the Context of Adversity." In *Handbook of Resilience in Children* (2nd ed.), edited by Sam Goldstein and Robert B. Brooks, 15–37. New York: Springer, 2013.

Zavaliy, Andrei G. "Dao De Jing: ca. 300–200 BCE." In *Milestone Documents of World Religions: Exploring Traditions of Faith Through Primary Sources, Vol. 1,* edited by David M. Fahey, 240–262. Ipswich, MA: Salem Press, Inc., 2010.

INDEX

Figures are indicated by *f* following the page number
For the benefit of digital users, indexed terms that span two pages (e.g., 52–53) may, on occasion, appear on only one of those pages.